QUAIN'S

ELEMENTS OF ANATOMY

EDITED BY

EDWARD ALBERT SCHÄFER, F.R.S.

PROFESSOR OF PHYSIOLOGY AND HISTOLOGY IN UNIVERSITY COLLEGE, LONDON,

AND

GEORGE DANCER THANE,

PROFESSOR OF ANATOMY IN UNIVERSITY COLLEGE, LONDON.

IN THREE VOLUMES.

VOL. II.—PART I.

OSTEOLOGY

By PROFESSOR THANE.

ILLUSTRATED BY 168 ENGRAVINGS.

Tenth Edition.

LONDON:
LONGMANS, GREEN, AND CO.,
1890.

CONTENTS OF PART I.

DESCRIPTIVE ANATOMY.

OSTEOLOGY.

DESCRIPTIVE ANATOMY.

DESCRIPTIVE ANATOMY may be treated of in two methods : viz., the *Systematic* and the *Topographical*.

In the first or Systematic Anatomy, the several organs and parts of the body are considered in a systematic order, according to their structure, their connection with each other, and their relation to the purposes of life ; while in the second, or Topographical Anatomy, the parts are described in the order of their position or association in any region of the body. The first method is best adapted for the elementary and complete study of the structure of organs, the second is more immediately useful in the study of particular regions in their relation to Medicine and Surgery. The object of the present work being mainly to serve as a guide for systematic study, the topographical details will for the most part be included under and combined with the general description of organs, and only some of the more important regions will receive separate notice.

The plan of construction of the body and the general arrangement of its chief parts have been explained in the Introduction at the beginning of Volume I. The several systems and regions now to be described will be treated of under the following heads :—

1. Osteology, the Bones.
2. Arthrology, the Articulations.
3. Myology, the Voluntary Muscles, with which will be combined the Fasciæ and Aponeuroses.
4. Angeiology, the Heart, the Blood-Vessels, and the Lymphatics.
5. Neurology, the Spinal Cord and Brain, the Nerves, and the Organs of the Senses.
6. Splanchnology, the Organs of Respiration, the Organs of Digestion, the Urinary Organs, and the Organs of Reproduction.
7. Superficial Anatomy, and Topographical Anatomy of some Regions.

Descriptive terms.—In anatomical descriptions the body is always supposed to be in the erect attitude, and terms of relation are employed strictly with reference to this position. Thus, *superior* and *inferior* correspond respectively to *cephalic* and *caudal*, *anterior* and *posterior* to *ventral* and *dorsal*. The body being bilaterally symmetrical, it might be divided into similar and nearly equal halves by a vertical plane directed from before backwards. This is known as the *median plane*, and the line along which the median plane meets the surface of the body is called the *middle* or *median line*. The words *internal* or *mesial* and *external* or *lateral* denote respectively nearer to or farther from the median plane. *Sagittal* indicates a dorso-ventral direction in or parallel to the median plane, and *coronal* or *frontal* a direction perpendicular to the foregoing in a transverse vertical plane. The terms *superficial* and *deep*, *central* and *peripheral*, *proximal* and *distal*, are often used, and need no explanation. In many cases precision may be obtained by reference to certain fixed relations of parts, such as the *vertebral* and *sternal* ends of the ribs, the *radial* and *ulnar*, or *tibial* and *fibular* borders, and the *flexor* and *extensor* surfaces of the limbs. *Preaxial* and *postaxial*, applied, for instance, to parts of the limb, signify, respectively, on the primitive cephalic or caudal aspect of the axis of the member.

OSTEOLOGY.

By G. D. THANE.

THE SKELETON.

THE **skeleton** or solid framework of the body is mainly formed of the bones, but is completed in some parts by the addition of cartilages. The bones are bound together by means of ligaments, and are so disposed as to support the softer parts, protect delicate organs, and give attachment to the muscles by which the different movements are executed.

In the lower animals the term skeleton has a wider signification than in man, comprehending two sets of parts, viz., 1st, those of the *endoskeleton*, or the deeper osseous and cartilaginous framework which corresponds to the human skeleton ; and 2nd, those of the *exoskeleton*, or *dermal skeleton*, comprising the integument and various hardened structures connected with it. All vertebrate animals possess an endoskeleton ; but in some of them the exoskeleton attains greater proportions than in others, and is combined by means of hardened parts more fully with portions of the endoskeleton. In most invertebrate animals the dermal or exoskeleton alone exists.

In man, as in the higher vertebrates, the greater part of the endoskeleton is formed of bone, a calcified animal tissue, which, when freed by putrefactive macera-tion from its fat and various soft adherent parts, and subsequently dried, is capable of remaining unchanged for a very long period of time. It is customary and con-venient thus to study the bones chiefly in the macerated and dried state, that is, deprived of their accessory soft parts.

The accessory soft parts connected with the fresh bones consist chiefly of the external fibrous and vascular covering termed *periosteum*, and of the *medulla*, marrow or fat, which fills their larger internal cavities. The bones are permeated by blood-vessels, and they are provided also with absorbent vessels and with nerves in small quantity.

The ends of the bones, when jointed moveably with others, are covered by a thin layer of dense permanent cartilage, called *articular cartilage;* and the adjacent bones are united together by fibrous ligaments which may be considered as con-tinuous with the periosteum covering the rest of the bones. In some instances distinct bones are directly united by means of ligament or cartilage without any joint-cavity intervening. Thus the osseous system as a whole may be considered to be enveloped by a fibrous covering.

The bones are originally formed by a process termed **ossification** from soft sub-stance. This process commences in the greater number of bones in cartilage ; in some it begins in fibrous tissue or membrane ; and in all instances the farther growth of the bone substance takes place largely in the latter way. The deposit of bone begins generally at one spot, which is therefore called the *primary centre* of ossification ; but there may be several of these from the first. The main part of the bone thus formed from the primary centre is sometimes named the *diaphysis*. In most bones, after considerable advance in growth by extension from the primary centre, ossification occurs at comparatively later periods in one or more separate points, forming *secondary* or *tertiary centres ;* and the portions of bones so formed, which remain united to the main part for a time by intervening cartilage, are termed *epiphyses.* In many instances entire consolidation of the bone by the osseous union of the epiphyses does not take place till the full size has been attained, and this may be as late as the twenty-third or even the twenty-fifth year of life.

In their **outward form** the bones present much diversity, but have been reduced by anatomists to the following classes :—1. Long or cylindrical, such as the chief bones of the limbs. These consist of a body or shaft, cylindrical or prismatic in shape, and two extremities which are usually thicker than the shaft, and have smooth cartilaginous surfaces for articulation with neighbouring bones. The shaft is generally hollow and filled with marrow, by which sufficient size and strength are attained without undue increase of weight. 2. Tabular or flat bones, like the scapula, ilium, and the bones forming the roof and sides of the skull. 3. Short bones, which are more or less cubical or oblong, as in the carpus and tarsus. 4. Irregular or mixed bones, mostly situated symmetrically across the median plane of the body, and often of a complex figure, such as the vertebræ.

In these differently shaped bones the osseous substance occurs in two forms, viz., the compact and the spongy. There is, however, no essential difference in structure or properties between these beyond that of thickness or thinness of the component material.

The surfaces of bones present various eminences, depressions, and other marks, to designate which the following terms are in common use. Any marked bony prominence is called a *process* or *apophysis ;* a slender, sharp, or pointed eminence is named a *spine,* or *spinous process ;* a blunt one a *tuberele ;* a broad and rough one a *tuberosity.* The terms *crest, line,* and *ridge* are usually applied to a prominent border, or to an elevation running some way along the surface of a bone. A *head* (caput, capitulum, or capitellum) is a rounded process usually supported on a narrower part named the *neck* (cervix). The term *condyle,* somewhat variously applied by anatomists, is most frequently employed to denote an eminence bearing a rounded articular surface.

The cavities and depressions of bones are very variously named. An aperture or perforation, when short, is a *foramen ;* when continued some way as a passage it is a *canal* or *meatus.* A narrow slit is a *fissure,* an open excavation or hollow in one bone or in several together is a *fossa.* This term is also sometimes applied to the socket of a joint, as in the *glenoid* or shallower, and the *cotyloid* or deeper form of joint-cavity. *Sinus* and *antrum* are names applied to considerable cavities in the interior of certain bones. Besides these, various other terms are employed which do not require explanation, such as *notch* (incisura), *groove,* *furrow* (sulcus), &c.

The number of bones in the skeleton varies at different periods of life, some which are originally distinct becoming united together as the process of ossification advances. The following is a statement of the number usually reckoned as distinct in middle life :—

		Single bones.	Pairs.	Total.
Axial Skeleton.	The vertebral column	26	...	26
	The skull	6	8	22
	The hyoid bone	1	...	1
	The ribs and sternum	1	12	25
Appendicular Skeleton.	The upper limbs	...	32	64
	The lower limbs	...	31	62
		34	83	200

Besides the bones included in the above enumeration, there exist likewise the three pairs of auditory ossicles, and various bones formed in tendons and called *sesamoid,* the most constant of which are, besides the patella and pisiform bone, reckoned in the table above as limb-bones, a pair in each thumb and great toe.

I.—THE VERTEBRAL COLUMN.

The vertebral column is composed of a series of bones called *vertebræ*, which are united together, for the most part, by joints and elastic substance in such a manner that, although the amount of motion allowed between each pair is slight, the aggregate is sufficient to give the column very considerable flexibility. The *vertebræ* are originally thirty-three in number. Of these, the upper twenty-four remain separate in the adult, retaining their mobility, and are hence called *moveable* or *true* vertebræ. They are succeeded by five others, which rapidly diminish in size from above downwards, and which are united into one mass called the *sacrum*; beyond the sacrum are four dwindled terminal members of the series, which as age advances, likewise become more or less united, and form the *coccyx*. These sacral and coccygeal vertebræ are known as the *fixed* or *false* vertebræ.

General characters of the vertebræ.—The general characters are best seen in the vertebræ placed near the middle of the column, of which the tenth dorsal vetebra, shown in fig. 1, may serve as an example. Each has more or less the form of a ring, and presents for consideration a body, arch, processes, and the enclosed spinal foramen.

The *body* or *centrum* is a short cylinder or disc, which forms the anterior part of the vertebra. Its superior and inferior surfaces are flattened and connected to the next vertebræ by strong and elastic intervertebral discs. On the front and sides it is convex horizontally, but slightly concave from above downwards; its posterior surface forms part of the ring, and is slightly concave from side to side. These vertical surfaces are pierced by numerous small foramina for the passage

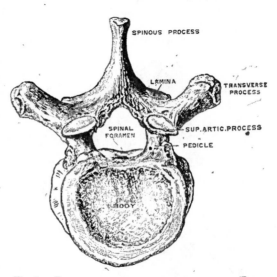

Fig. 1.—Tenth dorsal vertebra, from above. (Drawn by D. Gunn.)

of blood-vessels, and near the middle of the posterior surface are one or two much larger than the others.

The *arch* (*neural*) consists of two symmetrical portions which spring, one on each side, from the posterior surface of the body, and meet in the median plane behind. The anterior part of each half, thick and narrow, is called the *pedicle*; the posterior part is broad and flat, and is called the *lamina*. The concavities on the upper and lower borders of the pedicles are named *vertebral notches* (fig. 2, B), and constitute, by the apposition of those of contiguous vertebræ, the *intervertebral foramina*, a series of rounded apertures, which communicate with the vertebral canal, and transmit the spinal nerves and blood-vessels.

The *spinous process* (neural spine) projects backwards from the arch in the median plane. The *transverse processes*, placed one on each side, project outwards from the arch at the junction of the pedicle with the lamina. The *articular processes* (zygapophyses), two superior and two inferior, project upwards and downwards opposite the attachment of the transverse processes; their articular surfaces, coated with cartilage, in the superior pair look backwards, and in the inferior forwards, so that the former face the latter in adjoining vertebræ.

The *foramen* is bounded anteriorly by the body, posteriorly and laterally by the arch. The series of *rings* thus formed, united by ligaments, constitutes the *spinal* or *neural canal*, which lodges the spinal cord.

Texture.—The bodies of the vertebræ are almost entirely composed of spongy substance, the principal lamellæ being vertical ; on the surface is a thin layer of compact tissue. Venous canals, commencing at the larger foramina behind, traverse the cancellated structure. The arch and processes contain a much smaller proportion of spongy substance, being covered with compact tissue of considerable density in some places.

GROUPS OF VERTEBRÆ.

The vertebræ are divided into five groups, named from the regions which they occupy, *cervical, dorsal, lumbar, sacral,* and *coccygeal.*

Cervical vertebræ.—These are seven in number ; they are the smallest of the moveable - vertebræ, and are specially characterized by the presence of foramina in the transverse processes. The first and second are so peculiar in form, as to require a separate description. The following are the common characters of a cervical vertebra.

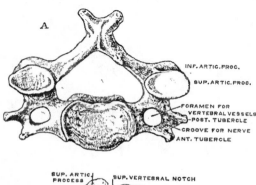

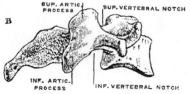

Fig. 2.—Fourth cervical vertebra : A, from above ; B, from the right side. (Drawn by D. Gunn.)

The *body* is small, and much broader from side to side than from before backwards ; in depth nearly the same in front and behind. Its upper surface is transversely concave from the upward projection of its lateral margins, and is sloped down in front. The under surface, on the contrary, is rounded off at the sides, while its anterior margin forms a marked projection downwards.

The *pedicles* spring from the body about midway between the upper and lower borders, and are directed outwards and backwards ; the *laminæ* are slender, long and flat. The superior and inferior *notches* are nearly equal in depth.

The *spinous process* is short, only slightly depressed, and bifid.

The *transverse processes* are short, and present at their extremities two tubercles, anterior and posterior. Each process is deeply grooved above for a spinal nerve, and its base is perforated vertically by a round foramen (vertebrarterial), through which in the upper six the vertebral artery and vein pass. It is united with the rest of the vertebra by two parts ; by the posterior, at the place of junction of the pedicle and lamina, like a dorsal transverse process ; by the anterior, to the body of the vertebra, in the same position as the heads of the ribs.

The *articular processes* are placed at the extremities of a short, stout, vertical column of bone ; their articular surfaces are nearly flat and oblique, the superior looking backwards and upwards, the inferior forwards and downwards.

The *foramen* is triangular, with rounded angles, and larger than in the dorsal or lumbar vertebræ.

The **first cervical vertebra,** or **atlas,** differs remarkably from the others in the absence of a body and spinous process, having the form merely of a large ring with articular and transverse processes.

The interior of the ring is wider behind than in front. Its posterior part cor-

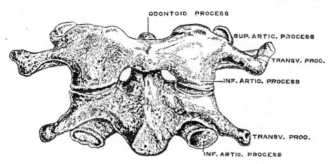

Fig. 3.—ATLAS AND AXIS, FROM BEFORE. (Drawn by D. Gunn.)

responds to the foramina of the other vertebræ ; its narrower anterior part is occupied by the odontoid process of the axis, and in the recent state is separated from the posterior by the transverse ligament. In front of the ring is the *anterior arch*, on the anterior aspect of which is a small tubercle, and on the posterior a smooth surface for articulation with the odontoid process. At the sides of the ring are the *lateral masses*, which are thick and strong, bearing the articular processes above and below, and extending outwards into the transverse processes. The *articular*

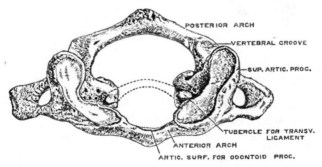

Fig. 4.—ATLAS, FROM ABOVE. (Drawn by D. Gunn.)
The position of the transverse ligament is indicated by dotted lines.

processes differ from those of other vertebræ in being situated in front of the places of exit of the nerves. The superior, larger than the inferior, are oval, and converge in front ; their articular surfaces are concave for the reception of the condyles of the occipital bone, and look upwards and inwards ; they are frequently divided by a transverse groove into two. Below the inner margin of each, towards the front, is a smooth rounded tubercle, to which the transverse ligament is attached. The inferior articular processes are smaller than the superior, flat, nearly circular, looking downwards and slightly inwards.

The *posterior arch* presents in the middle line a rough elevation, the rudiment of a spinous process ; at its junction with the lateral masses, it is hollowed out above so as to form a smooth transverse groove—the *vertebral groove*, in which lie the vertebral artery and first spinal (suboccipital) nerve ; the groove corresponds to the superior notches of the other vertebræ.

The *transverse processes* are larger and project farther outwards than those of the subjacent vertebræ. They are flattened from above downwards, and have a large foramen. Their extremities are not bifid, but broad and rough.

Varieties.—The posterior arch of the atlas is sometimes imperfect, the gap in the bone being bridged across by a fibrous band. A similar defect in the anterior arch is comparatively rare, but its complete absence has been observed.[1] The transverse process, especially the anterior bar, may also be the seat of defective ossification, and the foramen of the vertebral artery is then completed by ligament. A bony arch over the vertebral groove is frequently met with. Less common is the formation of a canal for the vertebral artery on the outer side of the superior articular process.

The **second vertebra** or **axis** (vert. dentata) forms a pivot on which the first vertebra rotates carrying the head.

The *body* is characterized by the presence of a large blunt tooth-like process called

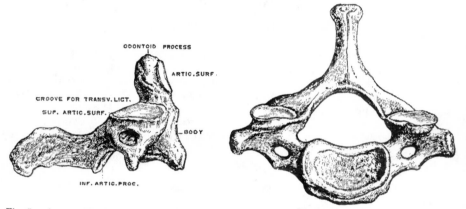

Fig. 5.—Axis, from the right side. (Drawn by D. Gunn.)

Fig. 6.—Seventh cervical vertebra, from above. (Drawn by D. Gunn.)

odontoid (proc. dentatus). This consists of an enlarged part termed the *head*, and a lower part or *neck*. It has in front a smooth surface for articulation with the atlas, and behind a smooth groove to receive the transverse ligament. The lower surface of the body resembles that of the succeeding vertebræ. Its anterior surface is marked by a low median vertical ridge, with a depression on each side.

The superior *articular surfaces*, placed like those of the atlas in front of the notch, lie close to the base of the odontoid process, partly on the body and partly on the pedicles of the vertebra. These surfaces look upwards and slightly outwards. The inferior articular processes are similar in form and position to those of the succeeding vertebræ.

The *spinous process* is very large, rough, deeply bifid, and grooved on its inferior surface. The *laminæ* are very thick and strong.

The *transverse processes* are short, and the anterior tubercle almost obsolete. The foramen for the vertebral artery is inclined obliquely upwards and outwards.

The **seventh cervical vertebra** has a long spinous process, which is not bifurcated, but ends in a broad tubercle projecting under the skin, whence the name

---

[1] Dwight, Journ. Anat., xxi, 539.

of *vertebra prominens* has been given to this bone. The transverse processes are massive, and only slightly grooved, with a small foramen; their posterior tubercle is large and prominent, while the anterior is but faintly marked.

In most cases the spinous process of the sixth cervical vertebra is also undivided; and in the dark races of man the spinous processes of the third, fourth and fifth vertebræ are more frequently simple than bifid. (D. J. Cunningham, Journ. Anat., xx, 637.)

Dorsal or thoracic vertebræ.

—These are twelve in number, and support the ribs.

The *body* as seen from above is somewhat heart-shaped; its anteroposterior and transverse diameters are nearly equal; its depth is greater behind than before.

It is specially characterized by the presence, at the place where it joins the arch, of articular surfaces for the heads of ribs. In the greater number of instances there are two costal surfaces on each side,—one at the upper, the other at the lower border,—so placed that each completes, with that of the adjacent vertebra, a cavity for the head of one rib.

The *laminæ*, broad and flat, are imbricated or sloped one pair over another like tiles on a roof. The superior *notches* are very shallow, the inferior deep.

The *spinous process*, described as bayonet-shaped, is three-sided, and terminates in a slight tubercle. It is longest and has the greatest downward inclination in those toward the middle of the series.

The *transverse processes* are strong, directed outwards and backwards, and terminate in a rough

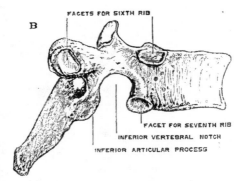

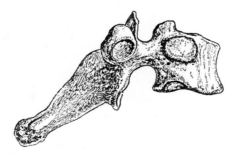

Fig. 7.—Sixth dorsal vertebra: A, from above; B, from the right side. (Drawn by D. Gunn.)

Fig. 8.—First dorsal vertebra, from the right side. (Drawn by D. Gunn.)

knob which presents anteriorly a smooth surface for articulation with the tuberosity of a rib.

The *articular processes* have their cartilaginous surfaces nearly vertical. Those of the superior processes look backwards, slightly upwards and outwards; those of the inferior look forwards, slightly downwards and inwards.

The *foramen* is nearly circular, and is smaller than in the cervical or the lumbar region.

The first, tenth, eleventh, and twelfth dorsal vertebræ present certain characters by which they may be individually distinguished.

The **first dorsal vertebra** in its general conformation approaches very closely

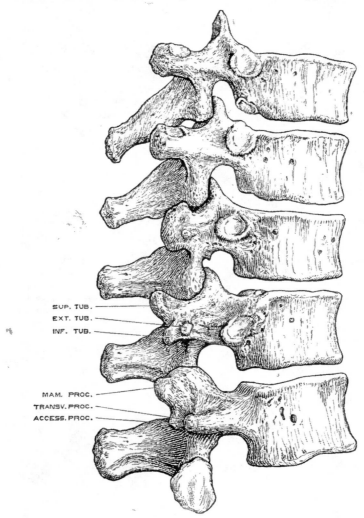

SUP. TUB.
EXT. TUB.
INF. TUB.

MAM. PROC.
TRANSV. PROC.
ACCESS. PROC.

Fig. 9.—NINTH, TENTH, ELEVENTH, AND TWELFTH DORSAL, AND FIRST LUMBAR VERTEBRÆ, FROM THE RIGHT SIDE. (Drawn by D. Gunn.)

the seventh cervical. The body is elongated transversely and concave on the upper surface; the superior vertebral notches are of considerable depth; the upper articular surfaces are oblique; and the spinous process is long and nearly horizontal. On each side of the body is a circular facet close to the upper border for the first rib, and a very small facet below for the second.

The **tenth dorsal vertebra** touches only one rib on each side, and has a single nearly complete articular surface, mainly on the pedicle. There is usually a small facet on the transverse process.

The **eleventh dorsal vertebra** has a complete articular surface on each side for the head of the rib, but no facet on the transverse process.

The **twelfth dorsal vertebra** has also only a single facet on each side ; the inferior articular processes have their surfaces turned outwards, resembling those of a lumbar vertebra ; the transverse processes are short and present three elevations, the *external, superior,* and *inferior tubercles,* which correspond to the transverse, mamillary, and accessory processes of the lumbar vertebræ. Indications of these tubercles may often be seen also upon the tenth and eleventh vertebræ.

Varieties.—The ninth dorsal vertebra frequently wants the lower facet on the side of the body. The tenth dorsal vertebra sometimes has no facet on the transverse process. The change from the dorsal to the lumbar type of articular processes occasionally takes place between the eleventh and twelfth dorsal vertebræ.

Lumbar vertebræ.—These are five in number, the largest of the moveable vertebræ, and are distinguished by the absence of costal articular surfaces.

The *body* has a greater diameter transversely than from before backwards,

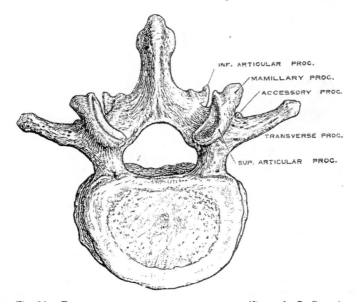

INF. ARTICULAR PROC.

MAMILLARY PROC.

ACCESSORY PROC.

TRANSVERSE PROC.

SUP. ARTICULAR PROC.

Fig. 10.—THIRD LUMBAR VERTEBRA, FROM ABOVE. (Drawn by D. Gunn.)

and viewed from above or below its surface presents a reniform outline ; the depth is generally slightly greater in front than behind.

The *laminæ* are shorter, deeper, and thicker than those of the dorsal vertebræ. The superior *notches* are shallow, the inferior deep.

The *spinous process* projects horizontally backwards. It has considerable breadth from above downwards, and is thickened and rough along its posterior edge.

The *transverse processes,* slender and somewhat spatula-shaped, project directly outwards ; they are shortest in the first, longest in the third vertebra. Their extremities lie in series with the external tubercles of the lower dorsal transverse processes, and with the ribs. Behind each at its base is a small process pointing downwards, which corresponds to the inferior tubercle of the dorsal transverse process, and is called the *accessory process* (anapophysis).

The *articular processes* are thick and strong. Their articular surfaces are vertical ;

the superior, concave, look backwards and inwards; the inferior, convex, look forwards and outwards. The superior pair are farther apart than the inferior, and embrace the inferior pair of the vertebra above them. From each superior articular process a tubercle projects backwards, which corresponds to the superior tubercle of the dorsal transverse process, and is called the *mamillary process* (metapophysis).

The *foramen* is large and triangular, or widely lozenge-shaped.

The **fifth lumbar vertebra** is massive, the body is much deeper in front than behind, the transverse processes are broad and conical, the lower articular processes are wider apart than the upper, and the laminæ project into the spinal foramen on each side.

While in the European the bodies of the lumbar vertebræ are collectively deeper in front than behind, in conformity with the curvature of this part of the column, the individual

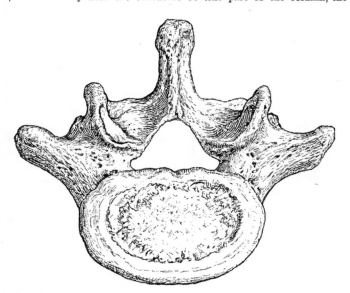

Fig. 11.—Fifth lumbar vertebra, from above. (Drawn by D. Gunn.)

segments show some difference in this respect. Thus, the first lumbar vertebra is deeper behind than in front ; in the second the anterior and posterior vertical diameters are nearly equal ; and the third, fourth and fifth are characterized by a preponderance of the anterior depth, which increases progressively from above downwards. In the dark races of man (Australian, Bushman, Andamanese, Negro) the depth of the five lumbar bodies together is greater behind than in front, and the fifth is the only one in which the anterior depth notably exceeds the posterior. It does not appear probable, however, that this conformation of the vertebral bodies is accompanied by a less marked degree of lumbar curvature, since the latter is determined mainly by the intervertebral discs. (W. Turner, Journ. Anat., xx, and "Challenger" Reports, Zoology, xvi ; D. J. Cunningham, "The Lumbar Curve in Man and Apes," Dublin, 1886, and Proc. Roy. Soc., 1889.)

Varieties in number of the moveable vertebræ.—The number of the cervical vertebræ is remarkably constant. The dorsal and lumbar vertebræ may vary reciprocally, the total remaining the same, according to the number of ribs present. Thus, if there are only eleven pairs of thoracic ribs, the twelfth vertebra will have lumbar characters; while in the more frequent case of a thirteenth pair of ribs being developed, the corresponding vertebra might be regarded as dorsal, although, in general conformation, it usually more resembles the lumbar type. The whole number of true vertebræ may be diminished or increased by one. In the former state the first sacral vertebra will be the 24th, as is the case generally in the orang, and, if the number of the ribs remain normal, there will be only four lumbar vertebræ. In the case of increase, the first vertebra to articulate with the hip-bone will be the 26th, and there may be twelve dorsal and six lumbar vertebræ, or thirteen dorsal and five lumbar. Sometimes an intermediate or transitional form is met with, as in the so-called *lumbo-sacral vertebra*, in which one side is united to the sacrum, while the other has a free transverse process (fig. 23, 11) ; such a vertebra may be the 24th or 25th. The study of the development of the vertebral column throws light on the origin of these varieties. It appears from the researches of Rosenberg that in the foetus the 26th vertebra is originally the first sacral, and that in the course of growth the hip-bones move headwards so as to become attached also to the 25th, which consequently becomes incorporated in the sacrum. This shifting may proceed farther, so that the 24th vertebra is included ; or it may be unsymmetrical, giving rise to a lumbo-sacral vertebra. Similarly, a thirteenth rib arises from the persistence and growth of a cartilaginous rudiment which is regularly present in the embryo, but usually becomes incorporated in the transverse process of the first lumbar vertebra. (J. Struthers, "Variations of Ribs and Vertebræ," Journ. Anat., ix ; P. Topinard, "Anomalies de nombre de la colonne vertébrale," Rev. d'Anthropol., 1877 ; E. Rosenberg, "Entwickelung der Wirbelsäule," Morph. Jahrb., i.)

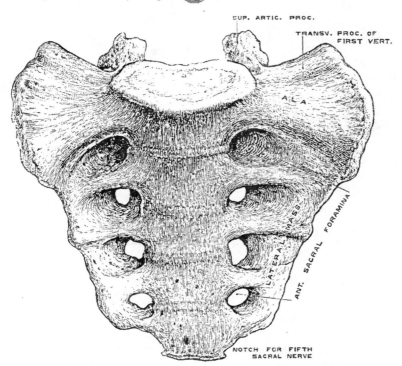

Fig. 12.—THE SACRUM, FROM BEFORE. (Drawn by D. Gunn.) ¾

Sacral vertebræ.—These by their union in the adult form the *os sacrum*, but in youth they present the elements of five distinct vertebræ. The sacrum is placed below the last lumbar vertebra, and articulates laterally with the two hip-bones, thus completing, together with the coccyx, the wall of the pelvis above and behind. The uppermost vertebra is the largest, those which follow become rapidly smaller, and the fifth is rudimentary. Hence the sacrum has the form of a triangle with its base directed upwards. It is concave and smooth in front, convex and uneven behind. The direction of its surfaces is very oblique, its ventral aspect looking considerably downwards, and forming above, at the place where it joins the last lumbar vertebra, the projection termed the *promontory*. The dorsal or posterior surface looks upwards as well as backwards.

The ventral surface is concave from above downwards, and slightly so from side to side. It is traversed horizontally by four ridges, which indicate the places of union of the bodies of the five sacral vertebræ, and at the extremities of which are situated on each side four *foramina* called *anterior sacral*. These foramina lead externally into grooves, and diminish in size from above downwards.

The dorsal surface is convex, very uneven, and somewhat narrower than the ventral. It presents along the median line three or four small eminences, the spinous processes, usually more or less connected, so as to form a ridge. Below the spinous process is a triangular opening, the termination of the spinal canal, the lateral margins of which are formed by the imperfect laminæ of the fourth and fifth sacral vertebræ, and are produced downwards into a pair of tubercles, the *sacral*

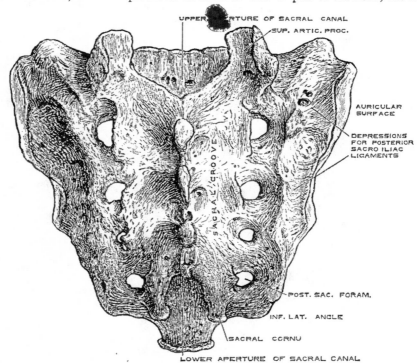

Fig. 13.—The sacrum, from behind. (Drawn by D. Gunn.) ¾

cornua, which represent the inferior articular processes of the last sacral vertebra, and are connected to the cornua of the coccyx. On each side of the ridge of spines the surface formed by the united laminæ is slightly hollowed, thus giving rise to the *sacral groove*, which prolongs the vertebral groove of the moveable part of the column ; and beyond this are the four *posterior sacral foramina*, opposite to, but smaller than the anterior. Immediately internal to each foramen is a slight eminence, which represents the articular and mamillary processes of the vertebræ above, while external to the foramen a more strongly marked elevation corresponds to the transverse process.

The part of the sacrum external to the foramina constitutes the *lateral mass*, and is broad and thick above, but narrowed below. The outer aspect of the upper part presents in front a large uneven surface, covered in the recent state with cartilage, which articulates with the ilium, and is called from its shape the *auricular surface :* behind this the bone is rough and marked with strong depressions for the attachment of ligaments. Lower down, the margin becomes narrowed and sinuous, terminating in the projection called the *inferior lateral angle*, below which the breadth of the bone is suddenly contracted so as to form a notch with the adjacent part of the coccyx.

The *base*, or upper surface of the first sacral vertebra, bears considerable

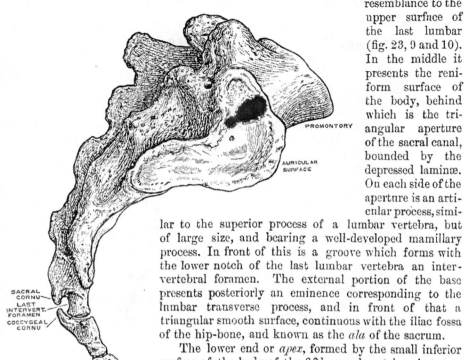

resemblance to the upper surface of the last lumbar (fig. 23, 9 and 10). In the middle it presents the reniform surface of the body, behind which is the triangular aperture of the sacral canal, bounded by the depressed laminæ. On each side of the aperture is an articular process, similar to the superior process of a lumbar vertebra, but of large size, and bearing a well-developed mamillary process. In front of this is a groove which forms with the lower notch of the last lumbar vertebra an intervertebral foramen. The external portion of the base presents posteriorly an eminence corresponding to the lumbar transverse process, and in front of that a triangular smooth surface, continuous with the iliac fossa of the hip-bone, and known as the *ala* of the sacrum.

The lower end or *apex*, formed by the small inferior surface of the body of the fifth sacral vertebra, is transversely oval, and articulates with the coccyx.

The *sacral canal* is curved with the bone, and gradually narrows as it descends ; in transverse section it is three-sided above, but flattened and rather semilunar below. It terminates on the posterior surface of the bone between the sacral cornua, where the laminæ

Fig. 14.—Sacrum and coccyx, from the right side. (Drawn by D. Gunn.) ¾

of the last two sacral vertebræ are imperfect. From this canal there pass outwards in the substance of the bone four pairs of intervertebral foramina, closed externally by the lateral masses, but opening on the surfaces by the anterior and posterior sacral foramina.

The sacrum of the female is broader in proportion to its length, and usually flatter than that of the male ; but the curvature varies greatly in different skeletons.

The sacrum of man is charac-

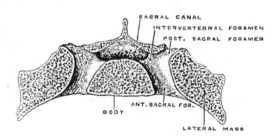

Fig. 15. — Transverse section of sacrum, passing through the first pair of foramina. (G. D. T.) ½

terized by its great breadth in comparison with its length. This proportion is expressed by the *sacral index*, which is ascertained by the following calculation, $\dfrac{100 \times \text{breadth}}{\text{length}}$. The average sacral index in the male European is 112, in the Negro 106, in the Australian 99, and in the Andamanese 94. In the European female it is about 116. The anthropoid apes have a sacral index varying from 87 in the orang to 72 in the gorilla. (Turner, Journ. Anat., xx, and "Challenger" Reports, Zoology, xvi.)

Varieties.—The sacrum not unfrequently consists of six pieces, a condition which is generally due to the inclusion of the first coccygeal vertebra. More rarely there are only four sacral vertebræ. Occasionally the bodies of the first and second vertebræ are not united, though complete union has taken place in every other part ; or the first vertebra may present on one side the usual sacral form, while on the other it has the form of a lumbar vertebra, and is not united to the next (see fig. 23, 11, *l'*), a peculiarity connected with the oblique form of pelvis. Instances also occur in which it presents, on both sides, characters intermediate between those of sacral and lumbar vertebræ. The sacral canal may be open below to a greater extent than usual ; it has even been found open throughout.

Coccygeal vertebræ, coccyx.—These are very rudimentary vertebræ, commonly four, sometimes five, seldom only three in number. The first of the series is considerably broader than the others. It presents superiorly, on the part corresponding to the body, an oval concave surface, which articulates with the lower end of the sacrum. From its posterior surface two small processes, termed *cornua of*

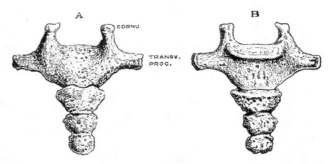

Fig. 16.—THE COCCYX : A, FROM BEHIND ; B, FROM BEFORE. (Drawn by D. Gunn.) ¾

the coccyx, project upwards ; they represent the pedicles and superior articular processes of the vertebræ generally, and are connected at their extremities to the sacral cornua, with which they enclose an aperture—the last intervertebral foramen (fig. 14) for the passage of the fifth sacral nerve. On each side the short transverse process projects, and usually bounds, with the lowest part of the lateral margin of the sacrum, a notch for the anterior division of the same nerve ; but in some cases it is united by bone to the lower lateral angle of the sacrum, so as to form a fifth anterior sacral foramen.

The remaining three coccygeal vertebræ are much smaller than the first. The second piece, when separate, has upper and lower flattened surfaces for articulation with the vertebra above and below ; on each side is a rudiment of the transverse process in the form of a slight tubercle ; and on the posterior aspect there may sometimes be seen two small eminences in series with the cornua of the first piece, and representing the last traces of a neural arch. The third and fourth pieces are mere rounded nodules, slightly compressed from above downwards, and corresponding solely to vertebral bodies. In middle life the first piece is usually separate, while the three lower pieces are united into one, the original separation being indicated by transverse grooves.

In advanced life the coccygeal vertebræ, having been previously joined into one bone, may become also united to the sacrum. This union occurs at an earlier age and more frequently in the male than in the female, but it is subject to much variation. The first piece often joins the sacrum before the union of the rest of the bone.

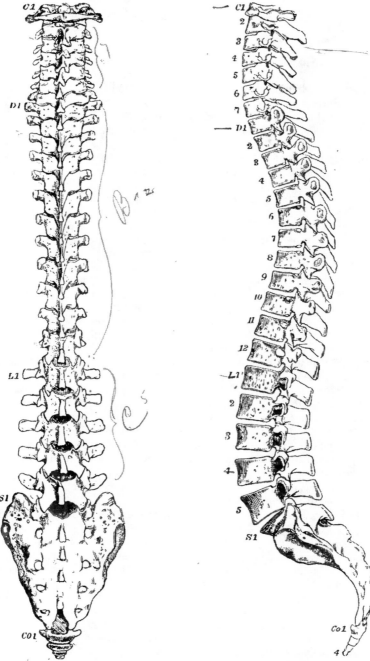

Fig. 17.—VERTEBRAL COLUMN OF AN ADULT MALE, FROM BEHIND. (Allen Thomson.) ¼

C 1, first cervical vertebra ; D 1, first dorsal vertebra ; L 1, first lumbar vertebra ; S 1, first sacral vertebra ; CO 1, first coccygeal vertebra. The transition in the form of the transverse processes and tubercles in the lower dorsal and first lumbar vertebræ is well marked in this specimen.

Fig. 18.—VERTEBRAL COLUMN, FROM THE LEFT SIDE. (Allen Thomson.) ¼

The letters and numbers indicate the several vertebræ. The antero-posterior curves of the column are shown, together with the shape and size of the vertebræ and intervertebral spaces.

According to the observations of E. Steinbach there are in most cases five coccygeal vertebræ in the male, four or five with about equal frequency in the female. ("Die Zahl der Caudalwirbel beim Menschen," Diss., Berlin, 1889.)

The vertebral column as a whole.—The vertebral column may be regarded as a central axis upon which the other parts of the skeleton are arranged. Superiorly it supports the skull, laterally the ribs, through which also it receives the weight of the upper limbs, and near its lower extremity it rests upon the hip-bones, by which the weight of the body is transmited to the lower limbs. It is a pillar of support to the rest of the skeleton, and protects the spinal cord by enclosing it in a bony canal. Its average length is about 28 inches in the male, 27 inches in the female.

When seen in profile the column presents four curves, directed alternately forwards and backwards,—forwards in the cervical and lumbar regions, backwards in the dorsal and sacral. The upper curves pass imperceptibly into one another, but at the junction of the last lumbar vertebra with the sacrum a considerable angle is formed, known as the *lumbo-sacral* or *sacro-vertebral angle*, causing the promontory to overhang the cavity of the pelvis. The dorsal and sacral curves are primary curves affecting those parts of the column which enter into the formation of the bony-walled cavities, the thorax and pelvis ; they make their appearance at an early period of fœtal life, and are due to the conformation of the vertebral bodies : the cervical and lumbar curves are secondary or compensatory curves, necessary to the upright posture, only developed after birth, and dependent mainly on the shape of the intervertebral discs ; in these regions also the principal movements of the spine take place. The curves obviously confer upon the column greater elasticity and security from injury than it would have were it perfectly straight. In the upper dorsal region there is also very frequently a slight degree of lateral curvature, the convexity of which, in most cases, is directed towards the right side, and which is probably connected with the greater use made of the right than of the left arm.

Viewed from the front, the bodies of the vertebræ are seen to become broader from the axis to the first dorsal, then slightly narrower to the fourth dorsal, and from this vertebra they gradually widen to the base of the sacrum. The width between the extremities of the transverse processes is considerable in the atlas ; small in the axis, it becomes greater as far as the first dorsal vertebra ; thence it is again gradually contracted as far as the last dorsal, and becomes suddenly much greater in the lumbar region.

In the lateral view, the antero-posterior diameter of the bodies increases in descending through the dorsal and lumbar regions.

Viewed from behind, the spines occupy the middle line. On the sides are the *vertebral grooves*, corresponding to the laminæ, and bounded externally in the cervical and dorsal regions by the transverse processes, and in the lumbar by the mamillary processes. Along each groove is a series of spaces between the laminæ, which, in the natural condition, are filled up by the yellow ligaments. The extent of these intervals is very trifling in the neck and in the greater part of the back ; it increases in the lower third of the dorsal, and still more in the lumbar region. The interval between the occipital bone and the arch of the atlas is considerable, and so is that between the last lumbar vertebra and the sacrum.

The only part of the vertebral column that appears on the surface of the body is the row of spinous processes, and these are subcutaneous from the seventh cervical to the third sacral. The upper cervical spines are deeply placed and can be felt with difficulty in the median interval between the muscular masses of the back of the neck ; the sixth is sometimes long and in such cases may project. The seventh cervical and the following one or two dorsal spines are prominent ; the others lie at the bottom of the long *spinal furrow* produced by the eminence of the spinal muscles on each side.

OSSIFICATION OF THE VERTEBRÆ.

The vertebræ in general.—The ossification of each vertebra proceeds in cartilage from three principal centres, one for the main part of the body, and one on each side for the arch and processes, together with a small part of the body. The lateral centres appear about the 7th week of fœtal life, that of the body very soon afterwards. From these centres the ossification extends gradually, so as to form the greater part of the vertebra. The central ossification does not pass, however, in the dorsal vertebræ the place of articulation of the head of the rib, but leaves on each side a portion of the body which is formed from the lateral ossification, and is separated up to the third year by a narrow cartilaginous interval—the *neuro-central synchondrosis*. It would appear farther, that while ossification in the arches commences first in the cervical vertebræ, the osseous centres of the bodies appear earliest in the lower dorsal vertebræ.

At the time of birth most of the vertebræ consist of three osseous pieces, corresponding to the three original centres. In the first year of infancy the laminæ of opposite sides become united in a number of the vertebræ, but not in all. The spinous processes, remaining

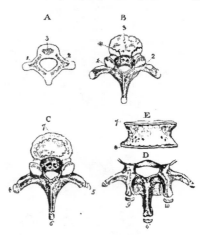

Fig. 19.—Ossification of the Vertebræ.
(R. Quain.)

A, fœtal vertebra, showing the three primary centres ; 1, 2, neural ossifications ; 3, central ossification.

B, dorsal vertebra from a child of two years ; 1 & 2 are seen to have encroached upon the body at * the neuro-central synchondrosis, to have extended into the articular and transverse processes, and to have united behind in the spinous process, leaving the ends cartilaginous.

C, dorsal vertebra at about seventeen years, showing epiphyses on the transverse processes, 4 & 5, and spinous process, 6, and the upper epiphysial plate of the body, 7.

D & E, parts of a lumbar vertebra of about the same age, showing, in addition to the foregoing, 8, the lower epiphysial plate of the body ; 9 & 10, the epiphyses of the mamillary tubercles.

cartilaginous for a time, are gradually completed by the growth of the cartilage and the extension of the bone into them, and at the same time, by the ossific extension of the transverse processes and other parts, the vertebræ gradually attain to nearly their full size and shape about the age of puberty. At different periods subsequent to this, five epiphyses, or supplementary centres of ossification, are added. Three of these are small portions of bone, placed on the tips of the spinous and transverse processes : the other two are thin annular plates on the upper and lower surfaces of the body at its circumference. In the lumbar vertebræ two other epiphyses surmount the mamillary processes. These epiphyses appear from the sixteenth to the twentieth year, and are not wholly united to the rest of the vertebra before the twenty-fifth year. The transverse process of the first lumbar vertebra is sometimes developed from a separate centre. The anterior divisions of the cervical transverse processes are for the most part ossified by the extension into them of osseous substance from the neighbouring posterior part of the process and from the arch ; but there are usually separate osseous nuclei for those of the seventh, sometimes also of the sixth, and even the fifth or second vertebræ.

Atlas and axis.—The ossification of the atlas and axis differs considerably from that of

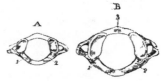

Fig. 20.—Ossification of the atlas. (R. Quain.)

A, before birth ; B, in the first year ; 1 & 2, lateral centres of ossification ; 3, ossific centre in the anterior arch.

the other vertebræ. In the atlas the anterior arch is formed by a strip of cartilage in which ossification, commencing by one or two centres, only appears in the course of the first year after birth. The posterior arch, together with the lateral masses, is formed from two centres which correspond to the neural ossifications of the other vertebræ, and which begin to ossify about the seventh week. Their union posteriorly occurs in the third year, and is frequently preceded by the formation of a distinct spinal nucleus. Their union with the anterior arch does not take place till the fifth or sixth year.

In the axis, the arch and processes are formed from two centres corresponding to those of the other vertebræ, and appearing about the seventh or eighth week. Ossification begins in

Fig. 21.—Ossification of the axis. (R. Quain.)

A, from a fœtus of seven months ; 3, centre for the body ; 4, 5, two centres in the base of the odontoid process.

B, shortly after birth ; 1, 2, neural ossifications ; 3, central ossification ; 6, odontoid ossification.

the body about the fourth month, from one or sometimes two centres, occupying the lower part of the common cartilage of the body and odontoid process. In the upper part of this cartilage, a little later, two collateral centres appear for the odontoid process ; these soon unite into one, so that at birth the axis is composed of four pieces of bone. About the fourth year the odontoid process becomes joined to the body and the fore part of the neural arch of the axis on each side, and a little later union occurs in front and behind. In the centre, however, a small disc of cartilage remains until advanced age.[1] The apex of the odontoid process is formed from a distinct centre which appears in the second year, and joins about the twelfth year. There is the usual annular epiphysis on the lower surface of the body.

Sacral vertebræ.—Each of the sacral vertebræ has three primary centres of ossification. one in the body and a pair in the arch. The centres of the bodies of the first three vertebræ appear about the eighth or ninth week, those of the two following vertebræ somewhat later.

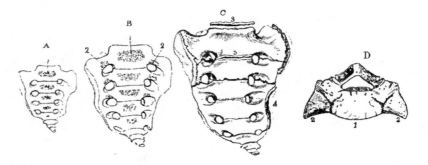

Fig. 22.—Ossification of the sacrum. (R. Quain.)

A, sacrum of a fœtus before six months seen from the front, showing the ossific centres in the bodies of the vertebræ.

B, at birth ; 2, 2, additional centres for the lateral masses.

C, about twenty-three years ; 3, 3, epiphysial plates still visible above and below the first vertebral body ; 4, 4′, lateral epiphysial plates.

D, upper surface of first sacral vertebra at four or five years ; 1, and 2, as in A and B. (Allen Thomson.)

A & B, nearly full size ; C, one-fourth ; D, one-third.

The laminæ begin to ossify about the sixth month, but the time of union with the bodies differs in the different vertebræ, taking place as early as the second year in the lowest, but not till the fifth or sixth year in the uppermost. In each of the first three vertebræ (sometimes however only in two, sometimes in four) the anterior part of the lateral mass on each side is formed from an additional nucleus which appears at the outer margin of the anterior sacral foramen from the sixth to the eighth month. These unite to the bodies later than the arches. In the case of the lower two vertebræ the lateral masses are formed by extension of ossification from the primary lateral nuclei. On the body of each vertebra epiphysial plates are formed after puberty, as in other vertebræ ; and two irregular plates of bone are added on each side of the sacrum, the uppermost of which extends over the auricular surface, and the

[1] D. J. Cunningham, Journ. Anat., xx, 238.

lower over the sharp edge below. These appear from the eighteenth to the twentieth year, and are united about the twenty-fifth. The bodies of the sacral vertebræ are at first separated by intervertebral discs, but about the eighteenth year, in the case of the lower vertebræ, ossification begins to extend through these discs and the epiphyses, so as completely to unite the adjacent bodies. The ossific union of the first and second bodies does not take place till the twenty-fifth year or later. Previous to this, the lateral masses have coalesced in the same order as the bodies.

Coccygeal vertebræ.—Each of the coccygeal vertebræ is ossified from a distinct piece of cartilage, and usually from a single centre, but in the upper sometimes from two centres. Ossification commences in the first generally about the time of birth ; in the second, from the fifth to the tenth year ; in the third, some time before, and in the fourth, some time after puberty. The ossific union of the three lower coccygeal vertebræ occurs before middle life ; their union with the first, and the union of this with the sacrum, belong to the later periods of life.

Variations may occur in the mode of ossification of the vertebræ, as is shown by the nature of certain malformations. Thus, instances are recorded in which a vertebral body is represented by two pieces of bone, separated by a median interval : here ossification must have proceeded from two centres, as is the case normally in the odontoid process, and sometimes in the body of the axis : probably this is the reappearance or persistence of a primitive condition. Similarly, the neural arch of the fifth lumbar vertebra (very rarely of one of the other vertebræ) may have a double origin, being divided by a cleft passing obliquely between the superior and inferior articular processes : according to Rambaud and Renault[1] there are always two nuclei in each half of the neural arch.

SERIAL HOMOLOGY OF THE VERTEBRÆ.

It is evident from the foregoing descriptions that the different segments of the vertebral column are generally similar in construction ; and this similarity is for the most part so marked that there can be no doubt of the homodynamy of the several constituent parts of successive vertebræ. In certain instances, however, there are peculiarities of arrangement which offer some difficulty in tracing the precise correspondence, and in explanation of these chiefly the following brief sketch of the serial homology of the vertebræ is given. The accompanying views of the vertebræ and some of their varieties (fig. 23) will also assist the reader in comparing their forms.

1. The series of centra or bodies, surrounding the primary axis of the notochord, is complete in man, from the odontoid process of the second vertebra to the caudal extremity. It must, however, be remembered that the part called the body of a vertebra includes not only the proper central ossification, but also the ventral extremity of the neural ossification on each side. The body is apparently absent in the atlas, but the part corresponding to the central ossification of that vertebra is united with the body of the axis in the odontoid process ; while the anterior arch of the atlas probably belongs to the series of subcentral parts or *hypapophyses*. The proofs of this view are derived mainly from, 1st, the remains of the notochord having been traced in the fœtus through the odontoid process (and not through the anterior arch of the atlas) into the base of the skull ; 2nd, the separate ossification in cartilage of the odontoid process ; and 3rd, the existence in some animals, as the ornithorhynchus and some reptiles, of a bone corresponding to the odontoid process, in a separate condition, without any other part representing the centrum of the atlas.

2. The series of neural arches is complete in the whole vertebral column of man, with the exception of the lower three coccygeal vertebræ, and in part of the first coccygeal and lower sacral vertebræ. The neural spines are also complete in nearly the same vertebræ as the arches. The spine is absent or little developed in the atlas, bifid at its extremity in the next four or five cervical vertebræ, but simple in all the remaining vertebræ in which it is present.

3. The articular processes or zygapophyses, superior and inferior (preaxial and postaxial), correspond in their relations throughout the whole of the vertebræ in which they exist, with the exception of both of those of the atlas and the superior of the axis. In these vertebræ the articular processes are not in the series of zygapophyses, being situated in front of the place of exit of the spinal nerves, instead of behind it, and therefore in a position which corresponds to that of the part of the vertebral body formed from the neural ossification. The joints which they form must accordingly be looked upon as homologous with the lateral portions of the articulations between the bodies of the succeeding vertebræ. In the sacral vertebræ the articular processes, existing as such in early life, come to be in the adult united by anchylosis. In the lower three coccygeal vertebræ they are absent.

[1] "Origine et Développement des Os," Paris, 1864. This work may be referred to for more detailed information concerning the ossification of the vertebræ, as well as of the bones generally.

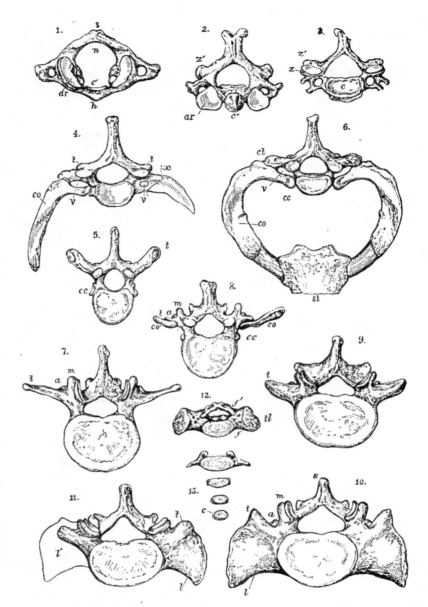

Fig. 23.—Views of different vertebræ from above to illustrate their homologies and some of their varieties. (Allen Thomson.)

1, atlas ; 2, axis ; 3, fifth cervical ; 4, seventh cervical with supernumerary ribs ; 5, middle dorsal ; 6, first dorsal, with costal arch and sternum attached ; 7, third lumbar ; 8, first lumbar with supernumerary ribs ; 9, fifth lumbar ; 10, first sacral ; 11, lumbo-sacral vertebra ; 12, fourth sacral vertebra in a young subject ; 13, four coccygeal vertebræ. In the several figures the parts are indicated by letters as follows, viz , in 1, *s*, spine ; *n*, neural arch ; *c'*, the space occupied by the odontoid process, or displaced centrum ; *h*, anterior arch ; *ar*, superior articular process : in 2, *c''*, odontoid process ; *ar*, superior articular surface ; *z'*, inferior articular process : in 3, *c*, centrum ; *z*, *z'*, superior and inferior articular processes : in 4, *t*, transverse process ; *r*, vertebrarterial foramen ; *co*, moveable right supernumerary or cervical rib ; *x*, with a dotted line marking the place where an anchylosed rib on the left side may be considered to be superadded to the transverse process of the vertebra : in 5, *t*, transverse process with costal facet ; *cc*, costo-central facet : in 6, *v*, vascular interval; *ct*, costo-transverse, and *cc*, costo-central articulations ; *co*, first rib : in 7, *m*, mamillary, and *a*, accessory tubercles ; *t*, transverse process : in 8, *co, co'*, supernumerary ribs : in 10, *l*, lateral mass : in 11, *l'*, place of the lateral mass, remaining undeveloped in this instance : in 12, *tl*, the transverse process and lateral mass which unite with the corresponding parts above ; *f, f'*, anterior and posterior sacral foramina thus formed : in 13, *c*, the centrum, which alone remains in the lower coccygeal vertebræ.

4. It is in the comparison of the parts known in human anatomy under the general name of **transverse processes** that the main difficulty of establishing homologies exists. In the cervical vertebræ the processes so called are pierced by a vertebrarterial foramen, and most of them have two tubercles. Those of the dorsal vertebræ are for the most part simple, but articulate with the tubercles of the ribs, whence they are known in comparative anatomy as the *tubercular processes* (diapophyses). At the place of articulation of the head of the rib with the vertebra there is in some animals a projection, called the *capitular process* (parapophysis) ; this is represented in man only by the articular facet on the body, which is separated however from the proper central ossification by the neuro-central synchondrosis. It is generally admitted that the part of the cervical transverse process in front of the vertebrarterial foramen corresponds to the first part of a rib, as is illustrated by the separate ossification of that piece of bone in the seventh cervical vertebra in man, and by the occasional occurrence of a more fully developed cervical rib in that situation (fig. 23, 4).

In the lumbar vertebræ the transverse processes are elongated laterally, and at their root two other processes become apparent, viz., the mamillary or *metapophysis* directed preaxially, and the accessory or *anapophysis*, directed postaxially. Several circumstances in the anatomy of the bones and muscles indicate that the outer part of the lumbar transverse processes is serially homologous with the first part of the ribs, but so intimately combined with both capitular and tubercular processes, and the part lying between them, as to leave no arterial passage. This view receives confirmation from the presence of a costal element in connection with the transverse process of the first lumbar vertebra in the fœtus, and its occasional development to form a supernumerary rib (p. 13 ; fig. 23, 8).

In the sacral part of the column still greater departure from the form of the transverse process of the upper vertebræ takes place by the large development and ossific union of the lateral parts. Throughout the whole five vertebræ recognised as sacral in man, this may be looked upon as occurring to some extent in portions of the bones which are serially homologous with the combined capitular and tubercular processes ; but in the upper sacral vertebræ, another element is interposed between the transverse process and the iliac surface of articulation, constituting the greater portion of the lateral mass of the sacrum. This element is generally regarded as serially homologous with part of a rib, and those vertebræ which are thus connected to the ilium by means of a costal element are distinguished as *true sacral*, the remaining anchylosed vertebræ being called *pseudo-sacral*.

With the exception of the anterior arch of the atlas already referred to, there are no parts developed in the human skeleton corresponding to the *hypapophyses* which occur in connection with the vertebral column of animals, such as the "chevron" bones below the caudal vertebræ of cetacea, and the hæmal arches enclosing the main artery of fishes.

II.—THE THORAX.

The skeleton of the thorax consists of the dorsal vertebræ already described, the sternum, the ribs, and the costal cartilages.

THE STERNUM OR BREAST-BONE.

The **sternum** is situated in the median line at the fore part of the thorax. It is connected with the rest of the trunk by the cartilages of the first seven ribs on each side ; and at the upper end it gives attachment to the clavicles. It consists originally of six segments. The first of these usually remains separate from the rest, and is called the *manubrium* : the succeeding four are united into one in the adult, and form the *body* : the sixth generally remains cartilaginous for some years after birth, and often partially so even to advanced age, constituting the *ensiform process* ; in middle life it is most frequently united by bone to the body.

The sternum is flattened from before backwards, and presents a slight longitudinal curve with the convexity in front. It is of unequal width, being broad at the upper part of the manubrium, considerably narrower at the lower end of that portion and

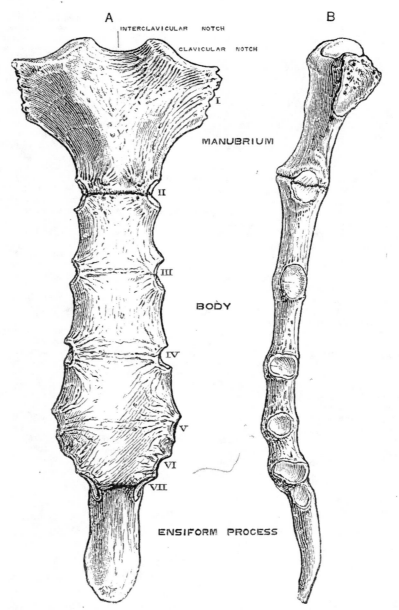

A

INTERCLAVICULAR NOTCH

CLAVICULAR NOTCH

MANUBRIUM

BODY

ENSIFORM PROCESS

B

Fig. 24.—The sternum: A, from before; B, from the left side. (Drawn by D. Gunn.) ¾

The Roman numerals indicate the articular surfaces for the corresponding rib-cartilages.

in the first segment of the body, somewhat wider near the lower end of the body, and finally narrowed at the junction with the ensiform process. It consists of light cancellated tissue, with a thin covering of compact bone.

The **manubrium** (*presternum*) is the thickest part of the bone. Its anterior surface presents a slight median elevation; its posterior surface is smooth and somewhat concave. Its upper border is divided into three deep notches; the middle one is named the *incisura semilunaris*, or *interclavicular notch;* the lateral ones form two depressed articular surfaces, directed upwards, outwards and backwards, for articulation with the clavicles, and called the *clavicular notches.* Each lateral border presents superiorly, close to the clavicular notch, a rough triangular surface, which unites with the cartilage of the first rib. Below this the bone slopes inwards, and at its inferior angle presents a small surface, which with a similar one on the body forms a notch for the cartilage of the second rib. The lower margin is straight and united by cartilage to the upper margin of the body.

The **body** (*gladiolus, mesosternum*) is marked on its anterior surface by three slight transverse elevations at the lines of junction of its four component parts. Its posterior surface is comparatively smooth. Each lateral margin presents five notches for the reception of costal cartilages, and a small surface above, which, with the similar depression on the manubrium, forms the notch for the second costal cartilage. The notches for the third, fourth, and fifth costal cartilages are opposite the lines of junction of the four segments of the body of the sternum; those of the sixth and seventh are placed close together on the sides of the inferior segment, that for the seventh being completed by the ensiform process.

The **ensiform** or **xiphoid process** (*metasternum, xiphisternum*) is a thin spatula-like process projecting downwards between the cartilages of the seventh ribs. It is subject to frequent varieties of form, being sometimes bent forwards, sometimes backwards, often forked, and occasionally perforated.

The sternum is subcutaneous in the middle line, forming the floor of the *sternal groove* between the pectoral muscles, which cover the lateral portions of the anterior surface. The upper end is marked by the deep *suprasternal notch;* and the ensiform process lies at the bottom of the *infrasternal depression,* the latter being due to the prominence of the body and the seventh costal cartilages beyond the surface of the ensiform process.

The length of the sternum and the proportions of its parts differ somewhat in the two sexes. In the male the body is as a rule slightly more than twice as long as the manubrium; while in the female the whole bone is relatively shorter, and the body is usually less than twice the length of the upper segment. Individual variations are, however, frequent and great. (M. Strauch, Diss., Dorpat, 1881; T. Dwight, Journ. Anat., xv, 327, and xxiv, 527; F. Petermöller, Diss., Kiel, 1890.)

Varieties.—The sternum is subject to many varieties of form. It is not unfrequently much shorter than usual, and indented at its lower part, as occurs especially from the pressure of the cobbler's last. Occasionally the lower part of the body is perforated by the so-called *sternal foramen* (fig. 30, E); and in rare cases the sternum has been found divided to a greater or less extent, constituting the malformation of *fissura sterni,* and connected in some instances with ectopia cordis.

Two small nodules of bone, *ossa suprasternalia,* have been found in some rare cases at the upper border, close to the clavicular notches, united by cartilage and ligament to the sternum. Their position is indicated by the asterisks (**) in figure 30, E. They appear to be vestiges of the episternal bone of monotremata and lizards, the lateral parts of which are represented normally in the interarticular fibro-cartilages of the sterno-clavicular articulations.

THE RIBS.

The **ribs** (*costae*), twelve in number on each side, constitute a series of arched and highly elastic bones, which extend outwards and forwards from the vertebral column, and form the lateral walls of the thorax. Their anterior extremities give attachment to cartilaginous prolongations—the *costal cartilages,* the first seven pairs of which pass inwards to the sternum. On this account the first seven pairs of ribs are called *sternal,* also *true,* and the remaining five pairs *asternal* or *false* ribs. Of these asternal ribs, each of the upper three has its cartilage attached along its superior border to the cartilage of the rib above it; while the two last are entirely free from such attachment, and are thence called *floating* ribs.

General characters of the ribs.—These are best marked in the ribs near the middle of the series. The posterior extremity is thickened, and is termed the *head*

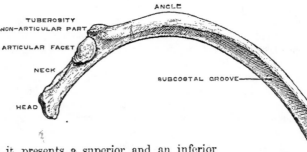

or *capitulum;* it presents a superior and an inferior oblique articular surface for articulation with the bodies of two vertebræ, and, between them, a slight ridge, to which the interarticular ligament is attached. At a little distance from the head, and separated from it by the slightly constricted neck, is the *tuberosity,* an oval eminence which is divided into two parts by an oblique groove; the inner part is smooth and articulates with the transverse process of the lower of

Fig. 26.—FIFTH RIB OF THE RIGHT SIDE, FROM BEHIND.
(Drawn by D. Gunn.) ¾

the two vertebræ with which the head is connected, while the outer part is rough and serves for the attachment of the posterior costo-transverse ligament. The whole extent beyond the tuberosity constitutes the body. It is laterally compressed, and broader from above downwards towards the anterior extremity. Outside the tuberosity, over the most convex part of the body, is a rough line which corresponds to the outer border of the erector spinæ muscle, and marks the *angle,* so called because at this point the rib takes a more sudden curve, its direction being now forwards and outwards. The inferior border presents on its inner aspect the *subcostal groove,* in which lie the intercostal vessels and nerve, and which is best marked opposite the angle and disappears in front.

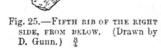

Fig. 25.—FIFTH RIB OF THE RIGHT SIDE, FROM BELOW. (Drawn by D. Gunn.) ¾

The anterior extremity of each rib is hollowed at its tip into an oval pit, in which the costal cartilage is implanted.

Inclination and curves.—There is a general inclination of the ribs downwards from the head to the anterior extremity, the slope being greatest between the head and angle. The curve of the ribs is more marked towards the back part than in front, especially near the angle. Besides the main curves now mentioned, the rib is slightly twisted on itself, so that while its surfaces are vertical behind, they are placed somewhat obliquely in front.

Special characters of certain ribs.—The ribs increase in length from the first to the seventh or eighth, and decrease to the twelfth, so that the last is little

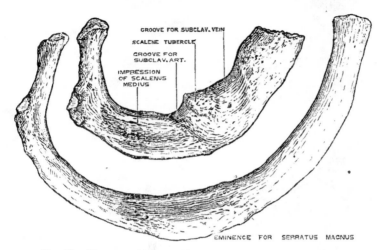

Fig. 27.—First and second ribs of the right side, from above. (Drawn by D. Gunn.) ⁴⁄₄

longer, often even shorter, than the first. The first rib is the broadest, and after it the middle ones ; the twelfth is the narrowest. The distance of the angle from the tuberosity increases gradually from above down.

The **first rib** is not twisted, and is so placed that its surfaces look nearly upwards and downwards. The head is small, and presents a single articular surface for the first dorsal vertebra. The neck is slender, and the angle coincides with the tuberosity. On the superior surface are two slight smooth depressions with an intervening rough mark, and a considerable rough surface behind. The rough surface marks the attachment of the scalenus medius muscle, the posterior depression the position of the subclavian artery, the anterior depression the subclavian vein ; and the intervening slight elevation, frequently terminating in a sharp spine on the inner edge—the *scalene tubercle*—indicates the attachment of the scalenus anticus muscle. There is no subcostal groove on the first rib.

The **second rib**, longer than the first, presents externally a prominent roughness which marks the attachment of the serratus magnus.

In the **eleventh** and **twelfth ribs** the articular facet on the head is single, and the tuberosity is represented only by a slight elevation or roughness, without an articular facet. The subcostal groove is faintly marked on the eleventh, and is absent, together with the angle, from the twelfth.

Varieties.—The number of the ribs is sometimes increased to thirteen on one or both sides. The supernumerary rib is usually short, and is most frequently formed in connection with the transverse process of the first lumbar vertebra, or occasionally with the seventh cervical ; in the latter case the additional rib has generally a double attachment, viz., to the body, and to the transverse process of the vertebra outside a vertebrarterial foramen (see fig. 23, 4, *r*, *r*, and 8, *co*). In rare instances the additional rib is associated with a thirteenth dorsal vertebra (see p. 13). The tenth rib frequently articulates only with one vertebra; and it may want the articular facet for the transverse process. The twelfth rib varies in length from 8 inches to less than an inch; complete suppression is very rare.

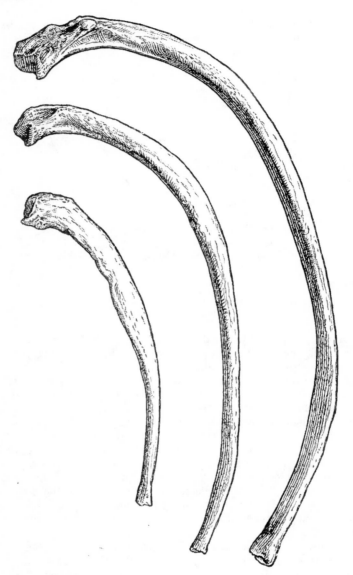

Fig. 28.—TENTH, ELEVENTH, AND TWELFTH RIBS OF THE RIGHT SIDE, FROM BELOW. (Drawn by D. Gunn.) ¾

The **costal cartilages** prolong the ribs towards the sternum. Their breadth diminishes gradually from the first to the last, while their length increases as far as the seventh, after which they become gradually shorter. Their line of direction varies considerably. The first descends a little, the second is horizontal, and all the rest, except the last two, ascend more and more from the rib towards the sternum as they are situated lower down. The external or costal extremity, convex and uneven, is implanted into and united with the end of the corresponding rib. The internal extremities of the cartilages of the true ribs (except the first, which is directly united to the sternum without articular cavity) are smaller than the external, and fit into the corresponding notches on the side of the sternum. Each of the cartilages of the first three false ribs becomes slender towards its extremity, and is attached to the lower border of that which is next above it. The eleventh and twelfth are pointed and unattached. The fifth, sixth, seventh, and eighth cartilages form a series of *inter-chondral articulations*, by means of a broad process sent down from the rounded angle of the one meeting a less salient projection from the upper border of the next.

Varieties.—The eighth costal cartilage not unfrequently articulates with the sternum. Occasionally the seventh costal cartilage fails to reach the mesosternum (owing to reduction of the latter), and meets its fellow in front of the ensiform process. The articulation between the fifth and sixth cartilages is sometimes wanting, and then one may be formed between the eighth and ninth.

THE THORAX AS A WHOLE.

The bony thorax is of a somewhat conical shape, flattened from before back, and much longer behind than in front. The posterior wall, formed by the dorsal

Fig. 29.—FRONT VIEW OF THE THORAX.

1, manubrium ; 2, is close to the place of union of the first costal cartilage ; 3, clavicular notch ; 4, body of the sternum ; 5, ensiform process ; 6, groove on the lower border of the ribs ; 7, the vertebral end of the ribs ; 8, neck ; 9, tuberosity ; 10, costal cartilage ; 12, first rib ; 13, its tuberosity ; 14, first dorsal vertebra ; 15, eleventh rib ; 16, twelfth rib.

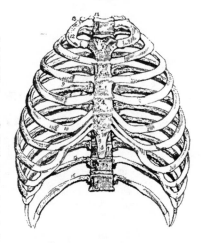

vertebræ and the ribs, is convex from above down, and, the ribs being directed backwards from the vertebræ as far as their angles, a broad furrow is produced on each side of the spines, which lodges the erector spinæ muscle. The anterior wall, formed by the sternum and costal cartilages, is only slightly convex, and is inclined at an angle of 20° to 25° with the vertical. In the condition of expiration the upper border of the sternum is opposite the disc between the second and third dorsal vertebræ, the junction of the manubrium and body opposite the middle of the fifth dorsal vertebra, and the xiphi-sternal articulation about opposite the interspace between the ninth and tenth dorsal vertebræ.

The sides are sloped outwards to about the ninth rib, are slightly convex from above down, and strongly arched from before back. The upper aperture is contracted, reniform, nearly plane, and much sloped downwards ; the lower is irregular ; the margin ascends on each side from the tenth rib to the xiphi-sternal articulation, and thus gives rise to the *subcostal angle*, in the centre of which the ensiform process projects. The form of the cavity corresponds generally to that of the exterior, but in the median plane the antero-posterior diameter is much reduced by the projection of the bodies of the vertebræ ; as a consequence of this and the backward direction of the hinder ends of the ribs, a deep hollow is formed on each side, into which the posterior portions of the lungs are received, and thus the weight of the body is thrown farther back and is more equally distributed around the vertebral column.

The intercostal spaces are eleven in number, and somewhat wider above than below, but varying with the elevation or depression of the ribs.

In man the transverse diameter of the thorax exceeds the antero-posterior, whereas in quadrupeds the dorso-ventral diameter is usually the greater. In the human fœtus also the sagittal diameter preponderates, and at the time of birth it is but little less than the coronal. In the female the thorax is relatively shorter, and more rounded than in the male.

OSSIFICATION OF THE STERNUM AND RIBS.

The ossification of the **sternum** begins about the sixth month, and usually by a single centre in the manubrium. The next centre appears at the seventh month in the upper

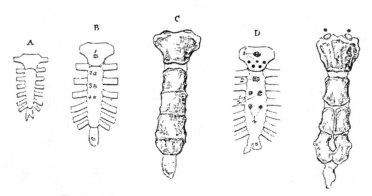

Fig. 30.—OSSIFICATION OF THE STERNUM. (R. Quain.)

A, the cartilaginous sternum before the middle of fœtal life.
B, the sternum at birth. 1, 2, 3, & 4, the nuclei for the manubrium and upper three pieces of the body.
C, the sternum soon after puberty, showing cartilage between the manubrium and body, and imperfect union of the first, second and third pieces of the body, while the third and fourth are united.
D, a sternum at birth with an unusual number of ossific centres, six in the manubrium, 1′, which is very uncommon; two pairs in the lower pieces of the body 3′ & 4′, which is not unusual; 2, the single centre of the first piece of the body.
E, Example of perforated sternum; this figure also shows two suprasternal bones, * *. C and E are reduced below the size of nature.

segment of the body, and ossification follows in the next two segments shortly before birth. In the lower segment ossification begins in the first year or later, in the xiphisternum usually not before the sixth year, and often much later. In the manubrium there are sometimes two

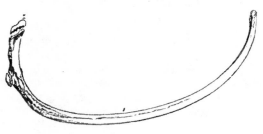

Fig. 31.—ONE OF THE MIDDLE RIBS AT ABOUT TWENTY YEARS OF AGE. (R. Quain.)

1, body; 2, epiphysis of the head; 3, that of the tuberosity.

centres of ossification, one above the other, and occasionally several are met with. In the upper segment of the body the centre is most commonly single, but in each of the following segments there are frequently two, placed one on each side of the middle line. The lower segments of the body unite together after puberty, but the upper one often remains separate till after the twenty-fifth year. The xiphisternum is united to the body in middle life; the manubrium and body are only exceptionally joined by bone. The bony parts formed from the lateral centres of the lower segments of the body not unfrequently remain separate for a considerable time, and occasionally, by defect of ossification or non-union across the middle line, leave the permanent median aperture referred to on p. 25.

The ossification of the **ribs** begins in cartilage posteriorly about the eighth or ninth week of foetal life, and extends rapidly forwards, so as to reach the permanent cartilage about the fourth month. After puberty the centres of two small epiphyses appear in the cartilage of the head and tuberosity. These become united with the main bone by the twenty-fifth year. The epiphysis of the tuberosity is wanting in the eleventh and twelfth.

In the adult the first costal cartilage usually becomes the seat of a superficial ossification, which may proceed so far as to form a complete sheath around it; and in advanced life the other cartilages are frequently more or less covered by bone, especially on their anterior surface. The tendency to bony deposit is as a rule stronger in the male than in the female, but the age at which the ossification begins, and the extent to which it proceeds, are subject to great variation. The cartilage itself is but seldom ossified.

III.—THE BONES OF THE HEAD.

The skull, comprising the bones of the head, is of a spheroidal figure, compressed on the sides, broader behind than before, and supported on the vertebral column. All its bones, with the exception of the lower jaw, are immoveably united together by lines and narrow surfaces, more or less uneven, termed *sutures*. The skull is divided by anatomists into two parts, the *cranium* and the *face*. The cranium protects the brain; the face surrounds the mouth and nasal passages, and completes with the cranium the orbits or cavities for the eyes. The cranium is composed of eight bones, viz.: the *occipital*, two *parietal*, the *frontal*, two *temporal*, the *sphenoid*, and the *ethmoid*. The face is composed of fourteen bones, of which twelve are in pairs, viz.: the *superior maxillary, malar, nasal, palate, lachrymal*, and *inferior turbinate bones*; and two single, viz.: the *vomer*, and the *inferior maxilla*. The *hyoid bone*, suspended by ligaments from the under surface of the cranium, may also be classed with the bones of the head.

THE OCCIPITAL BONE.

The **occipital bone** is situated at the lower and back part of the cranium. In general form it is flattened and lozenge-shaped, with the longest diameter directed from behind, forwards and downwards. It is much curved, so that one surface is concave and looks forwards and upwards, while the other is convex and looks backwards and downwards. At the lower and fore part it is pierced by a large oval aperture, the *occipital foramen* or *foramen magnum*, which forms the communication between the cranial cavity and the spinal canal. The portion of the bone behind the foramen is *tabular*, the narrower part in front forms a thick mass named *basilar process*, and the parts on the sides of the foramen, bearing the condyles or articulating processes by which the head is supported on the atlas, are the *condylar portions*.

The two superior borders are deeply serrated, and articulate with the parietal bones in the lambdoid suture. By its two inferior borders, which are uneven but not deeply serrated, it articulates with the mastoid and petrous portions of the temporal bone; while the extremity of its basilar process is united to the body of the sphenoid, in the young condition by cartilage, but after the age of twenty years by continuous osseous substance. The rhombic form generally given by the meeting of these borders at the four angles is not unfrequently somewhat changed to the octagonal, by the projection of subordinate obtuse angles between the upper and lateral, and between the lateral and lower angles.

The **tabular portion**, on its *posterior surface*, presents about the centre a prominence—the *external occipital protuberance*, from which the *superior curved line* arches outwards on each side towards the lateral angle of the bone, thus dividing the surface into two parts, an upper and a lower. The protuberance varies greatly in its development in different skulls; when well marked it can be readily felt beneath the skin at the back of the head. A little above the superior curved line there may generally be seen the less distinct *highest curved line*[1]; and between the two is a narrow semilunar area in which the bone is denser and smoother than either above or below. The part of the surface above this is regularly convex, and is covered by the hairy scalp. The lower part is more uneven: it is divided into two lateral portions by a median ridge called the *external occipital crest;* and each of these is

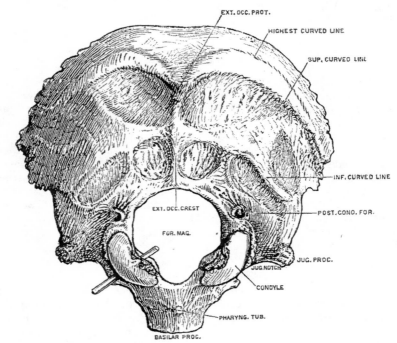

Fig. 32.—OCCIPITAL BONE, FROM BELOW. (Drawn by D. Gunn.) ¾

On the left side a probe is passed through the anterior condylar foramen.

again divided into an upper and a lower surface by the *inferior curved line*, which can be followed outwards to the extremity of the jugular process. The curved lines and the areas thus marked out give attachment to the numerous muscles of the back of the neck.

Along the highest curved line the epicranial aponeurosis is fixed to the bone. To the upper curved line are attached, internally the trapezius, and externally parts of the occipitalis, sterno-cleido-mastoid, and splenius capitis muscles. Below the upper line is a large impression for the complexus; and more externally, immediately above the outer part of the lower line, is a smaller mark where the obliquus capitis superior is inserted. The inferior curved line forms the upper limit of two impressions, the inner one for the rectus capitis posticus minor, and the outer one for the rectus posticus major. To the lower part of the protuberance and the external occipital crest the ligamentum nuchæ is attached.

The *deep surface* of the bone is marked by two smooth ridges which cross one another, one extending from the upper angle to the foramen magnum, and the other transversely between the two lateral angles; at the point of intersection of these

[1] F. Merkel, "Die Linea nuchæ suprema." Leipzig, 1871.

ridges is the *internal occipital protuberance*. Separated by the ridges are four hollows, the *superior* and *inferior occipital fossæ*, which lodge respectively the posterior cerebral and the cerebellar lobes. The superior part of the longitudinal and the transverse ridges are grooved in the course of the longitudinal and lateral venous sinuses respectively. The wider space where the longitudinal groove is continued into one of the lateral grooves (more frequently the right) by the side of the internal occipital protuberance lodges the torcular Herophili. The inferior part of the

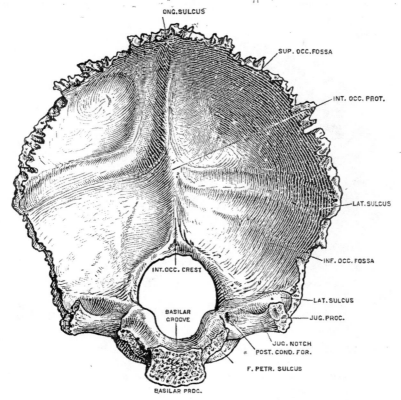

Fig. 33.—Occipital bone, from before. (Drawn by D. Gunn.) ¾

longitudinal ridge is sharp, and is named the *internal occipital crest*. The margins of the tabular portion are deeply serrated above the lateral angles for articulation with the parietal bones ; below that level, they unite with the mastoid portions of the temporal bones.

The **condylar portions** bear the articulating condyles on their lower part, close to the margin of the foramen magnum in its anterior half. The condyles are elliptical, and converge somewhat in front ; their surfaces are convex from behind forwards and from side to side, and somewhat everted. On the inner side of each is a rough impression for the attachment of the lateral odontoid ligament of the axis. Perforating the bone at the base of the condyle is the *anterior condylar foramen*, running from the interior of the cranium immediately above the foramen magnum outwards and forwards, and transmitting the hypoglossal nerve. Behind the condyle is a pit, *posterior condylar fossa*, containing usually the *posterior condylar foramen* ; this gives passage to a vein, but it varies greatly in size, and is often absent on one or both sides. Externally to the condyle is a projecting portion of bone known as the *jugular process ;* this lies over the transverse process of the atlas, and is continuous behind with the tabular part, while in front it has a free excavated margin, the *jugular notch,* which contributes, with a notch in the temporal bone, to form the jugular foramen. Its extremity presents a small irregular surface, which articulates with the jugular facet of the petrous part of the temporal bone by synchondrosis, passing into osseous union at about twenty-five years of age. The upper surface of the jugular process is marked by a deep groove for the lateral sinus

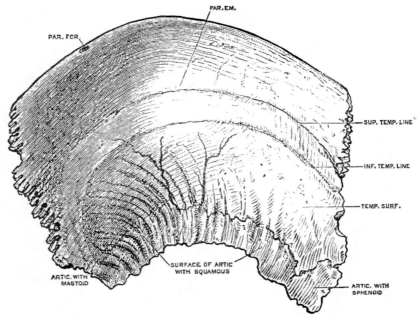

PAR.EM.

PAR. FOR.

SUP. TEMP. LINE

INF. TEMP. LINE

TEMP. SURF.

SURFACE OF ARTIC WITH SQUAMOUS

ARTIC. WITH MASTOID

ARTIC. WITH SPHENOID

Fig. 34.—RIGHT PARIETAL BONE : EXTERNAL SURFACE. (Drawn by D. Gunn.) ¾

leading to the jugular notch, and here is seen the inner opening of the posterior condylar foramen ; the under surface is rough for the insertion of the rectus capitis lateralis muscle.

The basilar process projects forwards and upwards in the middle of the base of the skull. It increases in thickness and diminishes in breadth towards its extremity. On the inferior surface in the mid-line is a small elevation, *pharyngeal tubercle,* for the attachment of the fibrous raphé of the pharynx, and on each side of this are impressions for the rectus capitis anticus major and minor muscles. Its superior surface presents a central smooth hollow, the *basilar groove,* which supports the medulla oblongata, and close to each lateral margin a shallow groove for the inferior petrosal sinus.

Varieties.—The portion of the bone above the superior curved lines, which represents the interparietal bone of lower animals, is in rare cases separated from the rest by a suture running transversely from one lateral angle to the other ; partial separation by lateral fissures is often met with (p. 73). The area between the superior and highest curved lines is occasionally very prominent, constituting the *torus occipitalis transversus.* In some bones there is a groove along the internal occipital crest for the occipital sinus. The anterior condylar foramen is not unfrequently double. An *intrajugular process* is often seen in the form of a small projection at the fore part of the jugular notch ; occasionally it is longer, and meets the petrous portion of the temporal bone (p. 71). A projection from the under aspect of the jugular process represents the *paramastoid process* of many mammals : it may be so long as to meet the transverse process of the atlas. In rare cases an additional articulation is formed between the basilar process and the anterior arch of the atlas, or the tip of the odontoid process.

THE PARIETAL BONE.

The **parietal bones** form a considerable part of the roof of the skull. They have the shape of quadrilateral plates, convex externally, concave internally. They are a little broader and thicker above than below ; the anterior inferior angle is the

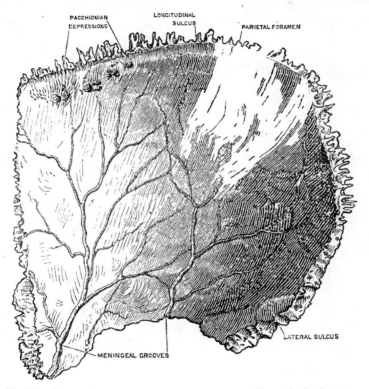

Fig. 35.—RIGHT PARIETAL BONE : INTERNAL SURFACE. (Drawn by D. Gunn.)

most projecting. They articulate with each other in the middle line above, with the frontal bone anteriorly, the occipital posteriorly, and the temporal and sphenoid below.

On the *outer surface*, near its middle, a more marked convexity exists, forming the *parietal eminence*. Passing through or close below this are the *superior* and *inferior temporal lines*, enclosing between them a narrow curved portion of the surface, which is usually smoother and more polished than the rest. Below the inferior temporal line is the *temporal surface*, somewhat flattened, forming part of the temporal fossa, and giving origin to the temporal muscle. The surface above the upper line is covered only by the scalp. Close to the upper border, and nearer to the posterior angle, is the small *parietal foramen*.

The *inner surface* is concave, the deepest part, opposite the parietal eminence, being known as the *parietal fossa ;* it is marked by shallow depressions corresponding with the convolutions of the brain, and by narrower furrows, branching upwards and backwards from the lower border, for the meningeal vessels. The largest of these grooves, running from the anterior inferior angle, is sometimes converted into canal for a short distance. A slight depression along the inner part of the superio border forms, with the one of the opposite side, the groove of the longitudinal sinus and a depression at the posterior inferior angle forms a small part of the groov of the lateral sinus. Near the upper border there are in most skulls, but particularl in those of old persons, small irregular pits, lodging the Pacchiónian bodies.

Borders.—The anterior, superior, and posterior borders are deeply serrated. Th inferior border presents in the greater part of its extent a sharp or squamous edge with a slightly fluted surface directed outwards, and overlapped at its anterio extremity by the great wing of the sphenoid, and behind that by the squamous par

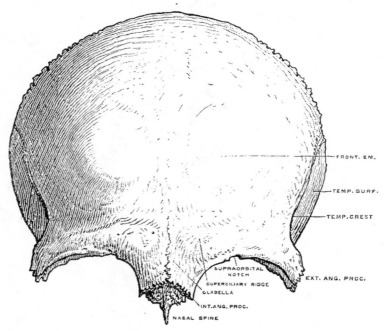

Fig. 36.—Frontal bone, from before. (Drawn by D. Gunn.) ¾

of the temporal bone ; its posterior part is serrated, and articulates with the mastoid portion of the temporal. The anterior border is slightly overlapped by the frontal bone above, but overlaps the edge of that bone below.

Varieties.—The parietal foramen varies greatly ; frequently it is absent on one or both sides ; in extreme cases it has been seen more than half an inch in diameter. As a rare occurrence the parietal bone is divided by a suture into an upper and a lower part. In senile bones considerable depressions of the outer surface are sometimes met with, the floor of which is not thicker than paper ; usually on both sides and symmetrical (Humphry, Med. Chir Trans., 1890).

THE FRONTAL BONE.

The **frontal bone**, arching upwards and backwards above the orbits, forms the fore part of the cranium ; it likewise presents inferiorly two thin horizontal laminæ. the *orbital plates*, which form the roofs of the orbits, and are separated by a median excavation, the *ethmoidal notch*. It articulates with twelve bones, viz., posteriorly with the parietals and sphenoid ; outside the orbits with the malars ; and between the orbits, from before backwards, with the nasal, superior maxillary, lachrymal, and ethmoid bones.

Anterior surface.—The part forming the greatest convexity of the forehead on each side is called the *frontal eminence.* It is separated by a slight depression below from the *superciliary ridge,* a curved elevation of varying prominence above the

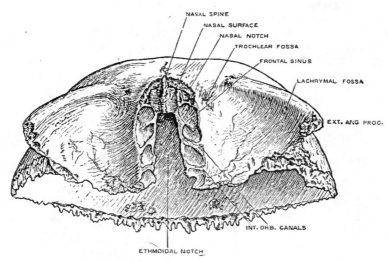

FIG. 37.—FRONTAL BONE, FROM BELOW. (Drawn by D. Gunn.) ¾

margin of the orbit. Between the superciliary ridges is the surface called *glabella.* The margin of the orbit, the *orbital arch,* is most defined towards its outer part ; it presents towards its inner third the *supraorbital notch,* sometimes a foramen, which transmits the supraorbital nerve and artery. The extremities of the orbital arch point downwards, and form the *internal* and *external angular processes :* the internal is but slightly marked ; it meets the lachrymal bone : the external is strong and projecting, and articulates with the malar bone. The *temporal crest* springs from the external angular process, and arches upwards and backwards to be continued into the temporal lines of the parietal bone : it separates the temporal from the frontal part of the outer surface of the bone.

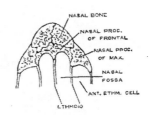

Fig. 38.—TRANSVERSE SECTION OF THE BRIDGE OF THE NOSE. (G. D. T.)

Inferior surface.—The *orbital surfaces* are somewhat triangular, their internal margins being parallel, while the external are directed backwards and inwards. Close to the external angular process is the *lachrymal fossa,* which lodges the lachrymal gland ; and close to the internal angular process is a small depression, *trochlear fossa,* where the pulley of the superior oblique muscle is attached. Between the orbits in front is the *nasal notch,* bounded by a narrow semilunar serrated surface which articulates with the upper ends of the nasal bones and the nasal processes of the superior maxillæ. Occupying the concavity of the notch is the *nasal process* (Henle), which projects beneath the nasal and maxillary bones, supporting the bridge of the nose. On the posterior aspect of the nasal process are a small grooved surface on each side, which enters into the formation of the roof of the nasal fossa, and a

median ridge, which is continued into a sharp process of variable length, the *nasa*
spine. The latter descends in the septum of the nose, between the crest of the nasa
bones in front and the vertical plate of the ethmoid behind.   Between th
ethmoidal notch and the inner margin of the orbital surface is an irregular are
occupied by depressions forming the roofs of cells in the ethmoid bone.   Traversin
this surface are two grooves, which complete, with the ethmoid, the *anterio*
and *posterior internal orbital canals* ; the anterior transmits the nasal nerve and th
anterior ethmoidal vessels ; the other, the posterior ethmoidal vessels.   Farthe
forward is the opening of the *frontal sinus*, a cavity which extends within the bon
for a variable distance behind the superciliary ridges.   Outside and behind th

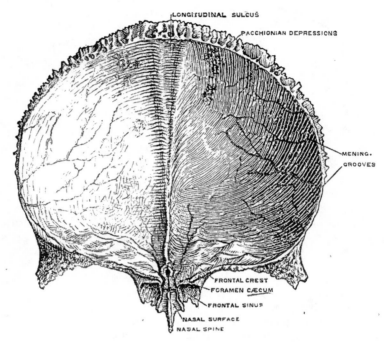

Fig. 39.—Frontal bone, from behind.   (Drawn by D. Gunn.)   ¾

orbital surface there is a large rough triangular area which articulates with the gre
wing of the sphenoid.
      Cerebral surface.—This surface forms a large concavity, except over the roo
of the orbits, which are convex.   Upon it are seen the impressions of the cerebr
convolutions, which, with the intervening ridges, are strongly marked over the orbi
A groove, the *frontal sulcus*, lodging the superior longitudinal sinus, descends from th
middle of the upper margin of the bone, and is succeeded by the *frontal crest*, a rid
which runs down nearly to the lower margin.   A small foramen, usually formed
part by the crista galli of the ethmoid, is situated at the base of the frontal cres
it is known as the *foramen cæcum*, being generally closed below, but it may transm
a minute vein from the nasal fossæ.   On each side small ramifying furrows, whi
lodge branches of the middle meningeal vessels, run inwards from the lateral marg
of the bone ; and at the upper part, in the neighbourhood of the longitudinal groov
are some depressions for Pacchionian bodies.   The upper and greater part
the edge encompassing the cerebral surface of the bone is serrated, and articulat

with the parietal bones in the coronal suture in the manner before described ; the lower transverse part is thin and uneven, and articulates with the greater and lesser wings of the sphenoid.

Varieties.—The trochlear fossa is often faintly marked or absent ; on the other hand there may be a small prominence, the *trochlear spine*, by the side of the depression (10 per cent., Merkel). The frontal bone is at times divided by a median *frontal* or *metopic suture*, the two parts of the infantile bone having failed to unite. This condition, which is termed *metopism*, was found by Anutschin to exist in 8·7 per cent. of European skulls, in 5·1 per cent. in Mongolian races, in 1·2 per cent. of Negro, and 1 per cent. of Australian skulls. A trace of the metopic suture is to be seen in nearly all adult frontal bones above the root of the nose (fig. 36).

THE TEMPORAL BONE.

The **temporal bone** takes part in the formation of the side and base of the skull, and contains in its interior the organ of hearing. It is usually described in three parts, viz., an expanded anterior and superior part, the *squamous* portion, including

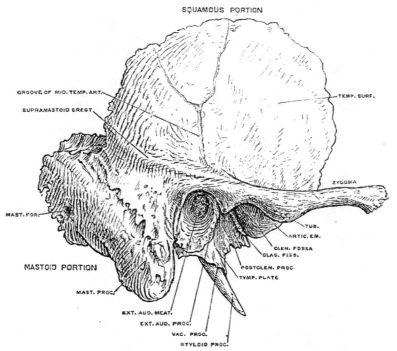

Fig. 40.—Right temporal bone : outer view. (Drawn by D. Gunn.)

the zygomatic process, a thicker posterior portion, the *mastoid*, and below and between these the *petrous* portion, a three-sided pyramid, exhibiting at its base externally the aperture of the ear, and projecting forwards and inwards into the base of the skull.

It articulates posteriorly and internally with the occipital bone, superiorly with the parietal, anteriorly with the sphenoid, by the zygomatic process with the malar, and by the glenoid cavity with the inferior maxillary bone.

The **squamous portion,** or squamo-zygomatic, extends forwards and upwards from its connection with the other portions, and is limited superiorly by an arched border which describes about two-thirds of a circle.

The *inner surface* is marked by cerebral impressions, and by meningeal grooves. At its upper border the outer table is prolonged considerably beyond the inner, forming a thin scale with the fluted surface looking inwards and overlapping the corresponding bevelled edge of the parietal bone. But in front, at its lower part, the border is thicker, looks forwards and inwards, is bevelled slightly on the outer side, and serrated for articulation with the great wing of the sphenoid.

The *outer surface* is in its greatest extent vertical, with a slight convexity, and

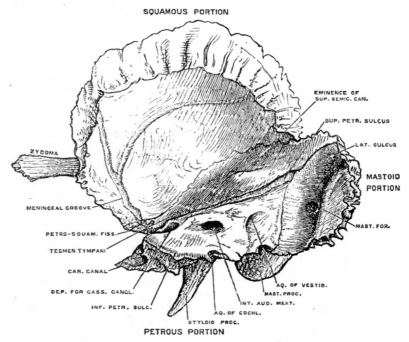

SQUAMOUS PORTION

EMINENCE OF
SUP. SEMIC. CAN.

SUP. PETR. SULCUS

LAT. SULCUS

ZYGOMA

MASTOID
PORTION

MENINGEAL GROOVE

PETRO-SQUAM. FISS.

TEGMEN TYMPANI

CAR. CANAL

DEP. FOR CASS. GANGL.

INF. PETR. SULC.

MAST. FOR.

AQ. OF VESTIB.

MAST. PROC.

INT. AUD. MEAT.

AQ. OF COCHL.

STYLOID PROC.

PETROUS PORTION

Fig. 41.—RIGHT TEMPORAL BONE : INNER VIEW.   (Drawn by D. Gunn.)

The bone is rotated slightly about a sagittal axis, the upper border being moved inwards.

forms part of the temporal fossa. Above the aperture of the ear it is marked by a small, nearly vertical furrow for the middle temporal artery. From the lowest part of this surface a long process, the *zygoma*, takes origin.

The *zygoma*, or zygomatic process, is connected with the lower and outer part of the squamous portion, and is of considerable breadth at its base, which projects outwards. It then turns forwards, becomes narrower, and is twisted on itself so as to present outer and inner surfaces and upper and lower borders. The superior margin is thinner, and prolonged farther forwards than the inferior. The extremity is serrated, and articulates with the malar bone. At its base the zygoma presents two roots : the *anterior*, continuous with the lower border, is a broad convex ridge, directed inwards on the under aspect of the bone : the *posterior*, also called the *supramastoid crest*, is prolonged from the upper border ; it passes backwards above the external auditory meatus, marking the line of division between the squamous and mastoid portions of the bone, and turning upwards posteriorly forms the boundary of the temporal fossa. At the place where the two roots diverge is a slight tubercle, which gives attachment to the external lateral ligament of the lower jaw. Between the two roots is the *glenoid fossa*, a considerable hollow, elongated from without inwards, and divided into two parts by the nearly transverse *fissure of Glaser*. The posterior part of the glenoid fossa is formed by the tympanic plate of the petrous division of the bone, is non-articular, and lodges a portion of the parotid gland : the anterior part of the fossa, together with the cylindrical elevation, *articular eminence*, formed by the anterior root of the zygoma in front of the hollow, is coated with cartilage, and forms the concavo-convex surface for articulation with the lower jaw ; the articular cavity is bounded behind by a small conical process which descends in front of the external auditory meatus, and is known as the *postglenoid process*. In front of the articular eminence, and separated from the temporal surface by a slight ridge, is a small triangular area which enters into the zygomatic fossa.

The **mastoid portion** is rough externally for the attachment of muscles, and is prolonged downwards behind the aperture of the ear into a nipple-shaped projection—the *mastoid process*. This process has on its inner side a deep groove, the *digastric fossa*, which gives attachment

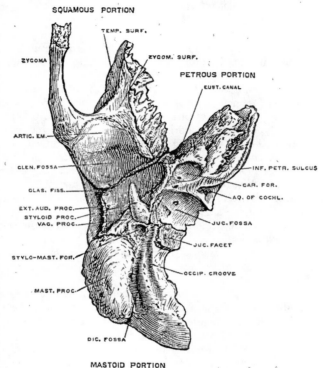

SQUAMOUS PORTION

TEMP. SURF.

ZYGOM. SURF.

ZYGOMA

PETROUS PORTION

EUST. CANAL

ARTIC. EM.

GLEN. FOSSA

INF. PETR. SULCUS

CAR. FOR.

GLAS. FISS.

AQ. OF COCHL.

EXT. AUD. PROC.

STYLOID PROC.

VAG. PROC.

JUG. FOSSA

JUG. FACET

STYLO-MAST. FOR.

OCCIP. GROOVE

MAST. PROC.

DIG. FOSSA

MASTOID PORTION

Fig. 42.—RIGHT TEMPORAL BONE, FROM BELOW. (Drawn by D. Gunn.)

to the digastric muscle ; and internal to that is the slight *occipital groove*, for the occipital artery. The internal surface of the mastoid portion is marked by a deep sigmoid depression, which is part of the groove of the lateral sinus. A passage for a vein, of very variable size, the *mastoid foramen*, usually pierces the bone near its posterior margin, and opens into the groove.

The **petrous portion,** so named from its hardness, contains the organ of hearing. It forms a three-sided pyramid, with its base directed outwards, one surface looking downwards, and the other two turned towards the interior of the skull.

Inferior surface, base, and apex.—At the base is the aperture of the ear. It forms a short canal, the *external auditory meatus*, directed inwards and a little forwards, narrower in the middle than at its extremities, and leading into the cavity of the *tympanum*, part of which is seen from the exterior in the macerated bone. The external orifice is bounded above by the posterior root of the zygoma, and in the remainder of its circumference chiefly by the *external auditory process*, a curved uneven border, to which the cartilage of the ear is attached. This process is the thickened outer extremity of the *tympanic plate*, a lamina one surface of which forms the anterior and inferior wall of the external auditory meatus and the tympanum, while the other looks towards the glenoid fossa. The upper margin of the tympanic plate sinks beneath the squamous, and forms the posterior boundary of the *fissure of Glaser;* while its lower margin descends as a sharp edge, the *vaginal process,* which partly surrounds the styloid process at its base. The *styloid process* is long and tapering, and is directed downwards and forwards. It is placed in front of the digastric fossa, and has immediately behind it the foramen which forms the outlet of the canal of the facial nerve, named *stylo-mastoid* from its position between the styloid and mastoid processes. Internal to the stylo-mastoid foramen is a small irregular surface, the *jugular facet,* which articulates by synchondrosis with the jugular process of the occipital bone. In front of this comes a smooth and deep depression, the *jugular fossa,* which forms with the jugular notch of the occipital bone the jugular foramen. In front of the jugular fossa is the *carotid foramen,* the inferior extremity of the carotid canal ; and internal to the carotid foramen is a rough, free surface which is continued into the inner extremity, or *apex* of the petrous bone. The *carotid canal* ascends at first perpendicularly, then turns horizontally forwards and inwards, and emerges at the apex, close to the anterior margin ; it transmits the internal carotid artery.

The *posterior surface* looks backwards and inwards, and forms part of the posterior fossa of the base of the skull. About the centre of this surface is a large orifice leading into a short canal which is directed outwards, the *internal auditory meatus.* This canal is terminated by a plate of bone named the *lamina cribrosa,* from the numerous minute apertures which it presents for the divisions of the auditory nerve, while in its upper and fore part is the beginning of the canal called *aqueduct of Fallopius,* which transmits the facial nerve. The aqueduct takes a somewhat circuitous course through the petrous bone, passing outwards and backwards over the labyrinth of the ear, and then downwards to terminate at the stylo-mastoid foramen.

The *anterior* or *upper surface* looks upwards and forwards, and forms part of the middle fossa of the base of the skull. A depression near the apex marks the position of the Gasserian ganglion. A narrow groove runs obliquely backwards and outwards to a foramen named the *hiatus Fallopii,* which leads to the aqueduct of Fallopius, and transmits the large superficial petrosal nerve. Farther back is a rounded eminence, indicating the situation of the superior semicircular canal.

The line of separation of this surface of the petrous from the internal surface of the squamous is marked by a narrow *petro-squamous fissure,* commencing anteriorly at the retiring angle between the two portions, and generally to be traced less distinctly to the posterior border of the bone. The portion of bone between this fissure externally and the eminence of the superior semicircular canal and the hiatus Fallopii internally is a thin lamina, often perforated, which roofs in the tympanum and the common canal of the Eustachian tube and tensor tympani muscle, and is known as the *tegmen tympani.*

The *superior border* is grooved for the superior petrosal sinus. The *anterior border* is very short, and forms at its junction with the squamous part an angle in which is situated the orifice of the *Eustachian canal,* the osseous portion of a tube of the same name, which leads from the pharynx to the tympanum ; and above this, partially separated from it by a thin lamella, the *cochleariform process,* is a small passage which lodges the tensor tympani muscle. The *posterior* or *inferior border* internal to the jugular fossa articulates with the basilar process of the occipital bone, and forms with that the groove for the inferior petrosal sinus.

Small foramina, &c.—The opening of the *aqueduct of the vestibule* is a narrow fissure, covered by a depressed scale of bone, and situated on the posterior surface of the petrous portion, about four lines outside the internal auditory meatus ; that of the *aqueduct of the cochlea* is a small foramen, beginning in a three-sided wider depression in the inferior margin, directly below the internal auditory meatus. In the plate between the jugular fossa and the carotid canal is the foramen by which the nerve of Jacobson passes to the tympanum. In the ascending part of the carotid canal is the minute foramen for the tympanic branch of the carotid plexus. In the jugular fossa are a groove and foramen for the auricular branch of the vagus nerve ; and parallel to the hiatus Fallopii, close to the canal for the tensor tympani muscle, are a groove and foramen for the small superficial petrosal nerve.

The so-called fissure of Glaser is in the inner portion of its extent a double cleft, the tympanic plate being here separated from the squamous division of the bone by a descending process of the tegmen tympani, which forms the greater part of the outer wall of the common canal of the tensor tympani and Eustachian tube. Between this process and the tympanic plate is a small orifice leading to the cavity of the tympanum, and lodging in the recent state the slender process of the malleus and the tympanic branch of the internal maxillary artery ; farther inwards is another small canal by which the chorda tympani nerve issues. The outer portion of the Glaserian fissure is entirely closed.

The fundus of the internal auditory meatus may be most conveniently studied in an infantile bone, where the canal is short and the apertures relatively wide. A horizontal ridge, named *crista falciformis*, runs from the anterior wall of the meatus across the lamina cribrosa, so as to separate a small superior from a large inferior fossa. At the bottom of the superior fossa is a collection of minute apertures giving passage to the filaments of the superior division of the auditory nerve, and constituting the *area cribrosa superior;* while the orifice of the aqueduct of Fallopius is placed on the anterior wall of the fossa. In the inferior fossa are seen— 1, the *area cribrosa media*, below the hinder part of the crest, for the nerve to the saccule ; 2, the *foramen singulare*, at

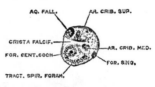

Fig. 43. — Semi-diagrammatic view of the fundus of the right internal auditory meatus of an infant. (G. D. T.) $\frac{2}{1}$

the lower and posterior part of the fossa, transmitting the nerve of the posterior semicircular canal ; and 3, the *tractus spiralis foraminulentus*, for the cochlear division of the auditory nerve, a series of minute holes beginning below the area cribrosa media, forming one turn and a half in a depression corresponding to the base of the cochlea, and ending at the *foramen centrale cochleæ*, the orifice of the central canal of the modiolus.

From the fore part of the superior border of the petrous portion, where there is often a small projection overhanging the upper end of the groove for the inferior petrosal sinus (fig. 69), a fibrous band, the *petro-sphenoidal ligament*, extends to the lateral margin of the dorsum sellæ of the sphenoid bone. This completes a foramen through which the inferior petrosal sinus and the sixth nerve pass. In rare cases the ligament is ossified.

The description of the Small Bones of the Ear, with the Tympanum and Internal Ear, will be found in the chapter on the Organs of the Senses in Vol. III.

THE SPHENOID BONE.

The **sphenoid bone** is placed across the base of the skull, near its middle. It enters into the formation of the cavity of the cranium, the orbits, and the nasal fossæ. It is of very irregular shape, and consists of a central part or *body*, a pair of lateral expansions called the *great wings*, a pair of smaller horizontal processes above, called the *small wings*, and a pair which project downwards, the *pterygoid processes*.

The sphenoid is articulated with all the seven other bones of the cranium and with five of those of the face, viz., posteriorly with the occipital and with the petrous portions of the temporals, anteriorly with the ethmoid, palate, frontal, and malars, laterally with the squamous portions of the temporals, the parietals, and frontal, and inferiorly with the vomer and palate bones ; sometimes it touches also the superior maxilla.

The **body** is hollowed out into two large cavities, the sphenoidal sinuses, separated by a thin median lamina, the *sphenoidal septum*, and opening anteriorly into the nasal fossæ by two rounded apertures. The *superior surface* presents in the middle a deep pit, the *pituitary fossa* or *sella turcica*, which lodges the pituitary body. In front of the fossa is an elevated portion of bone on a level with the optic foramina, the *olivary eminence*, on which the optic commissure rests in the slight *optic groove ;* and in front of this is a surface on a somewhat higher level, continuous with the superior surfaces of the small wings, and having a slight projection forwards of its anterior border, which articulates with the cribriform plate of the ethmoid, and is called the *ethmoidal spine*. Behind the pituitary fossa is a prominent lamella, the *dorsum sellæ*, the posterior surface of which is sloped upwards and forwards in continuation of the basilar groove of the occipital bone. The angles of this lamella project over the fossa, and are called the *posterior clinoid processes*. On each side of the body the surface descends obliquely to a considerably lower level than the fossa : it presents close to the margin of the fossa a superficial winding groove directed from behind forwards, marking the course of the internal carotid artery. Behind the commencement of the groove, and at the lower end of the lateral margin of the dorsum sellæ is a compressed projection, the *petrosal*

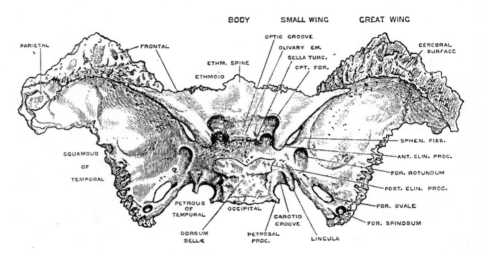

Fig. 44.—The sphenoid bone, from above. (Drawn by D. Gunn.)

process of the sphenoid, which fits against the apex of the petrous part of the temporal bone ; and opposite to this, on the outer side of the groove, the more slender tongue-like process termed *lingula sphenoidalis* projects backwards in the angle between the body and great wing.

The *posterior surface* is united to the basilar process of the occipital bone, in early life by cartilage, but in adult age by continuous bony substance.

The *anterior surface* is marked in the middle line by the *sphenoidal crest*, a thin projecting edge which descends from the ethmoidal spine, and articulates with the vertical plate of the ethmoid. The oblong surface on each side of the crest is divided into a mesial and a lateral part : the lateral part is irregularly excavated, and articulates with the lateral mass of the ethmoid and the orbital process of the palate bone : the mesial part is smooth and free, entering into the formation of the roof of the nasal fossa, and presenting near its upper end the rounded orifice of the sphenoidal sinus. The sphenoidal crest terminates below in the *rostrum*, a sharp vertical prominence which is continued back some distance on the *inferior surface*, and fits in between the alæ of the vomer. These last and the vaginal processes of the internal pterygoid plates cover the great part of the inferior surface of the body.

The **sphenoidal turbinate** or **spongy bones** (*cornua sphenoidalia, bones of Bertin*) form a considerable part of the anterior wall of the body of the sphenoid, bounding the foramen of each sinus. These bones have a triangular form, with the apex directed downwards and backwards, and are in the adult usually incorporated with the sphenoid, but as explained in the account of their development, were originally distinct. They are commonly united by earlier or stronger anchylosis with the ethmoid or palate bones, so as to come away, at least in part, with either of these in disarticulation of the skull, and thus lay open the sphenoidal sinuses. A small portion of these bones sometimes appears on the inner wall of the orbit, between the ethmoid, frontal, sphenoid, and palate bones (Cleland in Phil. Trans., 1862).

Each *lateral surface* of the body is for the most part occupied by the attachments of the two wings, but at the fore part, below the root of the small wing, there is a small free surface which bounds the sphenoidal fissure internally and forms the hindmost portion of the inner wall of the orbit (fig. 69, p. 66).

The **small** or **orbital wings** extend nearly horizontally outwards on a level with

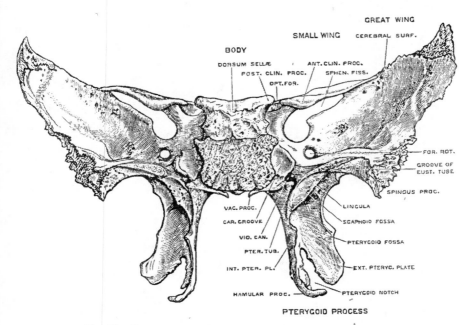

Fig. 45.—THE SPHENOID BONE, FROM BEHIND. (Drawn by D. Gunn.)

the fore part of the superior surface of the body. The extremity of each is slender and pointed, and comes very close to, but usually not into actual contact with, the great wing. The superior surface forms part of the anterior fossa of the base of the cranium; the inferior overhangs the sphenoidal fissure and the back of the orbit. The anterior border, thin and serrated, articulates with the orbital plate of the frontal bone. The posterior border is prominent and free, and forms the boundary between the anterior and middle cranial fossæ, terminating internally in a smooth rounded projection, the *anterior clinoid process*. Between the anterior clinoid process and the olivary eminence is a semicircular notch in which the carotid groove terminates; and in front of this is the optic foramen perforating the base of the wing.

The **great** or **temporal wings** project outwards and upwards from the sides of the body. The back part of each is placed horizontally, and occupies the angle between the petrous and squamous portions of the temporal bone; from its pointed extremity it sends downwards a short and sharp projection, the *spinous process*. The upper and fore part is vertical, and three-sided, lying between the cranial cavity the orbit, and the temporal fossa (fig. 66, p. 64). The *cerebral surface* of the great wing is concave, and forms part of the middle fossa of the base of the cranium. The *external surface* (temporo-zygomatic) is divided by a ridge, *infratemporal crest*, into an inferior part, which looks downwards into the zygomatic fossa, and an elongated superior part, looking outwards, which forms a part of the temporal fossa (fig. 68, p. 66). The *anterior surface* looks forwards and inwards, and consists of a quadri-lateral *orbital* portion, which forms the back part of the external wall of the orbit, and of a smaller inferior portion which overhangs the pterygoid process, looks into the spheno-maxillary fossa, and is perforated by the foramen rotundum. The *posterior border* in its mesial part bounds the foramen lacerum, in its lateral part articulates

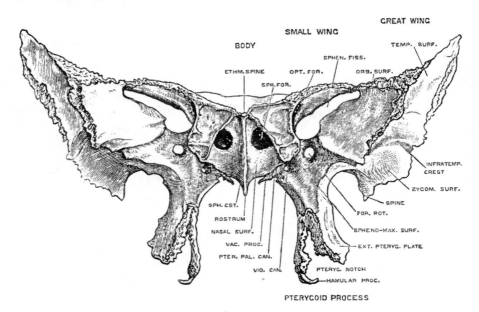

Fig. 46.—The sphenoid bone, from before. (Drawn by D. Gunn.)

with the petrous, and forms with that a groove on the under aspect for the carti-laginous part of the Eustachian tube. The *external margin* articulates with the squamous, and the extremity overlaps the anterior inferior angle of the parietal. In front of this comes a triangular surface, the sides of which are formed by the upper margins of the cerebral, orbital, and temporal surfaces respectively, for articulation with the frontal bone. The *anterior margin*, between the orbital and temporal surfaces, articulates with the malar bone ; and below this is a short horizontal free edge separating the zygomatic and spheno-maxillary surfaces. Above and internally the orbital and cerebral surfaces meet at the sharp border which forms the inferior boundary of the sphenoidal fissure, and which is frequently marked at its inner part by a small projection giving attachment to the lower head of the external rectus muscle of the eyeball.

The **pterygoid processes** project downwards and slightly forwards from the adjacent parts of the body and the great wings. Each consists of two plates united in front and diverging behind, so as to enclose between them the *pterygoid fossa*, in which the internal pterygoid muscle arises. The *external pterygoid plate*, broader than the internal, lies in a plane extending backwards and outwards ; its outer surface bounds the zygomatic fossa, and is impressed by the external pterygoid muscle. The *internal pterygoid plate* is longer and narrower than the external, and is prolonged below into the slender hook-like or *hamular process,* round which in a groove plays the tendon of the tensor palati muscle. Above, the internal plate turns inwards beneath the body, from which its extremity remains distinct as a slightly raised edge, known as the *vaginal process,* which articulates with the everted margin of the vomer ; externally to this it is marked by a small groove, which contributes with the palate bone to form the *pterygo-palatine canal.* Posteriorly, the internal pterygoid plate forms at its base a small blunt prominence, the *pterygoid tubercle,* to the inner side of and below the orifice of the Vidian canal ; between this and the pterygoid fossa is a slight depression, called the *navicular* or *scaphoid fossa,* occupied by the attachment of the tensor palati muscle ; and lower down, on the hinder margin of the plate, is a projection which supports the cartilage of the Eustachian tube. The interval between the lower ends of the pterygoid plates, *pterygoid notch,* is occupied by the pyramidal process of the palate bone.

Fissures and foramina.—Each lateral half of the bone presents a fissure, four foramina, and a canal. The *sphenoidal fissure* is the obliquely placed elongated interval between the great and small wings, closed externally by the frontal bone ; it opens into the orbit, and transmits the third, fourth, and sixth nerves, the ophthalmic division of the fifth nerve, and the ophthalmic veins. Above and to the inside of the sphenoidal fissure is the *optic foramen,* which is inclined outwards and forwards from the side of the olivary eminence, pierces the base of the small wing, and transmits the optic nerve and the ophthalmic artery. The *foramen rotundum* is directed forwards through the great wing, below the sphenoidal fissure ; it opens immediately below the level of the orbit, and transmits the superior maxillary nerve. The *foramen ovale* is large, and placed behind and a little external to the foramen rotundum, near the posterior margin of the great wing ; it is directed downwards, and transmits the inferior maxillary nerve and small meningeal artery. The *foramen spinosum* is a small foramen piercing the great wing, near its posterior angle, and transmits the large middle meningeal vessels.

The *Vidian* or *pterygoid canal* pierces the bone in the sagittal direction at the base of the internal pterygoid plate. It opens anteriorly into the spheno-maxillary fossa, and posteriorly into the foramen lacerum ; and through it pass the Vidian nerve and vessels.

Varieties.—A small tubercle is often seen on each side in front of the pituitary fossa, at the base of the olivary eminence, and immediately internal to the last part of the carotid groove ; this is known as the *middle clinoid process,* and is sometimes connected by a spiculum of bone to the anterior clinoid process, forming a *carotico-clinoid foramen.* Less frequently the anterior and posterior clinoid processes are similarly united. There are normally fibrous bands, *interclinoid ligaments,* beneath the dura mater in these situations (Gruber). In some cases a *superior petrosal process* projects from the lateral margin of the dorsum sellæ (fig. 69), giving attachment to the petro-sphenoidal ligament (p. 43). The outer pterygoid plate may be connected by a bridge of bone or of ligament (*pterygo-spinous*) with the spinous process. The foramen ovale and foramen spinosum are frequently incomplete at the posterior margin of the bone. The name of *foramen of Vesalius* is given to an aperture sometimes present on the inner side of the foramen ovale : it gives passage to an emissary vein. At the base of the spinous process, to the inner side of the foramen spinosum, there is occasionally a minute canal (*canaliculus innominatus*—Arnold) transmitting the small superficial petrosal nerve.

THE ETHMOID BONE.

The **ethmoid,** or sieve-like bone, projects downwards from between the orbital plates of the frontal bone, and enters into the formation of the cranium, the orbits, and the nasal fossæ. It is of a cuboid figure, and exceedingly light for its size, being composed of very thin plates of bone surrounding in great part irregular cells.

It consists of a central *vertical plate*; and of two *lateral masses*, united at their superior borders by the horizontal *cribriform plate*. It articulates with thirteen bones : the frontal, sphenoid and vomer, the nasal, lachrymal, superior maxillary, palate, and inferior turbinate bones.

The **vertical plate** lies in the median plane, and forms the upper third of the septum of the nose (fig. 71, p. 69). Its superior border appears in the cranial cavity, above the cribriform plate, in the form of a ridge, rising anteriorly into a thick process, the *crista galli*, to which the falx cerebri is attached. The posterior margin of the crista galli is thin and smooth. The anterior is in its lower part broadened out, and divided into two *alar processes*, which project laterally, and are rough in front for articulation with the frontal bone : between them there is usually a median groove completing the foramen cæcum. Below the level of the cribriform plate, the anterior border of the vertical plate slopes much forwards, and articulates with the nasal spine of the frontal and with the nasal bones. The inferior margin articulates in front, and sometimes even in its whole extent, with the septal cartilage of the nose : in its posterior half, in the adult, it is more or less completely joined by osseous union on one or both sides to the two plates of the vomer. The posterior margin is very thin, and is united to the crest of the

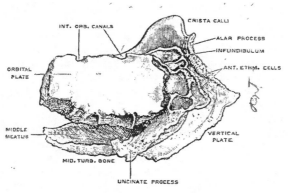

INT. ORB. CANALS

CRISTA GALLI

ALAR PROCESS

INFUNDIBULUM

ANT. ETHM. CELLS

ORBITAL PLATE

MIDDLE MEATUS

VERTICAL PLATE

MID. TURB. BONE

UNCINATE PROCESS

Fig. 47.—THE ETHMOID BONE, FROM THE RIGHT SIDE.
(Drawn by D. Gunn.)

sphenoid. This plate presents superiorly a number of grooves and minute canals, leading from the foramina of the cribriform plate, for the transmission of the olfactory nerves.

Each **lateral mass** or **labyrinth** encloses a number of spaces of irregular form, arranged in three sets, the *anterior, middle*, and *posterior ethmoidal cells*, which in the recent state are lined with prolongations of the mucous membrane of the nose. On its *external aspect* is a thin, smooth lamina, of an oblong form, the *orbital plate* or *os planum*, which closes in the middle and posterior ethmoidal cells, and forms a considerable part of the inner wall of the orbit (fig. 69, p. 66). The circumference of the orbital plate articulates in front with the lachrymal, behind with the sphenoid, above with the frontal, and below with the superior maxillary and palate bones, which often complete two or three ethmoidal cells. At the lower part of this aspect is a deep groove, which belongs to the *middle meatus of the nose*, and is limited below by the rolled margin of the *inferior turbinate process*. Anteriorly, the groove curves upwards, and is continued into a passage named the *infundibulum*, which leads through the fore part of the lateral mass into the frontal sinus. Into the horizontal part of the groove the middle ethmoidal cells open, and into the ascending part the anterior ethmoidal cells. In front of the orbital plate, the lateral mass extends forwards under cover of the lachrymal bone, which closes over the open anterior cells seen in the disarticulated ethmoid bone ; and from this part descends the *uncinate process*, a long thin lamina, which curves backwards, downwards and outwards in the groove of the middle meatus. In the complete skull the uncinate process lies across the orifice of the antrum of the superior maxilla, and forms part of the inner wall of that cavity ; at its extremity it articulates, by means of one or two irregular projections, with the ethmoidal process of the inferior turbinate bone (fig. 69, p. 66).

The *internal aspect* of each lateral mass forms part of the external wall of the nasal fossa, and consists of a thin, uneven lamella, connected above with the cribriform plate, and exhibiting a number of canals and grooves for branches of the olfactory nerve. It is divided at its back part by a channel, directed forwards from its posterior margin to about its middle. This is the *superior meatus of the nose*, and communicates with the posterior ethmoidal cells. The short, thin plate which overhangs this channel, is the *superior turbinate process* or *spongy bone*. Below the groove is another plate, somewhat thickened and rolled outwards inferiorly, the *inferior turbinate process* or *middle spongy bone*. This is free also in front and

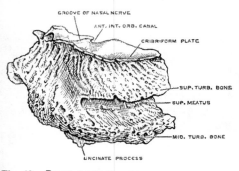
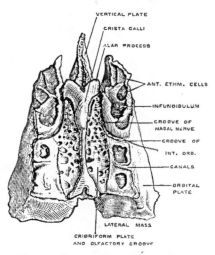

Fig. 48.—Right lateral mass of ethmoid bone : inner surface. (Drawn by D. Gunn.)

Fig. 49.—The ethmoid bone, from above. (Drawn by D. Gunn.)

behind, and, as has already been seen on the outer aspect, overhangs the *middle meatus of the nose.*

The superior margin of the lateral mass is covered, and the cells completed, by the projecting inner border of the orbital plate of the frontal bone ; two grooves are seen crossing it, which complete with the frontal bone the internal orbital canals. The inferior margin is formed by the rounded edge of the middle turbinate bone, and is free in the nasal fossa. The anterior extremity presents one or two open cells, which are closed by the nasal process of the superior maxilla ; and the posterior extremity fits against the front of the body of the sphenoid, where it is commonly anchylosed with the sphenoidal spongy bone.

The **cribriform plate** corresponds in size to the ethmoidal notch of the frontal bone, which it occupies. On each side of the crista galli it is depressed into the *olfactory groove* which lodges the olfactory bulb, and is pierced by numerous foramina for transmission of the filaments of the olfactory nerves. The foramina in the middle of the groove are few, and simple perforations ; the internal and external sets, more numerous, are the orifices of small canals which subdivide as they descend on the vertical plate and lateral mass. At the anterior extremity is a small fissure on each side of the crista galli, close to its base ; and externally to this is a notch or foramen, connected by a groove with the anterior internal orbital canal, which transmits the nasal branch of the ophthalmic nerve.

THE SUPERIOR MAXILLARY BONE.

The **upper jaw,** *superior maxilla,* is the principal bone of the face ; it supports all the teeth of the upper range, and takes part in the formation of the hard palate, the floor of the orbit, and the floor and lateral wall of the nasal cavity. It consists of a central part or *body,* and four processes. The body presents an external surface, which is again subdivided into anterior or *facial,* and posterior or *zygomatic* portions ; an internal or *nasal* surface, and a superior or *orbital* surface. The processes are—the *nasal* or *ascending,* projecting upwards from the fore part of the body, the *alveolar,* forming the lower border of the bone and containing the alveoli or sockets for the teeth, the *malar* on the outer aspect, separating the facial and

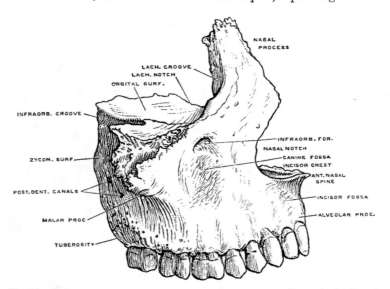

Fig. 50.—RIGHT SUPERIOR MAXILLARY BONE : OUTER VIEW. (Drawn by D. Gunn.)

zygomatic surfaces, and the *palate process,* projecting horizontally on the inner side. The body is farther excavated by a large sinus or *antrum,* which opens on the inner side into the nasal fossa. The superior maxillary bone articulates with its fellow, with the nasal, frontal, lachrymal, ethmoid, palate, malar, vomer, and inferior turbinate bones, and sometimes with the sphenoid.

The *facial surface* is marked at the lower part, where it is continuous with the outer surface of the alveolar process, by a series of eminences corresponding in position to the fangs of the teeth ; that of the canine is particularly prominent, and internal to this is a slight depression, the *incisor* or *myrtiform fossa ;* while between it and the malar process is the deeper *canine fossa.* Above the canine fossa, and close below the margin of the orbit, is the *infraorbital foramen,* by which the infraorbital nerve and artery issue. The inner margin of this surface is deeply excavated by the *nasal notch,* the sharp edge of which is produced below into the *anterior nasal spine.*

The *zygomatic surface* looks into the zygomatic and spheno-maxillary fossæ ; it is convex, and presents about the centre one, two or more apertures of the *posterior dental canals,* transmitting the vessels and nerves of that name ; the lower and posterior part of this surface is prominent and rough, and is distinguished as the *tuberosity.*

The *nasal surface* presents at the fore part a nearly horizontal ridge, the *inferior turbinate crest*, for articulation with the inferior turbinate bone ; below the crest is a smooth concave surface belonging to the inferior meatus of the nose ; and above the crest a smaller surface, extending on to the base of the nasal process, and bounding the atrium of the middle meatus. Behind the nasal process is seen the *lachrymal groove*, nearly vertical, but inclined slightly backwards and outwards, about half an inch in length, and leading into the inferior meatus ; the margins overhang the groove in front and behind, and the small interval left is closed by the lachrymal and inferior turbinate bones, thus completing the canal of the nasal duct. Behind the lachrymal groove is the large opening into the antrum ; and above this there are

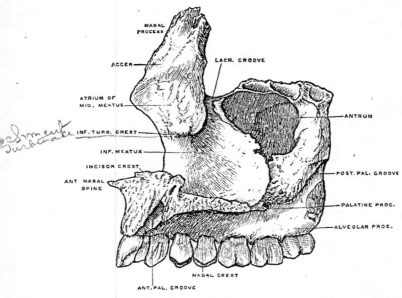

Fig. 51.—RIGHT SUPERIOR MAXILLARY BONE : INNER VIEW. (Drawn by D. Gunn.)

often one or two small hollows which complete the middle ethmoidal cells. Behind the opening of the antrum the surface is rough for articulation with the palate bone ; and traversing the lower part of this roughness is a smooth groove, directed downwards and forwards from the posterior margin, and completing with the palate bone the *posterior palatine* or *palato-maxillary canal.*

The *orbital surface* is triangular, flat, and smooth ; anteriorly it reaches the margin of the orbit for a short distance at the root of the nasal process ; externally it is bounded by the rough surface for the malar bone. The internal border presents, behind the nasal process, an excavation which receives the lachrymal bone, the *lachrymal notch*, and then a nearly straight margin for articulation with the ethmoid and palate bones. The posterior border is smooth, rounded and free, and bounds the spheno-maxillary fissure ; the *infraorbital groove* commences here, and leads forwards into the canal of the same name, which opens anteriorly by the infraorbital foramen. From the infraorbital are given off the *anterior* and *middle dental canals*, which run down in the substance of the facial portion of the bone, and convey the anterior and middle dental vessels and nerves.

The *nasal process*, slender and tapering, has an external surface, smooth and continuous with the facial surface of the body, and an internal surface, the hinder

E 2

part of which is irregular, and fits against the anterior extremity of the lateral mass of the ethmoid, completing the foremost cells of that bone ; in front of this the surface is free in the outer wall of the nasal fossa, and in its lower part is crossed by a smooth oblique ridge, called the *agger nasi*, which forms the upper boundary of the atrial surface of the body. The anterior border is rough, often grooved, for articulation with the nasal bone, and its summit is serrated for articulation with the frontal. Posteriorly, it presents a continuation of the *lachrymal groove*, which has already been seen on the nasal surface of the body, and which here lodges the lachrymal sac : the groove is bounded internally by a sharp linear edge, which articulates with the lachrymal bone, and externally by a smooth border which forms part of the orbital margin.

The *alveolar border* or *process*, thick and arched, is hollowed out into sockets or *alveoli*, corresponding in number, form, and depth to the roots of the teeth, which are fixed in them.

The *malar process* is thick and triangular : its anterior and posterior surfaces are continuous with the facial and zygomatic surfaces of the body ; the superior is

Fig. 52.—FRONT PART OF THE PALATE AND ALVEOLAR ARCH OF AN ADULT. ⅔

Showing the openings into the anterior palatine fossa. 1, 2, are placed on the palate plates of the superior maxillary bones ; 4, anterior palatine fossa, in which are seen four openings—the two lateral, with lines pointing to them from 1 and 2, are the incisor foramina ; the anterior and posterior, indicated by 3 and 4, are the foramina of Scarpa.

rough and grooved to support the malar bone. The inferior border runs down on the outer surface of the body in the form of a thick buttress opposite the first molar tooth.

The *palate process* or *plate*, along with that of the opposite side, forms about three-fourths of the hard palate. Its superior surface is smooth, and concave from side to side ; its inferior surface is vaulted and rough, and is marked laterally with grooves for nerves and vessels, which reach the palate through the posterior palatine canal. Its posterior extremity falls short of that of the alveolar arch and body of the bone, and articulates with the horizontal plate of the palate bone, which completes the hard palate. The mesial border, finely serrated, rises into a vertical ridge, which, with its fellow, constitutes the *nasal crest*—a grooved elevation receiving the lower margin of the vomer ; at the fore part this border rises suddenly to a considerable height, and the more elevated portion is distinguished as the *incisor crest ;* forwards this is prolonged into the anterior nasal spine, on its upper border rests the septal cartilage of the nose, and into the angle behind it the truncated anterior extremity of the vomer fits. Close by the side of the incisor crest on the upper surface of the palate plate is seen a foramen which is directed downwards to the mouth, but in the lower half becomes converted into a wider groove by deficiency of the inner wall. Thus, when the two bones are placed in apposition, one orifice of considerable size is formed on the palatal aspect, which divides above into right and left branches leading to the corresponding nasal fossæ ; the lower aperture is the *anterior palatine fossa* (or *canal*), the lateral branches are the *incisor foramina* (or *canals*) or *foramina of Stensen*. Farther, in the middle line are two other smaller foramina opening into the anterior palatine fossa, one before, the other behind ; these are the *foramina of Scarpa.*

The incisor foramina are placed between the two elements, the premaxilla and the maxilla proper, which make up the superior maxillary bone of human anatomy, and are the remains of a primitive communication between the nose and mouth. In the lower animals they are generally of large size, and open separately on the palate. A median anterior palatine fossa receiving the two incisor foramina is met with only in man and a few animals, and the deeply placed lamina which then bounds the incisor foramen on the inner side corresponds to the mesial palatine process of the premaxillary bone of other animals. The foramina of Scarpa lie in the suture between the laminæ referred to. They transmit the naso-palatine nerves, the nerve of the right side occupying, according to Scarpa, the posterior one, which is usually the larger, and that of the left side, the anterior; but they are very inconstant. (Scarpa, Annot. Anatom., lib. ii, cap. 5.)

The *maxillary sinus* or *antrum of Highmore* has an irregularly pyramidal form. Its walls are thin : the sides correspond to the facial, zygomatic and orbital surfaces of the body ; the base to the nasal surface ; and the apex extends into the malar process. The large aperture is closed to a considerable extent by the uncinate process of the ethmoid, the palate and inferior turbinate bones ; and in the fresh state it is reduced by the mucous membrane to a small orifice through which the cavity communicates with the middle meatus of the nose. Its extent below generally corresponds with that of the molar teeth, and the outer alveoli of one or more of these form prominences in its floor.

THE PALATE BONE.

The **palate bone** forms the back part of the hard palate and the lateral wall of the nose between the superior maxillary bone and the internal pterygoid plate. It consists of a *horizontal* and a *vertical plate* united at a right angle, and of three processes, viz., the *tuberosity* or *pyramidal process,* extending outwards and backwards from the junction of the horizontal and vertical plates, and the *orbital* and *sphenoidal processes,* surmounting the vertical plate.

The palate bone articulates with its fellow, and with the superior maxillary, ethmoid, sphenoid, vomer, and inferior turbinate bones.

The *horizontal* or *palate plate* presents a superior surface, concave and smooth, forming the back part of the floor of the nasal fossa, and an inferior surface, completing the vault of the hard palate, and marked near its posterior border by a transverse ridge to which some tendinous fibres of the tensor palati muscle are attached.

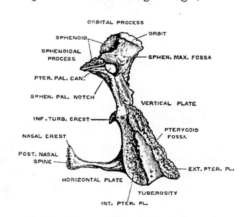

Fig. 53.—Right palate bone, from behind. (Drawn by D. Gunn.)

The anterior border articulates with the palate process of the superior maxilla ; the posterior is free, concave and sharp, giving attachment to the soft palate, and produced at its inner end into a sharp point, which with that of the other side forms the *posterior nasal* or *palatine spine ;* internally it articulates with its fellow by a thick serrated border, forming a continuation of the *nasal crest* of the superior maxillæ, and also supporting the vomer ; externally, at its junction with the vertical plate, it is grooved by the extremity of the posterior palatine canal.

The *vertical plate* is very thin. Its internal or nasal surface is divided into two parts, corresponding to the middle and inferior meatuses of the nose, by a nearly horizontal ridge, the *inferior turbinate crest,* which articulates with the inferior turbinate bone ; and at the upper end of the surface, crossing the roots of the two processes, is another less marked ridge, the *ethmoidal* or *superior turbinate crest*, which articulates with the middle turbinate bone. The external surface presents, nearer to the posterior border, a narrow smooth surface which forms the inner wall of the pterygomaxillary fissure, and leads down to a deep groove forming with the superior maxillary bone the *palato-maxillary* or *posterior palatine canal* for the transmission of the large palatine nerve and vessels ; in front of the groove the surface is applied against the superior maxillary bone, and overlaps the orifice of the antrum by a thin tongue-shaped projection, the *maxillary process*, which may attain a considerable size ; behind the groove it articulates inferiorly with the hinder border of the maxilla, superiorly with the inner surface of the pterygoid process.

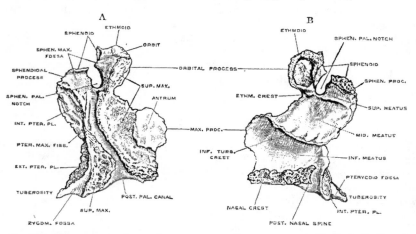

Fig. 54.—RIGHT PALATE BONE: A, OUTER VIEW; B, INNER VIEW. (Drawn by D. Gunn.)

The *pyramidal process* or *tuberosity* fits into the notch between the pterygoid plates. It presents posteriorly a triangular surface which is concave and smooth, and completes the pterygoid fossa : on each side of this is a narrow area, the internal deeply grooved, the external rough, for articulation with the anterior border of the corresponding pterygoid plate. Externally there is a small free surface which appears between the tuberosity of the superior maxillary bone and the pterygoid process in the zygomatic fossa (fig. 68). Inferiorly, close to its connection with the horizontal plate, are the orifices of the *posterior* and *external accessory palatine canals* which transmit the lesser palatine nerves ; the external is the smaller and less constant.

The *orbital process* surmounts the anterior margin of the vertical plate. It is somewhat pyramidal in shape, and has five surfaces, two of which, the superior and external, are free, and the rest articulated. The superior surface forms the posterior angle of the floor of the orbit (fig. 69), the external looks into the spheno-maxillary fossa, the anterior articulates with the maxillary, the internal with the ethmoid, and the posterior, which is small, articulates with the sphenoid. The process is generally hollow, and the cavity completes one of the posterior ethmoidal cells, or it may open behind into the sphenoidal sinus.

The *sphenoidal process* curves upwards and inwards from the posterior part of the vertical plate. Its superior surface is in contact with the body of the sphenoid and the base of the internal pterygoid plate, and is grooved for the completion of the pterygo-palatine canal ; its internal or under surface looks to the nasal fossa ; and at its base a third surface looks forwards and outwards into the spheno-maxillary fossa. Its inner extremity touches the ala of the vomer.

The two processes are separated by the deep *spheno-palatine notch*, which is closed above by the body of the sphenoid, and thus converted into the foramen of the same name. It leads from the spheno-maxillary fossa into the nasal cavity, and transmits the internal nerves from Meckel's ganglion and the nasal branch of the internal maxillary artery, with corresponding veins.

. **Varieties.**—The groove of the posterior palatine canal is sometimes closed in below, so that the opening on the palate is bounded solely by the palate bone. The spheno-palatine notch may also be converted into a foramen by the union of the upper ends of the sphenoidal and orbital processes ; or the foramen may be double from the development of an intermediate osseous bridge. The orbital process varies greatly in size ; its orbital surface is frequently enlarged from the union with the palate bone of a portion of bone ossifying from a separate centre, usually united with the ethmoid or sphenoid, and already described with the sphenoidal spongy bone (p. 45). The external accessory palatine canal is often wanting ; or it may be placed between the palate and superior maxillary bones.

THE VOMER.

The **vomer** is a thin median bone, irregularly quadrilateral, and placed vertically between the nasal fossæ. It articulates with the sphenoid, ethmoid, palate, and superior maxillary bones, and with the septal cartilage of the nose.

The surfaces are smooth and in the recent state covered by mucous membrane ; each is traversed by a faint groove running downwards and forwards, and conducting the naso-palatine nerve to the canal of Scarpa. The superior border is by far the thickest part of the bone, and is divided into two spreading *alæ*, which fit under the body of the sphenoid, receiving the rostrum into the groove between them ; the edge of each ala meets the vaginal process of the sphenoid and the sphenoidal

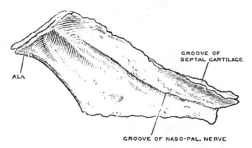

Fig. 55.—VOMER, FROM THE RIGHT SIDE. (Drawn by D. Gunn.)

process of the palate bone. The anterior border, sloping downwards and forwards, is grooved for the septal cartilage, and in the upper half is united by anchylosis on one or both sides with the perpendicular plate of the ethmoid.

The anterior extremity of the vomer forms a short vertical edge which fits in behind the incisor crest of the maxillaries, and from the upper end of which a process projects forwards in the groove of the crest, while from its lower end a point sometimes projects downwards between the incisor foramina. The inferior border articulates with the nasal crest of the maxillary and palate bones. The posterior border, thin, smooth, and unattached, separates the posterior nares.

THE MALAR BONE.

The **malar bone** forms the most prominent part of the cheek, and separates the orbit from the temporal fossa. It is quadrangular in shape, with the angles directed vertically and horizontally. The outer surface is convex, and presents a little below the centre a slight elevation called the *malar tuberosity* ; above this is the orifice of the malar canal. The inner surface is concave, and looks into the temporal and zygomatic fossæ. The upper angle, *frontal process*, is the most prominent, and is serrated at the extremity for articulation with the external angular process of the frontal bone. The border behind this, *temporal*, is sinuous and continuous with the upper edge of the zygoma. The posterior angle, *temporal process*, is serrated for articulation with the extremity of the zygoma, and the postero-inferior border, *masseteric*, thick and rough, completes the lower edge of the zygomatic arch. The antero-inferior border, *maxillary*, together with a rough triangular part of the inner surface, articulates with the malar process of the superior maxilla. The remaining border, *orbital*, is strongly excavated, smooth and rounded, and forms a great part of the orbital margin ; from this the *orbital process* projects backwards

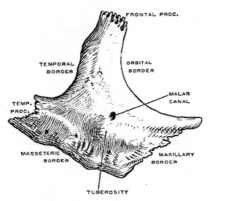

Fig. 56.—RIGHT MALAR BONE : OUTER VIEW.
(Drawn by D. Gunn.)

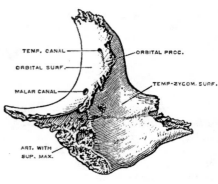

Fig. 57.—RIGHT MALAR BONE : INNER VIEW.
(Drawn by D. Gunn.)

and inwards, a triangular, curved plate, forming the fore part of the outer wall of the orbit, and articulating by its rough edge with the great wing of the sphenoid ; between the sphenoidal and maxillary articulations there is frequently a small free margin which closes the anterior extremity of the spheno-maxillary fissure. On the orbital surface of this process are seen two grooves leading to small canals, the *temporal*, opening on the temporal surface, and the *malar* leading to the facial surface of the bone ; they transmit the two divisions of the temporo-malar branch of the superior maxillary nerve.

Varieties.—The malar bone is rarely divided by a horizontal suture into an upper larger and a lower smaller part. The small canals are subject to great variation ; they may begin with a common opening on the orbital surface ; either may be double ; or one may fail entirely. There is often a well marked projection at the upper part of the temporal border, called the *marginal process ;* it gives attachment to a strong band of the temporal fascia In the numerous cases in which the malar bone does not enter into the formation of the spheno-maxillary fissure, it is excluded either by the articulation of the great wing of the sphenoid with the superior maxilla, or by a small Wormian bone.

THE NASAL BONE.

The **nasal bones** form the bridge of the nose. They are narrow and thick above, but gradually become wider and thinner below. The superior border of each is serrated, and articulates with the inner part of the nasal notch of the frontal bone : the inferior is free in the dried skull, but in the recent state it gives attachment to the lateral nasal cartilage ; it is generally marked by a small notch near its inner end. The external border is the longest, and articulates with the nasal process of the superior maxilla, being supported by small teeth which fit into depressions on the edge of that bone. The internal border is thicker above than below, and meets its fellow in the somewhat irregular internasal suture, which commonly deviates to one side at the upper end: the two bones form posteriorly a median crest, which rests from above down upon the nasal spine of the frontal bone, the vertical plate of the ethmoid (fig. 66), and the septal cartilage of the nose. The anterior or facial surface is concave from above down at its upper part, convex below, and presents a small vascular foramen. The posterior or nasal surface is rough for a short distance above, where it rests upon the nasal process of the frontal bone (fig. 38); in the rest of its extent it is concave and smooth, being lined by the

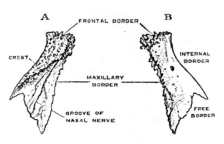

Fig. 58.—RIGHT NASAL BONE: A, INNER VIEW; B, OUTER VIEW. (Drawn by D. Gunn.)

mucous membrane of the nose; and a little external to its centre it is traversed by a small longitudinal groove which lodges the nasal nerve.

Varieties.—The form and dimensions of the nasal bones vary greatly in different individuals. They are in general relatively large and prominent in the white races, small and flat in the dark and yellow races. Fusion of the two bones, by obliteration of the internasal suture, is occasionally, though rarely, met with: this condition is usual in apes.

THE LACHRYMAL BONE.

The **lachrymal bone**, or *os unguis*, is a thin scale of bone placed at the anterior and inner part of the orbit (fig. 69). It articulates above with the frontal bone, behind with the orbital plate of the ethmoid, and in front with the nasal process of the superior maxilla.

The external surface is divided by a vertical ridge, the *lachrymal crest*, into two parts: the anterior is grooved, *lachrymal groove*, for the lachrymal sac, and this part is prolonged inferiorly beyond the orbit as the *descending process* which assists in bounding the canal of the nasal duct, and articulates with the inferior turbinate bone; the posterior part, broader, is flat, continuous with the orbital surface of the ethmoid, and is produced below into a hook-like projection, the *hamular process*, which curves forwards in the lachrymal notch of

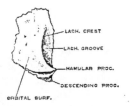

Fig. 59.—RIGHT LACHRYMAL BONE: OUTER VIEW. (Drawn by D. Gunn.)

the superior maxilla and bounds the orifice of the nasal duct on the outer side (fig. 66). The internal surface superiorly completes some anterior ethmoidal cells, and inferiorly looks into the middle meatus of the nose.

Varieties.—The lachrymal bone varies much in size: complete absence has been observed. It is sometimes perforated, or reticulate, or divided into two or more pieces. The hamular process is often very small, and sometimes wanting. On the other hand it may be unusually long, and reach the orbital margin, or even, in rare cases, extend slightly onto the face: this represents a more largely developed facial portion of the lachrymal bone in many mammals. Occasionally the place of the hamular process is taken by a separate ossicle. (Gegenbaur, Morph. Jahrb., vii.; Macalister, Proc. Roy. Soc., 1884.)

THE INFERIOR TURBINATE BONE.

The **inferior turbinate** or **spongy bone** is a slender lamina, attached by its upper margin along the lateral wall of the nose, and projecting into the nasal cavity, so as to divide the middle from the inferior meatus. It is slightly involuted, its convexity looking inwards, and its lower margin is free, somewhat thickened, and rolled upon itself. The attached margin articulates in its fore part with the inferior turbinate crest of the superior maxillary bone, then ascends abruptly, forming the *lachrymal process*, which completes the lachrymal canal and articulates with the

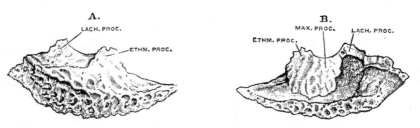

Fig. 60.—Right inferior turbinate bone : A, inner view ; B, outer view. (Drawn by D. Gunn.)

lachrymal bone ; behind this it is folded downwards in the *maxillary process*, forming part of the inner wall of the antrum below the entrance into that cavity (fig. 69) ; above and behind this, it presents a variable projection, the *ethmoidal process*, which articulates with the uncinate process of the ethmoid ; and posteriorly it is attached to the inferior turbinate crest of the palate bone. The posterior extremity is elongated, sharp and pointed ; the anterior flattened and broader.

This bone is marked by irregular pits, grooves and canals for vessels, which are directed for the most part longitudinally, but not, as the turbinal parts of the ethmoid are, with vertical grooves for the olfactory nerves.

THE INFERIOR MAXILLARY BONE.

The **lower jaw**, *inferior maxilla*, *mandible*, is the thickest and strongest bone of the face, and moves on the rest of the skull by means of a pair of condyles articulating with the glenoid fossæ of the temporal bones. It has the shape of an inverted arch bent forwards upon itself, and consists of a middle larger nearly horizontal part—the *body*, and of two ascending branches or *rami*.

The **body** is marked in the middle line in front by a faint vertical ridge, indicating the *symphysis* or place of union of the originally separate lateral parts : this expands below into the triangular elevation of the chin, or *mental protuberance*, the base of which is in well-marked bones slightly depressed in the centre, and prominent on each side, forming the *mental tubercle*. The superior or *alveolar* border of the body is hollowed out into sockets for the teeth. The inferior border or *base* is thick and rounded, and projects beyond the superior. On the outer surface, on each side of the symphysis, below the incisor teeth, is a shallow depression, the *incisor fossa* ; and more externally is the *mental foramen*, placed midway between the upper and lower borders, and under the interval between the two bicuspid teeth ; it is the anterior opening of the *dental canal*, and transmits the mental nerve and vessels. Close below the foramen is the somewhat indefinite *external oblique line*, running from the mental tubercle backwards and upwards to the anterior margin of the ramus. The deep surface is marked, on each side of the symphysis, along the inferior margin, by an oval depression, indicating the anterior attachment of the digastric muscle.

Above this are the *mental spines*, the *lower* being a small median ridge (often only a slight roughness), to which the genio-hyoid muscles are attached, and the *upper* a pair of more prominent tubercles, giving origin to the genio-glossi. Above the upper spines a small median foramen penetrates the bone, and continued upwards from this there is often to be seen a narrow groove marking the symphysis. Beginning below the mental spines, and passing backwards and upwards to the ramus, is the prominent *internal oblique line* or *mylo-hyoid ridge*, which gives origin to the mylo-hyoid muscle, and at its hinder end to a slip of the superior constrictor of the

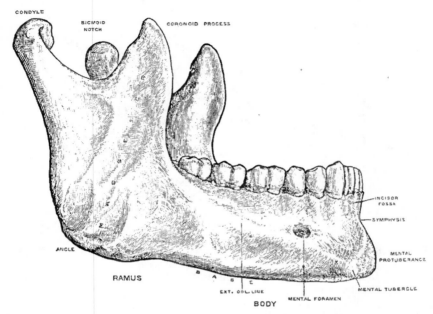

Fig. 61.—THE INFERIOR MAXILLARY BONE, FROM THE RIGHT SIDE. (Drawn by D. Gunn.)

pharynx. Above this line is a smooth depression for the sublingual gland, and more posteriorly beneath it another for the submaxillary gland.

The **ramus** is thinner than the body of the bone. Its posterior border in meeting the line of the base forms the *angle* of the jaw, which is more or less rounded off, and usually a little everted. The external surface is flat and impressed by the masseter ; towards the angle irregular oblique ridges mark the attachment of tendinous bundles of the muscle. The internal surface presents about its middle, and on a level with the crowns of the lower molar teeth, the *inferior dental foramen*, leading into the *dental canal*, which lodges the dental nerve and vessels. The inner margin of the foramen is sharp and prominent anteriorly, forming the *lingula*. Beginning at a notch behind the lingula is the *mylo-hyoid groove* (occasionally a canal for a short space), marking the passage of the mylo-hyoid nerve with companion vessels : it runs downwards and forwards to the body of the bone, and terminates below the hinder end of the mylo-hyoid ridge. Behind this, and reaching down to the angle, is a marked roughness for the internal pterygoid muscle.

The ramus is surmounted by two projections, the condyle and the coronoid process, which are separated by a deep excavation, the *sigmoid notch*. The *condyle* is continued upwards from the posterior part of the ramus. It is supported by a constricted portion, the *neck*, on the front of which is a depression for the insertion of the external pterygoid muscle. The condyle is a transversely elongated, convex articular process, the major axis of which is directed obliquely, so that if prolonged it would meet with that of its fellow near the anterior margin of the foramen

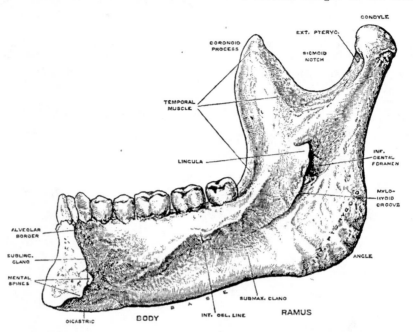

Fig. 62.—Right half of the inferior maxillary bone, inner view. (Drawn by D. Gunn.)

magnum. The coronoid process is continued upwards, with a slight inclination outwards, from the fore part of the ramus; it is beak-shaped, and compressed from side to side; by its sharp margins and somewhat roughened inner surface it gives insertion to the temporal muscle.

Fig. 63.—Transverse section of the lower jaw, passing through the socket of the last molar tooth. (G. D. T.)

The anterior border of the ramus is sharp and smooth, extending from the coronoid process to the posterior end of the external oblique line. To the inner side of this border is a grooved surface, which is bounded posteriorly by a ridge continued up from the internal oblique line to the mesial aspect of the coronoid process, and into which a part of the temporal muscle is inserted. At the lower end of the groove, and extending a short distance on the outer side of the alveolar process, there is sometimes to be seen a slight roughness marking the origin of the lower part of the buccinator muscle.

The lower jaw consists of a very thick shell of dense compact bone, enclosing cancellous tissue with slender trabeculæ. The dental canal lies close to the inner compact layer, and nearer to the lower than the upper border of the body: it has a thin wall of compact tissue, which becomes cribriform in the fore part of its extent. From the main passage small channels pass upwards to the sockets of the hinder teeth; and beyond the mental foramen a prolongation of the canal, with a less distinct wall, extends forwards, transmitting the nerves and vessels to the canine and incisor teeth.

The angle of the jaw is in the adult usually about 120°; in infancy it is as great as 140° or more; in strongly developed jaws it may be diminished to 110° or less; and in old and toothless jaws it is increased. These changes are connected with a variety of circumstances, among which may be noticed,—the development of the temporary and permanent teeth, the absorption of the alveolar arch after the loss of the teeth in advanced age, the elongation of the face and upper jaw towards adult life, and the varying state of development of the masseter muscles at different periods (see also p. 78).

THE HYOID BONE.

The **hyoid bone**, or *os linguæ*, is situated at the base of the tongue, and may be felt between the chin and the thyroid cartilage. It is shaped like the letter υ, and consists of a body and two pairs of cornua. It is suspended from the tips of the styloid processes of the temporal bones by a pair of slender bands, the *stylo-hyoid ligaments*, which in most animals form distinct bones.

The *body*, or central piece, is compressed from before backwards, and lies in a plane directed downwards and forwards. Its anterior surface is convex, and marked by a transverse ridge, with a slight median projection, on each side of which are depressions for muscular attachments. Its posterior surface is concave, and looks towards the epiglottis.

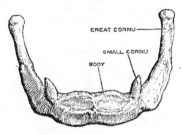

Fig. 64.—THE HYOID BONE, FROM ABOVE AND BEFORE. (Drawn by D. Gunn.)

The *great cornua* project backwards from the sides of the body. They are compressed from above down, are largest near their junction with the body, and terminate behind in slightly expanded and rounded extremities.

The *small cornua*, or *cornicula*, short and conical, project upwards and backwards from the places of junction of the body with the great cornua, and give attachment at their extremities to the stylo-hyoid ligaments. They are commonly in part, and not unfrequently entirely, cartilaginous.

The great cornua are connected to the body by synchondrosis, and after middle life usually by bony union; the small cornua by a synovial articulation which is seldom anchylosed. In some cases a synovial joint is formed also between the great cornu and body.

THE SKULL AS A WHOLE.

THE SUTURES.

With the exception of the lower jaw, which is moveably articulated with the temporal bone, the bones of the skull are closely fitted together by more or less uneven edges or surfaces, there being generally interposed only a small quantity of fibrous tissue, continuous with the periosteum; and to these lines of articulation the name *suture* is given. At the base of the cranium, however, in young subjects, the basilar process of the occipital is connected to the sphenoid, and the jugular process to the petrous, by a thin layer of cartilage; the articulation is therefore synchondrosis, and when adult age is reached it becomes converted into bony union.

The sutures are best named from the bones between which they lie, as, occipito-parietal, occipito-mastoid, fronto-ethmoidal, &c. Those around the parietal bones are the longest and most regular, and to them special names have been applied; thus, above, between the two parietal bones, is the *sagittal* or *interparietal suture;* posteriorly is the deeply serrated *lambdoid* or *occipito-parietal suture;* anteriorly is the *coronal* or *fronto-parietal suture*, most markedly serrated in the middle part of each lateral half, less so above where the frontal bone overlaps the parietal, and quite simple at the lower end where the parietal· overlaps the frontal ; inferiorly is the *temporo-parietal suture,* consisting of two parts, the *squamous suture,* arched in form, in which the squamous part of the temporal overlaps the parietal, and the *parieto-mastoid,* short and serrated ; while at the antero-inferior angle is the short *spheno-parietal suture,* about half an inch in length, absent only in rare cases when the frontal and temporal bones come into contact.

The cranial sutures are conveniently arranged in three groups, a *median longitudinal,* a *lateral longitudinal* and a *vertical transverse.* The first consists of the sagittal suture, which is continued in the infant, and frequently in the adult, by the frontal suture ; in the lateral longitudinal are included, on each side, the fronto-nasal, fronto-maxillary, fronto-lachrymal, fronto-ethmoidal, fronto-malar, fronto-sphenoidal, spheno-parietal, squamous, and parieto-mastoid sutures; the third comprises the coronal and spheno-squamous, the lambdoid and occipito-mastoid sutures ; and into this group also would fall the transverse articulations in the centre of the base between the ethmoid, sphenoid and occipital.

After adult life is reached the bones of the skull evince a disposition to unite, and many of the sutures thereby become closed ; but the period at which this commences, as also the order in which it proceeds, are subject to great variations, so that the condition of the sutures affords very little assistance in determining the precise age of a skull. The process commences generally about thirty years of age ; the union takes place first on the inner surface, and frequently the large sutures are quite obliterated internally while they are perfectly distinct on the external surface. The earliest points to close are commonly the part of the sagittal suture between the parietal forming, and the lower ends of the coronal suture ; the more dentated parts of these sutures and the lambdoid follow later. The squamous is very late in closing, and it is noteworthy that when the frontal suture fails to unite at the usual time it may remain unchanged even to very advanced age. (Dwight, "The Closure of the Cranial Sutures as a Sign of Age," Boston Med. and Surg. Journ., April, 1890.)

Wormian bones.—*Ossa triquetra, ossa suturarum.* These are irregular ossifications, found in many skulls, interposed between the cranial bones ; seldom in the face. They are of irregular form, with margins adapted to the character of the sutures in which they are situated, and usually of small size ; but they may exceed an inch in diameter. Their most frequent seat is in the occipito-parietal suture, where they sometimes occur in great numbers, more or less symmetrically arranged : in some cases one or several bones of considerable size occupy the place of the superior part of the occipital, more rarely of the antero-superior angles of the parietal bones : a scale-like ossification is often seen between the antero-inferior angle of the parietal and the great wing of the sphenoid (*epipteric bone,* Flower). They are much less frequent in the other sutures.

EXTERNAL SURFACE OF THE SKULL.

The external surface of the skull may be conveniently divided into superior, inferior, anterior, and lateral regions.

The **superior region,** extending from the supraorbital margins in front to the superior curved lines of the occipital bone behind, and bounded laterally by the temporal lines, is smooth and convex, covered only by the integument and by the muscular fibres and aponeurosis of the occipito-frontalis muscle. The skull as seen from above is of an oval form, broader in the parietal than the frontal region, flattened in front, and projecting somewhat in the middle behind. There is also a slight projection from the general curve at each of the frontal and parietal eminences.

The **anterior region** of the skull, below the forehead, presents the openings of the orbits, bounded by the frontal, malar, and superior maxillary bones ; and between the orbits, the bridge of the nose, formed by the nasal bones and ascending processes of the superior maxillaries. Below the nasal bones is the *anterior nasal aperture,* of an inverted heart-shape : its thin margin gives attachment to the nasal cartilages, and projects forwards in the middle line below as the anterior nasal spine. Below the nasal aperture are the incisor fossæ of the upper jaws ; below the orbits are the canine fossæ ; and external to the canine fossæ are the prominences of the cheeks, formed by the anterior inferior parts of the malar bones. The lower jaw completes the skeleton of the face. The foramina in this region, on each side, are the supra-orbital foramen or notch in the superior margin of the orbit, the infraorbital foramen below the inferior margin of the orbit, the mental foramen of the lower jaw, and the small malar canal of the malar bone.

The anterior nasal aperture is often markedly unsymmetrical, one half of the opening being broader and shorter, while on the other side it is narrower and more deeply excavated below. This is associated with a corresponding deviation of the cartilaginous part of the nose, which points towards the side on which the wider half of the aperture is placed. (H. Welcker, "Die Asymmetrien der Nase und des Nasenskeletes," Stuttgart, 1882.)

The **orbits** are pyramidal fossæ, irregularly quadrilateral, with their bases directed forwards and slightly outwards, their inner walls being nearly parallel, and

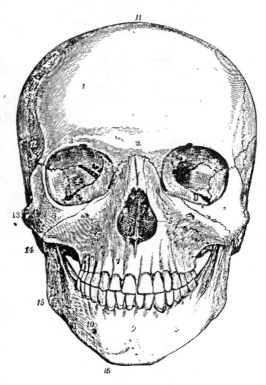

Fig. 65.—FRONT VIEW OF MALE SKULL AT ABOUT TWENTY YEARS. (Allen Thomson.) ½

1, frontal eminence; 2, glabella, between the superciliary ridges, and above the transverse suture of union with the nasal and superior maxillary bones ; 3, orbital arch near the supraorbital notch ; 4, orbital surface of great wing of sphenoid, between the sphenoidal and the spheno-maxillary fissures ; 5, anterior nasal aperture, within which are seen in shadow the vomer and the turbinate bones ; 6, superior maxillary bone at the canine fossa—above the figure is the infra-orbital foramen ; 7, incisor fossa ; 8, malar bone ; 9, symphysis of lower jaw ; 10, mental foramen ; 11, vertex, near the coronal suture ; 12, temporal fossa ; 13, zygoma ; 14, mastoid process ; 15, angle of the jaw ; 16, mental protuberance. In this skull there are fourteen teeth in each jaw, the wisdom teeth not having yet appeared.

their outer walls diverging so as to be nearly at right angles to each other. The roof of each orbit is formed by the orbital plate of the frontal and the small wing of the sphenoid ; the floor (fig. 66) by the malar and superior maxillary bones, and by the small orbital surface of the palate bone at the back part ; the inner wall (fig. 69) by the nasal process of the superior maxilla, the lachrymal, the ethmoid and body of the sphenoid ; and the outer wall by the orbital surfaces of the malar bone and great wing of the sphenoid. The *sphenoidal fissure* (foramen lacerum orbitale) at its inner extremity occupies the apex of the orbit, while its outer and narrower part lies between the roof and the external wall. The optic foramen is internal and superior to the sphenoidal fissure. In the angle between the external wall and the floor is the *spheno-maxillary fissure*, bounded by the sphenoid, palate, superior maxillary, and malar bones, and leading into the spheno-maxillary fossa at its back part, into the zygomatic fossa at its fore part. Passing forwards from the margin of the spheno-maxillary fissure is the commencement of the infraorbital canal, grooving the posterior part of the floor of the orbit. On the inner wall in front is the *lachrymal groove*, formed by the superior maxillary and lachrymal bones, and leading into the nasal duct ; farther back, between the ethmoid and frontal bones, are the *anterior* and *posterior internal orbital canals ;* on the roof, at its anterior margin, is the supraorbital foramen or notch ; within the external angular process is the fossa for the lachrymal gland ; and in the outer wall are the temporal and malar canals of the malar bone and one or two other minute foramina.

The **lateral region** of the skull presents in succession from behind-forwards the mastoid process, the external auditory meatus, the glenoid fossa, with the condyle

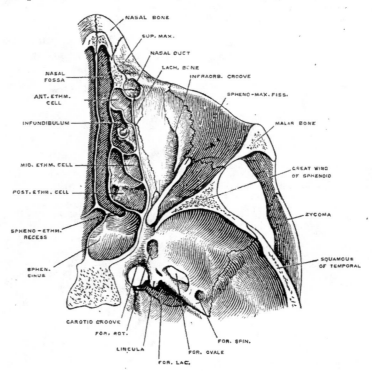

Fig. 66.—Fore part of a horizontal section of the skull, passing through the centre of the orbit.   (G. D. T.)

The right half of the lower portion is represented.

of the lower jaw, the *zygomatic arch,* formed by the zygomatic process of the temporal bone and the posterior part of the malar, and internal to this the coronoid process of the lower jaw.   Above the zygomatic arch is the temporal fossa, below is the zygomatic fossa, the two being separated by the infratemporal crest on the great wing of the sphenoid (fig. 68).

The **temporal fossa** is occupied by the temporal muscle, and the squamous part of the temporal, the parietal, frontal, sphenoid and malar bones take part in its formation.   It is bounded above by the temporal crest of the frontal bone and the lower temporal line of the parietal.   The latter turns down posteriorly to join the supramastoid crest of the temporal bone, which in front is continued into the upper edge of the zygomatic arch.   Along this line of bone is attached the temporal fascia, which in the complete state roofs in the temporal fossa.

The **zygomatic** or **infratemporal fossa** (fig. 68) is an irregular hollow, in part covered by the ramus of the lower jaw.   Its wall is formed internally by the external pterygoid plate; superiorly by the lower part of the great wing of the sphenoid, in which are seen the foramen ovale and foramen spinosum, and by a small part of the squamous of the temporal; and anteriorly by the zygomatic surface of the superior maxilla, presenting the orifices of the posterior dental canals, together with the lower part of the malar bone. Inferiorly, the external pterygoid plate approaches closely the superior maxillary bone, but the two are usually prevented from meeting by a thin portion of the pyramidal process of the palate bone; superiorly, they are separated by the *pterygo-maxillary fissure*, a vertical slit leading above into the spheno-

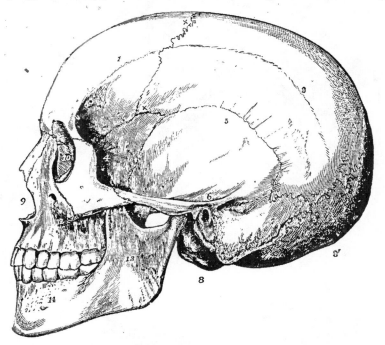

Fig. 67.—LATERAL VIEW OF THE SKULL REPRESENTED IN FIGURE 65. (Allen Thomson.) ½

1, frontal bone; 2, parietal bone at the upper temporal line; × ×, coronal suture; 3, on the occipital bone at the lower end of the lambdoid suture, near its meeting with the occipito-mastoid and parieto-mastoid sutures; 3', external occipital protuberance; 4, great wing of sphenoid; 5, squamous part of temporal; 6, the same at the root of the zygoma, immediately over the external auditory meatus; 7, mastoid portion of temporal, at the front of which is the mastoid process; 8, left condyle of occipital bone; 9, anterior nasal aperture; 10, on the lachrymal bone in the inner wall of the orbit; 11, malar bone, near its junction with the zygoma; 12, superior maxillary bone behind the canine fossa; 13, ramus of the lower jaw; 14, body of the lower jaw, near the mental foramen.

maxillary fossa, and closed internally by the vertical plate of the palate bone. At the upper part of the zygomatic fossa the horizontal spheno-maxillary fissure leads into the orbit.

The **spheno-maxillary fossa** is the space which lies in the angle between the pterygo-maxillary and the spheno-maxillary fissures. It is bounded behind by the pterygoid process and the lower part of the anterior surface of the great wing of the sphenoid bone; in front by the superior maxillary bone; and internally by the vertical plate of the palate bone with its orbital and sphenoidal processes. Into this narrow space five foramina open, viz., on the posterior wall, the foramen rotundum, the Vidian canal, and, between the sphenoidal process of the palate bone and the root of the internal pterygoid plate, the pterygo-palatine canal; on the inner wall, the

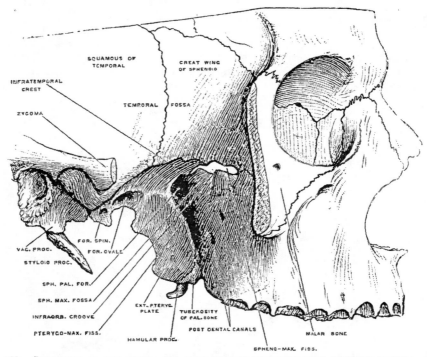

Fig. 68.—SIDE VIEW OF THE LOWER AND FORE PART OF THE SKULL, THE INFERIOR MAXILLA AND
ZYGOMATIC ARCH BEING REMOVED, TO SHOW THE ZYGOMATIC FOSSA.   (G. D. T.)

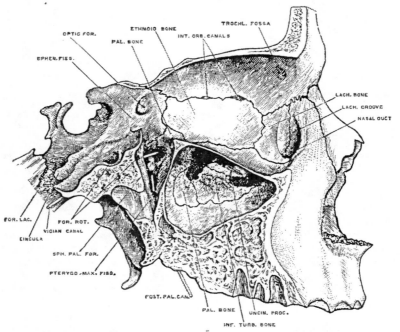

Fig. 69.—SAGITTAL SECTION OF THE FACIAL PORTION OF THE SKULL.   (G. D. T.)

The section passes through the right orbit a little internal to the centre, and opens up the antrum
and spheno-maxillary fossa.

spheno-palatine foramen formed by the palate bone and the sphenoid, and opening into the nasal cavity ; and inferiorly, the posterior palatine or palato-maxillary canal, which leads down to the roof of the mouth between the palate and superior maxillary bones.

The **external base of the skull**, excluding the lower jaw, is divisible into three parts, anterior, middle, and posterior.

The **anterior division** consists of the palate and the alveolar arch. It is traversed longitudinally by a median suture, and transversely by that between the maxillary and palate bones. Anteriorly, in the middle line, is the anterior palatine

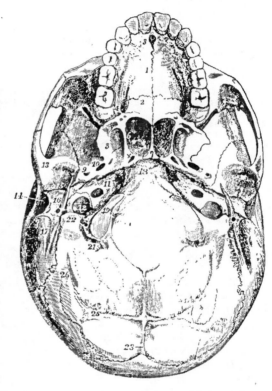

Fig. 70.—EXTERNAL BASE OF THE SKULL SHOWN IN FIGURE 65. (Allen Thomson.) ½

1, palate plate of the superior maxillary bone ; 2, palate plate of the palate bone ; 3, anterior palatine fossa ; 4, is placed outside the posterior palatine canal, inside the tuberosity of the superior maxilla, and in front of the smaller posterior palatine canals ; 5, inner surface of the external pterygoid plate ; 6, is placed within the posterior opening of the right nasal fossa on the internal pterygoid plate; 7, vomer ; ×, posterior opening of the pterygo-palatine canal in front of the foramen lacerum ; 8, spheno-maxillary fissure leading into the orbit ; 9, foramen spinosum ; 10, foramen ovale ; 11, placed on the apex of the petrous bone, between the foramen lacerum and the inferior opening of the carotid canal ; 12, jugular foramen ; 13, articular eminence of the temporal bone ; 14, external auditory meatus ; 15, glenoid fossa in front of the fissure of Glaser ; 16, tympanic plate or posterior part of the glenoid fossa, close to the styloid process, behind which is seen the stylo-mastoid foramen ; 17, mastoid process, and to its inside the digastric and occipital grooves ; 18, basilar process of the occipital bone, and in front the mark of the still incomplete union with the body of the sphenoid bone ; 19, condyle of the occipital bone ; 20, is placed in the foramen magnum, and points to the inner opening of the anterior condylar foramen ; 21, posterior condylar foramen ; 22, jugular process of the occipital bone ; 23, external occipital crest running down from the protuberance ; 24, superior curved line of the occipital bone ; 25, 26, inferior curved line.

fossa, with the four foramina opening into it (p. 52) ; posteriorly, on each side, at the base of the alveolar arch, is the opening of the posterior palatine canal, from which the palatine groove, lodging the large palatine nerve and vessels, runs forwards ; and farther back, on the under aspect of the tuberosity of the palate bone, are the apertures of the posterior and external small palatine canals. The palate is surrounded in front and on the sides by the alveolar arch bearing the teeth of the upper jaw.

The **middle division** extends back to the front of the foramen magnum. Its central portion has been called the *guttural fossa*. In the middle line is the basilar process of the occipital bone, and in front of that the body of the sphenoid, covered anteriorly by the alæ of the vomer. On each side, the petrous portion of the temporal bone reaches as far forwards as the extremity of the basilar process ; and between the petrous and squamous portions is the back part of the great wing of the sphenoid bone. Between this division of the base of the skull and the palate are the *posterior nares*, separated by the vomer, and bounded above by the body of the sphenoid bone, below by the horizontal plates of the palate bones, and laterally by the internal pterygoid plates. On each side of the posterior nares is the pterygoid fossa, completed below by the tuberosity of the palate bone ; and a line from the external pterygoid plate to the spine of the sphenoid forms the division between this region and the zygomatic fossa. Immediately behind or internal to this line is the groove for the cartilaginous part of the Eustachian tube, formed by the margins of the great wing of the sphenoid and the petrous, and leading to the osseous part of the tube in the temporal bone. Between the apex of the petrous, the basilar process, and the sphenoid is the foramen lacerum ; in a line proceeding backwards and outwards from this are the free surface of the petrous, the lower orifice of the carotid canal, the vaginal and styloid processes, and the stylo-mastoid foramen ; while internal to these are the jugular and anterior condylar foramina.

Between the basilar process of the occipital bone and the petrous portion of the temporal is an irregular cleft, extending from the foramen lacerum backwards and outwards to the jugular foramen, and called the *petro-basilar fissure*. This interval, together with the lower part of the foramen lacerum, is filled in the recent state by fibrous tissue which often contains one or two small Wormian ossicles. In front of the petrous portion, at the bottom of the groove of the Eustachian tube, is the *petro-sphenoidal fissure*, also continued outwards from the foramen lacerum.

The **posterior division** presents on each side of the foramen magnum, from within outwards, the occipital condyle, the under surface of the jugular process, the occipital groove of the temporal bone, the digastric fossa, and the mastoid process. Behind the foramen magnum is the tabular part of the occipital bone, with its ridges and muscular impressions.

THE INTERIOR OF THE CRANIUM.

The wall of the cranium consists of two layers of compact bony substance, the *outer* and *inner tables,* and an intervening cancellated substance, called *diploe.* The inner or *vitreous* table has a smooth, close-grained, shining appearance, is hard and brittle, and presents irregular digitate impressions corresponding to the convolutions of the cerebrum. The thickness of the skull-cap or *calvaria* is fairly uniform, and generally ranges from one-sixth to one-fourth of an inch : it is somewhat increased along the middle line, especially in front and behind, and diminishes below on each side, in the temporal fossa. The base of the skull varies greatly in this respect: the thickest parts are the basilar process, the petrous and mastoid portions of the temporal bones, and the occipital bone at the protuberances and ridges. The thinnest portions of the cranial wall are the cribriform plate of the ethmoid and the orbital plates of the frontal bone, in both of which the diploe is absent ; the bone is also thin and compact in the middle part of the inferior occipital fossæ, and in the lower part of the squama and the glenoid fossa of the temporal.

The upper part of the cranial cavity is enclosed by a single vaulted dome, formed by the frontal, parietal, and occipital bones. This is marked on its internal surface by the groove for the superior longitudinal sinus, by shallow cerebral impressions, by small ramified meningeal grooves, and by Pacchionian fossæ of varying depth. The only apertures in the roof of the skull are the inconstant parietal foramina, which open by the side of the longitudinal sulcus posteriorly ; they give passage to emissary veins, and occasionally a branch of the occipital artery.

The **internal base of the skull** is divided into three fossæ, named anterior, middle, and posterior.

The **anterior fossa**, formed by the orbital plates of the frontal bone, the cribriform plate of the ethmoid, and the small wings and part of the body of the sphenoid, supports the frontal lobes of the cerebrum. It is convex laterally above the orbits, but sinks into a hollow over the cribriform plate of the ethmoid, in the middle line of which the crista galli stands up, separating the deep olfactory grooves for the reception of the olfactory bulbs. In front of the crista galli is the foramen

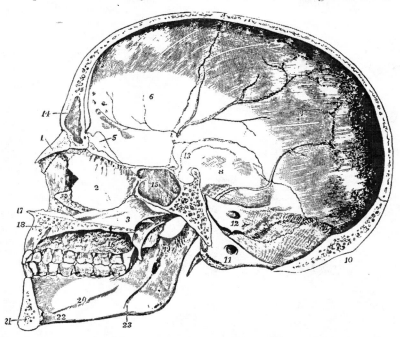

Fig. 71.—Sagittal section of the adult skull a little to the left of the median plane. (Allen Thomson.) ½

1, nasal bone ; 2, perpendicular plate of the ethmoid with olfactory foramina and grooves at its upper part ; 3, vomer ; 4, right superior maxillary bone, forming part of the wall of the right nasal fossa ; below this is the anterior extremity of the right inferior turbinate bone overhanging ×, which is the right inferior meatus of the nose ; 5, crista galli ; 6, inner surface of the frontal bone ; 7, of the parietal bone ; 8, squamous part of the temporal ; 9, on the occipital bone below the internal occipital protuberance ; 10, external occipital protuberance ; 11, on the condylar process below the anterior condylar foramen ; 12, on the posterior surface of the petrous below the internal auditory meatus ; between 9 and 12, the groove of the right lateral sinus ; 13, placed above the sella turcica ; 14, left frontal sinus ; 15, left sphenoidal sinus, the figure being placed on the sphenoidal septum ; 16, hard palate and alveolar arch—the figure is placed near the lower opening of the posterior palatine canal, and the grooves which extend forwards from it ; 17, anterior nasal spine ; 18, section of the left superior maxillary bone, and near the place to which the line points, the section of the anterior palatine fossa ; 19, on the inner surface of the ramus of the lower jaw, below the sigmoid notch, and above the inferior dental foramen ; 20, inner surface of the body of the jaw on the mylo-hyoid ridge ; 21, surface of section of the lower jaw to the left of the symphysis ; behind the symphysis, and between 21 and 22, the mental spines ; 23, mylo-hyoid groove.

cæcum ; on each side are the numerous apertures of the cribriform plate, the inner openings of the internal orbital canals, and the foramen by which the nasal nerve passes into the nose.

The foramen cæcum sometimes conveys a vein passing from the nose to the superior longitudinal sinus. The apertures of the cribriform plate are occupied by the olfactory nerve filaments. Through the anterior internal orbital canal the nasal nerve and the anterior ethmoidal artery enter the skull, and through the posterior, which is less constant, the posterior ethmoidal artery. The foramen for the exit of the nasal nerve is at the front of the cribriform plate, usually between that and the frontal bone, and is connected by a groove with the inner opening of the anterior internal orbital canal : the nerve is accompanied by the nasal division of the anterior ethmoidal artery.

The **middle fossa**, on a lower level than the anterior, consists of a median and two lateral parts. The median part is small, being formed by the olivary eminence and sella turcica of the sphenoid bone, and limited behind by the dorsum sellæ. The lateral part on each side, formed by the great wing of the sphenoid, the squamous part, and the anterior surface of the petrous part of the temporal, lodges the temporal lobe of the cerebrum. The foramina of the middle fossa are the optic foramen, sphenoidal fissure, foramen rotundum, foramen ovale, foramen spinosum, foramen lacerum and hiatus Fallopii.

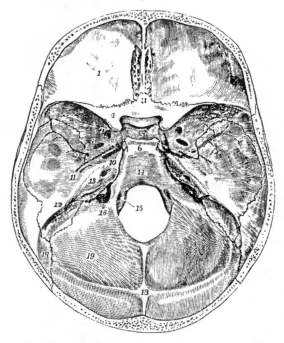

Fig. 72.—INTERNAL BASE OF THE SKULL. (Allen Thomson.) ½

1, anterior fossa and roof of the orbit, as formed by the frontal bone ; between 2 and 3, the foramen cæcum, crista galli and cribriform plate of ethmoid ; 3, ethmoidal spine of the sphenoid ; 4, lesser wing of sphenoid terminating posteriorly in the anterior clinoid process, inside which is the optic foramen ; 5, placed in the pituitary fossa, behind the olivary eminence and transverse groove of the optic commissure ; 6, dorsum sellæ, terminating in the posterior clinoid processes ; 7, foramen rotundum, in front of which, but not seen in the figure, is the sphenoidal fissure ; 8, foramen ovale ; 9, foramen spinosum ; 10, on the petrous bone, near its apex, and to the inside of the hollow occupied by the Gasserian ganglion ; in front of this is the foramen lacerum ; 11, in front of the eminence of the superior semicircular canal, and behind the hiatus Fallopii ; 12, upper border of the petrous, marked by the superior petrosal groove ; 13, the posterior surface of the petrous—to the inside, the internal auditory meatus, behind, the scale of bone covering the aqueduct of the vestibule ; 14, basilar groove ; 15, anterior condylar foramen ; 16, jugular foramen ; 17, groove of the lateral sinus ; 18, internal occipital protuberance, and running down from it the internal occipital crest ; between 17 and 18, the upper part of the groove of the lateral sinus, between 17 and 16, the lower part ; 19, cerebellar fossa.

Through the optic foramen the optic nerve and the ophthalmic artery enter the orbit. The sphenoidal fissure (foramen lacerum anterius) also opens into the orbit ; it gives passage to the third, fourth, ophthalmic division of the fifth, and the sixth nerves, and the ophthalmic veins. By the foramen rotundum the superior maxillary nerve passes into the spheno-maxillary fossa. The foramen ovale and foramen spinosum lead into the zygomatic fossa : the former transmits the inferior maxillary nerve, the small meningeal artery, and two or three emissary veins ; the latter, the large meningeal vessels.

The *foramen lacerum* (medium) is an irregular aperture between the apex of the petrous and the body and great wing of the sphenoid, and in the recent state is closed below by a mass of fibrous tissue ; the carotid canal opens on its external wall, the Vidian canal anteriorly. The lingula projecting backwards from the body of the sphenoid effects a partial, sometimes a complete subdivision of the space : by the inner part the carotid artery enters the cranial cavity ; and through the external, the large superficial petrosal nerve, coming from the hiatus Fallopii, reaches the posterior orifice of the Vidian canal.

The **posterior fossa**, deeper and larger than the others, extends back to the occipital protuberance, and lodges the cerebellum, medulla oblongata and pons.

The occipital bone, the petrous and mastoid portions of the temporal, the postero-inferior angle of the parietal, and the body of the sphenoid take part in its formation. In the centre of the fossa is the foramen magnum ; and on each side of this, in a nearly vertical line from below upwards, are the anterior condylar foramen piercing the condylar portion of the occipital bone, the jugular foramen between the occipital and petrous, and the internal auditory meatus on the posterior surface of the petrous. Behind the jugular foramen is the posterior condylar foramen (if present), and higher up the more constant mastoid foramen, both opening into the groove of the lateral sinus.

The foramen magnum is occupied in the recent state by the lower end of the medulla oblongata with its membranes, the vertebral arteries, and the spinal accessory nerves. The anterior condylar foramen transmits the hypoglossal nerve and a meningeal branch of the ascending pharyngeal artery. By the internal auditory meatus the facial and auditory nerves, with the portio intermedia and the auditory vessels, leave the cranial cavity. The posterior condylar and mastoid foramina transmit emissary veins, the latter also the mastoid branch of the occipital artery.

The *jugular foramen* (foramen lacerum posterius) is formed by the jugular notches of the petrous and occipital bones : somewhat pyriform in shape, two more or less marked constrictions indicate a division into three compartments ; most externally and posteriorly is a large rounded part in which the lateral sinus joins the internal jugular vein ; the middle part, corresponding to a distinct notch in the lower border of the petrous, transmits the glosso-pharyngeal, vagus, and spinal accessory nerves ; and the most anterior and internal, sometimes completely separated by a spiculum of bone (the intrajugular process; p. 34), gives passage to the inferior petrosal sinus. A meningeal branch of the ascending pharyngeal or occipital artery also enters the skull by the posterior compartment.

Grooves for blood-vessels.—The groove of the middle meningeal artery commences at the foramen spinosum, and ramifies principally on the squamous portion of the temporal bone and on the parietal. The groove of the internal carotid artery lies on the side of the body of the sphenoid, and extends from the foramen lacerum to the inner side of the anterior clinoid process. The groove of the superior longitudinal sinus, commencing at the frontal crest, passes backwards in the middle line of the roof of the skull, and terminates at the internal occipital protuberance. From that point the groove of the lateral sinus passes outwards on each side over the occipital bone, crosses the posterior inferior angle of the parietal bone, descends on the mastoid portion of the temporal bone, runs inwards again on the occipital, and turns forwards to terminate at the jugular foramen. The groove of the inferior petrosal sinus lies between the petrous portion of the temporal bone and the basilar process ; that of the superior petrosal sinus extends along the superior edge of the petrous portion.

THE NASAL CAVITIES AND COMMUNICATING AIR-SINUSES.

The **nasal cavities**, or **fossæ,** are placed one on each side of a median vertical septum. They open in front by the anterior nasal aperture and behind by the posterior nares already described, and communicate with the sinuses of the frontal, ethmoid, sphenoid, and superior maxillary bones. Their vertical extent, as well as that from before backwards, is considerable, but their transverse width is very limited, especially in the upper part.

The *internal wall*, or *septum nasi*, is formed by the central plate of the ethmoid, the vomer, the nasal spine of the frontal, the rostrum of the sphenoid, and the crests of the nasal, maxillary, and palate bones. It presents a great angular deficiency in front, which in the recent state is filled up by the septal cartilage. In most cases it deviates somewhat from the middle line to one side or the other.

The *roof* is horizontal in its middle part, but sloped downwards before and behind. The middle part is formed by the cribriform plate of the ethmoid, the fore part by the frontal and nasal bones, and the back part by the body of the sphenoid, the ala of the vomer and the sphenoidal process of the palate bone. In it are the apertures of the cribriform plate and the orifice of the sphenoidal sinus.

The *floor*, formed by the palate plates of the maxillary and palate bones, is smooth, and concave from side to side. Towards its anterior extremity is the orifice of the incisor foramen.

The *external wall* is the most extensive. The bones which take part in its formation are the nasal, superior maxillary, lachrymal, ethmoid, inferior spongy, and palate bones, and the internal pterygoid plate. The superior and inferior turbinate processes of the ethmoid bone, and the inferior spongy bone, projecting inwards, overhang the three hollows called *meatuses*. The *superior meatus*, very short, is placed between the superior and inferior turbinate parts of the ethmoid ; into it

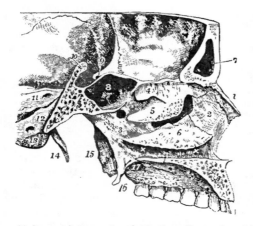

Fig. 73.—Sagittal section of a part of the skull, showing the outer wall of the left nasal fossa, &c. (Allen Thomson.) ½

1, nasal bone ; 2, nasal process of the superior maxillary bone ; 3, vertical plate of the palate bone ; 4, superior turbinate bone—below it the superior meatus, behind it the spheno-ethmoidal recess and the opening into the left sphenoidal sinus ; 5, middle turbinate bone—below it the middle meatus, into which opens the maxillary sinus ; superiorly and anteriorly, is the opening of the infundibulum ; behind it, and above 3, the spheno-palatine foramen ; 6, inferior turbinate bone—below it the inferior meatus × × ; below these marks the section of the palate plates of the left palate and superior maxillary bones ; 7, left frontal sinus ; 8, left sphenoidal sinus ; 9, left optic foramen in the root of the lesser wing of the sphenoid, and anterior clinoid process ; 10, dorsum sellæ divided ; and between 9 and 10, the sella turcica ; 11, posterior surface of the petrous, close to the internal auditory meatus ; 12, basilar process of the occipital bone, close to the jugular foramen ; 13, on the occipital condyle, below the anterior condylar foramen ; 14, styloid process ; 15, external, and 16, internal pterygoid plates ; 17, posterior palatine canal.

open anteriorly the posterior ethmoidal cells, and posteriorly the spheno-palatine foramen. The *middle meatus*, the space between the inferior turbinate part of the ethmoid and the inferior spongy bone, communicates with the anterior and middle ethmoidal cells, with the maxillary sinus, and at its fore part, by means of the infundibulum, with the frontal sinus. The *inferior meatus*, longer than the others, lies between the inferior spongy bone and the floor of the nasal cavity, and in its fore part is the orifice of the nasal duct. Above the superior meatus, in an angle of the roof formed by the cribriform plate and the front of the body of the sphenoid (fig. 73, behind 4), is a depression called the *spheno-ethmoidal recess* (G. H. Meyer), formed by the narrowing of the lateral mass of the ethmoid (fig. 66) ; on the posterior wall of the recess is the opening of the sphenoidal sinus.

The **air-sinuses** are hollows within the ethmoid, frontal, sphenoid, and maxillary bones, which communicate with the nasal cavities by narrow orifices. With the exception of the maxillary sinus these cavities are absent in the infantile skull. The maxillary sinus begins to be formed about the fourth month of foetal life ; the frontal, ethmoidal and sphenoidal first excavate the respective bones during childhood, but remain of small size up to the time of puberty, when they undergo a great enlargement. In advanced life they all increase in size by absorption of the cancellated tissue in their vicinity. The *ethmoidal sinuses* consist of several irregular spaces occupying the lateral mass of the ethmoid, and completed by the frontal, sphenoid, lachrymal, superior maxillary and palate bones. The *anterior* and *middle*, the larger and more numerous, open into the middle, the *posterior* into the superior meatus. The *frontal sinuses* are placed between the outer and inner tables of the frontal bone over the root of the nose. They extend outwards from behind the glabella to a variable distance over the orbit, being separated from each other by a thin bony septum. They open on each side into the middle meatus of the nose through the infundibulum. The *sphenoidal sinuses* occupy the body of the sphenoid, being formed in connection with the sphenoidal spongy bones. They are separated by a median septum, and open into the spheno-ethmoidal recess. The *maxillary sinus* has been described in connection with the superior maxillary bone ; it opens by a small aperture into the middle meatus.

The air-spaces of the temporal bone (tympanum and mastoid cells) are described in connection with the Anatomy of the Ear in Vol. III.

OSSIFICATION OF THE BONES OF THE HEAD.

The ossification of the bones of the base of the cranium takes place for the most part in cartilage, and in each case proceeds from several centres which represent distinct bones in lower vertebrate forms ; the bones of the roof are simpler in their development, and originate in

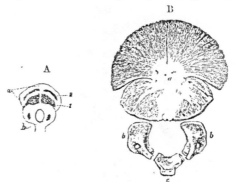

Fig. 74.—Ossification of the occipital bone. (R. Quain.)

A, in a fœtus of 10 weeks (from Meckel) ; *a*, tabular part ; 1 & 2, lower and upper pairs of centres ; *b*, lower part or basilar and condylar portions : ossific centres are seen in the condylar portions.

B, occipital bone at birth ; *a*, tabular part, in which the four centres have become united into one, leaving fissures between them ; *b*, *b*, condylar portions ; *c*, basilar portion.

membrane ; those of the face are also deposited in membrane, with the exception of the inferior turbinate bone and a small part of the lower jaw. In the expanded tabular bones the ossification spreads outwards from the centres, and the marginal portions, in the earlier stages, present more or less the form of radiated fibres or spicula. At birth the sutural edges, and especially the angles, are incomplete, the bones being united and the interspaces filled up by fibrous tissue. The diploe and air-sinuses are at first absent, some of the latter arising early in life, and others being formed at a comparatively late but variable period.

The occipital bone at birth consists of four separate pieces—a basilar, a tabular, and two condylar parts, united by intervening cartilage. The lines of junction of the basilar and condylar parts pass through the condyles near their anterior extremities ; those of the condylar and tabular parts extend outwards from the posterior margin of the foramen magnum. The basilar (*basioccipital*) and condylar parts (*exoccipitals*) arise each from one osseous nucleus, which appears from the eighth to the tenth week.[1] In the tabular part there appear, a few days earlier, usually four nuclei, an upper and a lower pair ; these speedily unite, but leave fissures running in from the upper and lateral angles, which remain for some time after birth. The upper pair of these differ from the other centres of this bone in being deposited in membrane, and while the lower portion of the tabular part is the proper *supraoccipital* element, the upper represents the *interparietal* bone of many animals ; it occasionally happens that this remains distinct in the human skull, the upper part of the occipital squama being separated from the rest by a suture running transversely from one lateral angle to the other, and by no means unfrequently a partial division exists, by persistence of the lateral fissures, which may

[1] In the descriptions of the mode of ossification of the bones, weeks and months refer always to periods of fœtal life.

even simulate fracture. The osseous union of the supra- and exoccipitals, beginning in the second or third, is completed in the fourth year; that of the basi- and exoccipitals, beginning in the third or fourth, is completed in the fifth or sixth year. The basioccipital is united to the basisphenoid by intervening cartilage up to about the twentieth year, after which ossific union begins and is completed in one or two years.

The **parietal bone** begins to ossify in membrane in the seventh week. According to Toldt [1] it has two nuclei, an upper and a lower, which speedily fuse into a single mass occupying the position of the future parietal eminence. The radiating ossification extends in such a way as to leave a notch or cleft at the upper part of the bone a little distance from the posterior angle, giving rise to the *sagittal fontanelle*—a space between the two bones, which gradually becomes closed in during the latter half of foetal life. Traces of the fontanelle are often to be recognized at the time of birth; and the parietal foramina are remains of the interval. [2] In rare cases a transverse *parietal fissure* persists. The parietal eminence is very conspicuous in the young bone, and gives a marked character to the form of the skull for a number of years in early life.

The **frontal bone** is ossified from two nuclei which appear, one on each side above the orbital arch, about the seventh week. At birth the bone consists of two separate lateral portions, which meet in a vertical median suture during the first year. This *frontal suture* usually

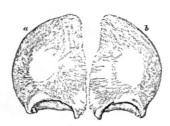

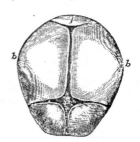

Fig. 75.—FRONTAL BONE OF A FŒTUS SHORTLY BEFORE BIRTH. (R. Quain.)

a & *b* indicate the two portions of the bone, in each of which the radiation of bony spicula from the frontal eminence is seen.

Fig. 76.—SKULL OF A CHILD AT BIRTH, FROM ABOVE. (Leishman.) ⅓

a, anterior fontanelle; *p*, posterior fontanelle; *b*, *b*, parietal eminences; for the lateral fontanelles, see fig. 83, p. 82.

becomes obliterated by osseous union taking place from below upwards, during the second year, though not unfrequently it persists throughout life (p. 39). The frontal sinuses appear about the seventh year, and continue to increase in size up to old age.

Fontanelles.—These are membranous intervals between the incomplete angles of the parietal and neighbouring bones, in some of which movements of the soft wall of the cranium may be observed in connection with variations in the state of the circulation and respiration. They are six in number, two median, anterior and posterior, and four lateral. The *anterior* fontanelle, situated between the antero-superior angles of the parietal bones and the superior angles of the ununited halves of the frontal bone, is quadrangular in form, and remains open for some time after birth. The *posterior* fontanelle, situated between the postero-superior angles of the parietal bones and the superior angle of the occipital bone, is triangular in shape. It is filled up before birth, but the edges of the bones, being united by membrane only, are still freely moveable upon each other. The *lateral* fontanelles, small and of irregular form, are situated at the inferior angles of the parietal bones. The fontanelles are gradually filled up by the extension of ossification into the membrane which occupies them, thus completing the angles of the bones and forming the sutures. The closure, especially of the posterior and lateral, is often assisted by the development of Wormian bones in these situations. All traces of these unossified spaces disappear before the age of four years. The *sagittal* fontanelle, existing before birth, has been noticed above.

The **temporal bone** in the later stages of foetal life consists of three principal pieces, the squamo-zygomatic, petro-mastoid or periotic, and tympanic. The *squamo-zygomatic* is ossified in membrane from a single nucleus, which appears in the lower part of the squamosal about the seventh or eighth week, and extends upwards into the squamosal, and outwards into the zygoma. From the hinder part of the squamosal a considerable *postauditory process* grows downwards below the supramastoid crest, separating the tympanic from the periotic, and

[1] "Lotos, Jahrbuch f. Naturw.," 1882.

[2] Broca, Bull. Soc. Anthrop. de Paris, 1875; Augier, "Rech. sur le développement des pariétaux à la région sagittale," Thèse, Paris, 1875.

forming the upper and fore part of the mastoid division of the bone.   Beneath this is an air-space continued backwards from the tympanum, and called the *antrum mastoideum*, from which the mastoid cells subsequently grow out.   During the third month an osseous nucleus appears in the lower part of the external membranous wall of the tympanum, and extends upwards forming the *tympanic ring*, an imperfect circle, open above, which encloses the tympanic membrane.   Before birth the extremities of this ring become united with the squamo-zygomatic.

Petro-mastoid or *periotic*.   It is only in the latter half of the fifth month that osseous deposits begin to be formed in the cartilaginous ear-capsule.   They extend rapidly, and the different ossifications are united by the end of the sixth month.   The first to appear is a nucleus on the promontory (*opisthotic*), which spreads round the fenestra rotunda, and forms the portion of the petrous below the internal auditory meatus and fenestra ovalis.   The second (*prootic*) arises over the superior semicircular canal, and forms most of the petrous seen in the interior of the skull, as well as the upper and inner part of the mastoid : it furnishes the upper boundaries of the internal auditory meatus and fenestra ovalis.   A little later, a third nucleus

Fig. 77.—SEPARATE PARTS OF THE TEMPORAL BONE OF A FŒTUS
        SHORTLY BEFORE BIRTH.   (R. Quain.)

a, squamo-zygomatic ; *b*, tympanic ; *c*, mastoid part of periotic ;
d, inner wall of tympanum ; *e*, mastoid antrum.

(*epiotic*), which is occasionally double, is developed in con-nection with the posterior semicircular canal, and extends into the lower part of the mastoid.   According to Sutton the tegmen tympani and covering of the external semi-circular canal are formed by a separate ossification (*pterotic*), appearing about the same time as the prootic.   Vrolik also described a special nucleus for the roof of the cochlea, and another in connection with the common crus of the superior and posterior semicircular canals.   (Huxley, "Lectures on Comparative Anatomy," 1864; Vrolik, Niederl. Arch. f. Zoologie, i, 291; Sutton, Journ. Anat., xvii, 498.)

At birth the petro-mastoid is separated from the squamosal by a thin plate of intervening cartilage, bony union taking place during the first year ; the mastoid portion also is flat, the glenoid fossa shallow, the articular eminence scarcely to be seen. and the tympanic ring and membrane are even with the outer surface of the bone.   The anterior and inferior walls of the external auditory meatus consist at first of fibrous tissue, in which the tympanic plate is formed after birth.[1]   The latter is developed from the outer margin of the slender tympanic ring, commencing in the form of two small tubercles at the fore and hinder parts respectively ; these increase in size and meet in the floor of the meatus, enclosing a foramen which is gradually closed.   The foramen is completed as a rule in the second year, and is seldom obliterated before five years of age.   The part of the wall of the meatus which was occupied by the foramen is commonly thin, and sometimes a small aperture persists through life. On the posterior surface of the petrous at birth is a considerable depression which extends into the arch of the superior semicircular canal, and represents the floccular fossa of the lower animals ; in the adult bone a vestige of this is always present as a small fissure above and outside the internal auditory meatus, between that and the aqueduct of the vestibule.   The mastoid process is developed about the second year, but the air-cells are not formed till near puberty.

The styloid process is formed by two small ossifications in cartilage—the *tympanohyal* at the base, commencing before birth and speedily joining the bone, and the *stylohyal* commencing usually after birth, but remaining very small until the period of puberty ; this only joins after adult age is reached, and often remains permanently separate.   (Flower, Brit. Ass. Rep., 1870.)

The **sphenoid bone** is divided in the fœtus into a posterior or *postsphenoid* part, to which the sella turcica and great wings belong, and an anterior or *presphenoid* part, including the body in front of the olivary eminence and the small wings,—a division which is found in many animals persistent through life.   The first osseous nuclei of the postsphenoid division appear about the eighth week in the great wings (*alisphenoids*), between the foramen rotundum and foramen ovale, and spread thence outwards into the wing and downwards into the external pterygoid plate.   About the same time also two granules appear in the post-sphenoid part of the body (*basisphenoid*), placed side by side in the sella turcica ; these unite

---

[1] See J. Symington, Journ. Anat., xix, 284, and "The Topographical Anatomy of the Child," 1887, p. 46.

in the fourth month, and after their union two others appear (*sphenotics*),[1] from which are formed the lingulæ and adjoining parts of the carotid grooves. The internal pterygoid plates, corresponding to the *pterygoid* bones of animals, are ossified from distinct nuclei, which appear in the fourth month ; they unite with the external pterygoid plates in the fifth month. The great wings are united to the body in the first year.

In the presphenoid division the first pair of nuclei appears in the ninth week outside the optic foramina, and extends by their growth into the small wings (*orbitosphenoids*) : another pair of granules appears on the inner sides of the foramina, and the presphenoid portion of the body either results from the union of these, or is an independent growth. The presphenoid ossifications are united to the body of the postsphenoid in the seventh or eighth month. At birth the place of union is marked on the under aspect of the body by a wide notch, which sometimes opens above by a small hole on the olivary eminence. The body of the presphenoid

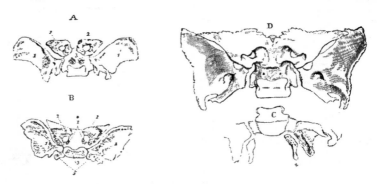

Fig. 78.—Ossification of the sphenoid bone.   (R. Quain.)

A, sphenoid bone at an early period, seen from above ; 1, 1′, the greater wings ossified ; 2, 2′, the lesser wings, in which the ossification has encircled the optic foramen, and a small suture is distinguishable at its posterior and inner side ; 3, nuclei of basisphenoid.

B, copied from Meckel (Archiv. vol. i, tab. vi, fig. 23), and stated to be from a fœtus of six months ; 2*, nuclei of presphenoid ; 5, separate lateral processes of the body (lingulæ) : the other indications are the same as in A.

C, back part of the bone shown in A ; 4, internal pterygoid plates still separate.

D, sphenoid at birth. The great wings are still separate. The presphenoid is now joined to the basisphenoid, and the internal pterygoid plates (not seen in the figure) are united to the external.

is for some years broad and rounded inferiorly ; it begins to be hollowed by the sphenoidal sinuses about the sixth year, and then becomes gradually narrower and more prominent, being ultimately reduced to the thin sphenoidal septum.

The *sphenoidal spongy bones* begin to ossify in the fifth month. At birth each consists of a small sagittal lamina, resting against the presphenoid, and continued posteriorly into a lateral projection, which is hollowed in front for the sphenoidal sinus, the latter having been formed as a recess of the mucous membrane of the nose at the end of the third month. By the third year the bone has entirely surrounded the sinus, forming an osseous capsule with an anterior opening—the *sphenoidal foramen*. About the fourth year the upper and inner parts of this capsule begin to be absorbed, and the presphenoid then forms the wall of the sinus, which in its farther extension excavates the body of the bone. At the outer and fore part also absorption takes place, and the cavity there comes to be bounded by the ethmoid and palate bones. The anterior projections of the sagittal plates meet in front of the presphenoid, and uniting with the vertical plate of the ethmoid form the rostrum. The spongy bones are anchylosed first to the lateral mass of the ethmoid (about the fourth year), whence they are often regarded as parts of that bone. They join the sphenoid from the ninth to the twelfth year. (Toldt, "Die Entstehung und Ausbildung der Conchæ und der Sinus sphenoidales beim Menschen," Lotos, 1882.)

In the ethmoid bone ossification begins in the lateral masses during the fifth month, first in the orbital plate, and then in the middle turbinate bone. In the first year a nucleus appears in the vertical plate, and the cribriform plate is formed by ossification extending from this internally and from the lateral masses externally. The three parts are united in

[1] J. B. Sutton, "On the Development and Morphology of the Human Sphenoid Bone," Proc. Zool. Soc. Lond., 1885.

the fifth or sixth year. The ethmoidal cells appear in the sixth month as depressions of the mucous membrane, but bony walls are not developed until after birth.

The **superior maxillary bone** begins to ossify immediately after the clavicle and the lower jaw. The osseous deposit takes place at several points, but the different parts speedily fuse, and the precise number of centres is by no means certain. It is probable, however, that the maxilla proper is developed in at least three pieces, a *malar* portion external to the infra-orbital canal, an *orbito-facial* portion between the foregoing and the nasal fossa, and a *palatine* portion including the palate process and the adjoining part of the nasal wall. The part of the bone which carries the incisor teeth, extending as far back as the incisor foramen, has an independent origin, corresponding to the *premaxillary* bone of the lower animals. In the young subject always, and often in the adult, there is to be seen a fine *incisor fissure* on the under surface of the palate process, passing outwards from the anterior palatine fossa to the alveolar border, internal to the canine socket; and on the upper surface a similar line may be seen, though less frequently, extending up some distance on the nasal surface of the body; but no trace of the line of union exists on the facial surface, as is the case in the lower animals. This is due to the development at the lower and fore part of the maxilla of an outgrowth, termed the *incisor process*, which forms the front wall of the incisor sockets;

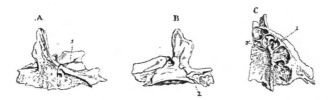

Fig. 79.—DIFFERENT VIEWS OF THE SUPERIOR MAXILLARY BONE OF A FŒTUS OF FOUR OR FIVE MONTHS. (R. Quain.)

A, external surface; a fissure, 1, is seen extending from the orbital surface into the infraorbital canal.

B, internal surface; the incisor fissure, 2, extends from the foramen upwards through the horizontal plate and some way into the nasal process.

C, the bone from below, showing the imperfect alveoli and the incisor fissure, 2', 1, which crosses the palate plate to the septum between the second and third alveoli.

behind this process, between it and the palate process, is a deep groove in which the pre-maxillary bone is formed, the latter being distinct up to the fifth month of fœtal life. (Callender, Phil. Trans., 1869; Th. Kölliker, "Os intermaxillare des Menschen," 1882; Sutton, Proc. Zool. Soc., 1884.)

The sockets of the teeth are formed by the downgrowth of an outer and an inner plate on the sides of the dental groove, and subsequently the partitions appear, those on each side of the canine tooth first. The antrum appears as a shallow depression on the inner surface of

Fig. 80.—THE VOMER AT THE TIME OF BIRTH. (R. Quain.)

1 & 2, the two plates forming a groove for the reception of the septal cartilage.

the bone at about the fourth month; this gradually extends, separating the orbital and palate portions of the bone, which at birth are still very close together. At its first appearance the antrum has a cartilaginous wall, which afterwards becomes absorbed. The infra-orbital canal begins as a groove on the orbital surface, which is gradually closed by the growing over of the outer margin; but a fine suture remains indicating the line of meeting.

The **palate bone** is ossified from a single centre, which appears in the seventh or eighth week at the angle between its horizontal and vertical parts.

The **vomer** is ossified from a pair of nuclei which arise in membrane at the lower and back part of the cartilaginous nasal septum in the eighth week. They soon unite below, but growing forwards and upwards form the two laminæ which embrace the septal cartilage. These laminæ gradually undergo increased union from behind forwards till the age of puberty, thus forming a median plate, with only a groove remaining on its anterior and superior margins.

The **nasal** and **lachrymal bones** are each ossified from a single centre appearing about the eighth week. At the time of birth there is a layer of cartilage beneath the nasal bone, which is continuous above with the ethmoidal cartilage, and below with the lateral cartilage of the nose : this subsequently disappears.

The **malar bone** also commences to ossify about the eighth week. According to Rambaud and Renault it is developed from three points which have united by the fourth month of foetal life ; and to the persistent separation of one of these, the divided condition of the bone referred to on p. 56 may be due.

The **inferior turbinate bone** is ossified in cartilage from a single centre, which only appears in the fifth month.

The **inferior maxillary bone** is developed principally in the fibrous tissue investing Meckel's cartilage (see development of the head in Vol. I.), but to a less extent the cartilage itself participates in the ossification. At birth it consists of the lateral parts united at the symphysis by fibrous tissue : the osseous union takes place in the first or second year. The process of ossification commences very early, being preceded only by the clavicle, and proceeds rapidly : it takes place from several centres, which are united by the fourth month. The largest part of each half is formed from a deposit (*dentary*) in the membrane on the outer side of Meckel's cartilage ; and to this there is added a second smaller plate (*splenial*) which forms the inner wall of the tooth-sockets, terminating behind in the lingula. A small part of the body by the side of the symphysis results from the direct ossification of the anterior end of Meckel's cartilage ; and, posteriorly, the condyle and a portion of the ramus, including the

Fig. 81.—THE INFERIOR MAXILLA OF A CHILD AT BIRTH. (R. Quain.)

a & *b* indicate the two portions separate at the symphysis.

angle, are developed from another ossification in cartilage. The last, however, is not connected with Meckel's cartilage, which can be seen in a foetus of the fifth or sixth month to be prolonged up to the fissure of Glaser, where it becomes continuous with the slender process of the malleus, surrounded by fibrous tissue which eventually forms the so-called internal lateral ligament of the jaw. (Callender, Phil. Trans., 1869 ; Kölliker, " Entwickelungsgeschichte " ; Toldt, " Wachsthum des Unterkiefers," Prag, 1883 ; Sutton, Trans. Odont. Soc., 1883.)

At birth, the body of the jaw is shallow, the basal part is but little developed, and the mental foramen is nearer the lower than the upper margin ; the ramus is very short and oblique, the angle which it forms with the body being about 140° ; the neck of the condyle also is short and inclined backwards ; and the coronoid process projects above the condyle. During the succeeding years the body becomes deeper, thicker, and longer, the ramus and the neck of the condyle lengthen, and the angle at which the ramus joins the body becomes less obtuse, till in the adult it is nearly a right angle. In old age, consequent upon the loss of the teeth and the absorption of the alveolar margin, the body becomes shallower, the mental foramen opens at the upper border of the bone, and the angle is again increased.

The **hyoid bone** has five points of ossification—one for the body, and one for each of its great and small cornua. The ossification begins in the great cornua and body in the last month of foetal life, in the small cornua in the first year after birth. The great cornua and body unite in middle life, the small cornua only exceptionally in advanced age. The stylohyoid ligaments are occasionally ossified in some part of their extent.

GENERAL MORPHOLOGY OF THE BONES OF THE HEAD

The circumstances which contribute most to modify the form of the human skull and the condition of its component bones, as compared with that of other animals, are—1st, the proportionally large size of the brain and the corresponding expansion of the cranial bones which enclose it ; 2nd, the smaller development of the face as a whole, and especially of the jaws, which brings the facial bones almost entirely under the fore part of the brain-case, instead of in front of it, as occurs in all animals, with the partial exception of the anthropoid apes ; and 3rd, the adaptation of the human skeleton to the erect posture, which, as regards the head, is attended with the sudden bend of the basicranial axis at a considerable angle upon the line of the erect vertebral column ; and along with this the great development of the cranium in a backward direction, whereby the occipito-vertebral articulation comes to be placed approximately in the centre of the antero-posterior length of the skull, so that the head is nearly balanced on the upper extremity of the spine. The downward openings of the nostrils, the forward aspect of the orbits and eyes, the nearly vertical forehead and more or less oval-shaped face, are accompaniments of these human peculiarities in the form of the head, which, together with those already mentioned, strongly contrast with the smaller cranium and its strong crests of bone, the larger projecting face and jaws, and the other characteristic features of the skull in most animals.

As regards the condition of the individual bones, it is farther to be remarked that there is generally in the human skull a more complete consolidation or bony union of the osseous elements than in animals, so that the whole number of bones forming the cranium and face is least in man. Thus, to mention only some of the most marked examples of this difference among mammals; the frontal bone and the lower jaw frequently divided into two lateral portions; the premaxillary very generally a separate bone from the maxillary; the presphenoid in many separate from the postphenoid; the interparietal from the occipital; and the squamosal and styloid ossifications from the periotic. It is also worthy of observation that the conditions now referred to as permanent in animals exist as transitory stages of development in man.

Homologies.—It is not possible here to enter at any length into the consideration of the homologies of the bones of the human skull, but the diagrammatic representation of the bones of the fœtal head in fig. 82, and the following table will serve to indicate to some extent the

Fig. 82.—DIAGRAMMATIC VIEW OF THE BONES IN THE RIGHT HALF OF A FŒTAL SKULL, FROM THE INSIDE. (Allen Thomson.)

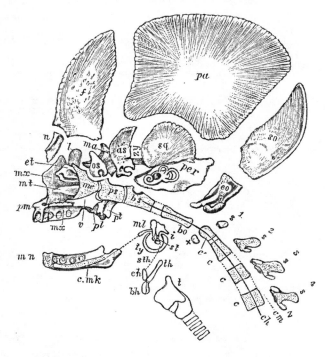

In this figure the bones have been slightly separated and displaced so as to bring the whole into one view : *f*, frontal ; *pa*, parietal ; *so*, supraoccipital ; *n*, nasal ; *l*, lachrymal ; *ma*, malar ; *os*, orbitosphenoid ; *as*, alisphenoid ; *sq*, squamosal ; *zy*, zygomatic ; *per*, periotic ; *eo*, exoccipital ; *et*, ethmoturbinal ; *mx*, maxilla ; *mt*, maxilloturbinal ; *pm*, premaxillary ; *me*, mesethmoid ; *v*, vomer ; *pl*, palatal ; *pt*, pterygoid ; *ps*, presphenoid ; *bs*, basisphenoid ; *bo*, basioccipital ; *c*, bodies of 2nd, 3rd, and 4th cervical vertebræ ; *c'*, odontoid process ; ×, anterior arch of atlas ; *s*, spinous processes of 1st, 2nd, 3rd, and 4th cervical vertebræ ; *cm*, neural canal ; *ch*, a line indicating the position of the notochord passing through the vertebral bodies into the base of the cranium ; *ty*, tympanic, along with *ml*, *i*, and *st*, displaced from its connection with *per* ; *ml*, malleus ; *c. mk*, cartilage of Meckel ; *mn*, mandible ; *i*, incus ; *st*, stapes ; *sth*, stylohyal ; *ch*, ceratohyal ; *th*, thyrohyal ; *bh*, basihyal ; *t*, thyroid cartilage.

morphological relations of the several bones to each other, and to those of other vertebrate animals, and to explain the origin of the constituent elements of the skull. Additional information as to the latter point will be found in the account of the development of the head in the chapter on Embryology in Vol. I. ; and for a fuller explanation of the homologies of the bones the reader is referred to works on Comparative Anatomy.

LIST OF THE TYPICAL COMPONENT PARTS OF THE BONES OF THE HEAD CLASSIFIED ACCORDING TO THEIR ORIGIN [1] :—

1. BONES DEVELOPED IN THE PRIMITIVE CARTILAGINOUS CRANIUM.

Basioccipital ; Basilar process of the occipital bone.
Exoccipitals ; Condylar portions of the occipital bone.
Supraoccipital ; Lower division of the tabular part of the occipital bone.

[1] The names first given, and printed in black type, are those received in comparative anatomy ; those usually employed in human anatomy follow, and are printed in common type.

Periotics ; Greater parts of the petrous and mastoid portions of the temporal bones.

Basisphenoid ; Posterior part of the body of the sphenoid bone, including the sella turcica.

Alisphenoids ; Great wings of the sphenoid with the external pterygoid plates.

Presphenoid ; Anterior part of the body of the sphenoid bone.

Orbitosphenoids ; Small wings of the sphenoid bone.

2. MEMBRANE-BONES COMPLETING THE CRANIAL WALL.

Interparietal ; Upper division of the tabular part of the occipital bone.

Parietals ; The parietal bones.

Frontals ; United in the single frontal.

Squamosals ; The squamous parts of the temporal bones with the zygoma.

3. BONES DEVELOPED IN THE CARTILAGINOUS NASAL CAPSULE.

Mesethmoid ; Vertical plate of the ethmoid bone, together with the cartilaginous part of the nasal septum.

Ethmoturbinals ; The lateral masses of the ethmoid, including the upper and lower turbinate bones.

Maxilloturbinals ; The inferior turbinate bones.

Sphenoidal turbinals ; The sphenoidal spongy bones.

4. MEMBRANE-BONES DEVELOPED AROUND THE NASAL CAPSULE AND FORMING THE GREATER PART OF THE UPPER FACE.

Lachrymals ; The lachrymal bones.

Nasals ; The nasal bones.

Maxillæ ; The superior maxillary bones, excepting the incisor part.

Premaxillæ or intermaxillæ ; The incisor parts of the superior maxillary bones.

Jugals or malars ; The malar bones.

Palatals ; The palate bones.

Pterygoids ; The internal pterygoid plates.

Vomer ; The vomer.

5. BONES DEVELOPED IN THE CARTILAGINOUS VISCERAL ARCHES OF THE HEAD.

Malleus, Incus, and Stapes ; The auditory ossicles or malleus, incus, and stapes.

Tympanohyals and Stylohyals ; The styloid processes of the temporal bones.

Epihyals ; The stylo-hyoid ligaments (occasionally ossified in man).

Ceratohyals ; The small cornua of the hyoid bone.

Thyrohyals ; The great cornua of the hyoid bone.

Basihyal ; The body of the hyoid bone.

6. MEMBRANE-BONES DEVELOPED IN CONNECTION WITH THE VISCERAL ARCHES.

Mandible ; The inferior maxillary bone (a small part is developed in the cartilaginous arch).

Tympanics ; The tympanic plate, forming the auditory and vaginal processes (developed in the periphery of the membrane closing the first visceral cleft).

The relations of the nerves at their passage out of the cranium to the osseous elements are remarkably constant, and afford considerable assistance in determining their homologies. Thus, the nerves of the principal sense-organs pass into their special capsules as follows, viz., the olfactory between the mesethmoid and ethmoturbinal divisions of the ethmoid bone ; the optic between the orbitosphenoid and the presphenoid ; and the auditory between the prootic and opisthotic divisions of the periotic mass.   Farther, the motor nerves of the orbital muscles (third, fourth and sixth), together with the ophthalmic division of the trifacial (fifth), pass through the sphenoidal fissure between the orbitosphenoid and alisphenoid, while the second division of the trifacial has a special foramen in the alisphenoid which has been separated off from the sphenoidal fissure by the growth of bone around the nerve.   Similarly, the foramen ovale for the third division of the trifacial has been cut off from the foramen lacerum between the alisphenoid and periotic.   The facial (seventh) nerve leaves the cranial cavity with the auditory between the divisions of the periotic, and then traverses a canal (aqueduct of Fallopius), the lower part of which is included between the outer surface of the periotic and the tympanic plate, while its Vidian branch occupies a canal surrounded by the basisphenoid, alisphenoid and pterygoid elements of the sphenoid bone. The glosso-pharygeal (ninth), pneumo-gastric (tenth) and spinal accessory (eleventh) nerves pass between the periotic and exoccipital; and the hypoglossal (twelfth) between the exoccipital and basioccipital. The internal carotid artery, it may be added, enters the skull by the foramen lacerum, a space between the basisphenoid, alisphenoid, and periotic, having previously traversed the carotid canal formed by the downgrowth of the opisthotic; and the jugular vein issues between the periotic and exoccipital.

A general review of the construction of the skull shows that it may be regarded as consisting mainly of three sets of parts, viz.—1st, **basal or central parts**, comprising the basioccipital, basisphenoid, presphenoid, and mesethmoid, which form a series prolonged forwards in the line of the vertebral axis, and constitute a *cranio-facial axis;* 2nd, **superior arches**, three in number, enclosing the brain, and consisting of more or less expanded bones, viz., the exoccipitals and supraoccipital together with the interparietal, the alisphenoids, squamosals and parietals, the orbitosphenoids and frontals; and 3rd, **inferior arches**, surrounding the visceral cavity as represented by the nose, mouth, and pharynx; these include the pterygoids, palatals and maxillæ in a first arch, the mandible and the malleus of the internal ear in a second, the cerato-, epi-, stylo- and tympanohyals in a third, while the thyrohyals are the rudiments of a fourth, and the basihyal is interposed between the last two. To these succeed in the lowest vertebrates the series of branchial arches, one, or perhaps two, of which may be in part represented by the thyroid cartilage of the larynx. Together with the foregoing there are associated other elements, viz.—1st, the periotic enclosing the organ of hearing, and the ethmo- and maxilloturbinals covering the organ of smell, which have been classed separately as **special sense-capsules**; and 2nd, the small bones of the face, malar, nasal, and lachrymal, supplementary to the maxillary arch, and the vomer, extending the cranio-facial axis.

There is thus a certain resemblance in the arrangement of the chief parts of the skull to that of the trunk-skeleton, and this resemblance has led to the conception of what is called the **vertebrate theory of the skull**, according to which the skull consists essentially of a series of vertebræ, the dorsal or neural arches of which have undergone great expansion, so as to predominate over the less developed ventral or visceral arches. Certain circumstances in the growth of the skull, especially the formation of a part at least of the cranio-facial axis around a prolongation of the notochord, appear at first sight to give support to this view; but the more complete knowledge of the mode of development of the skull which has been obtained of late years tends to show that there is no such homodynamous correspondence between the several bones of the skull and the vertebral segments of the trunk-skeleton. In explanation of this statement the following points of difference between the two may be specially referred to, viz.—1, a large part of the cranio-facial axis is prechordal, being formed beyond the cephalic extremity of the notochord, and therefore does not correspond to vertebral bodies; 2, the cartilage in which the bones of the cranio-facial axis and its lateral expansions are developed is not at any period segmented, as is the cartilage preceding the vertebræ; 3, the segmentation which is to be recognized in the bones of the skull does not agree with the segmentation which has been observed in the head of lower vertebrates at an early period of embryonic life; 4, the bones forming the dorsal and ventral arches of the head are in large part developed in membrane, and are probably dermal in origin, whereas the arches of the vertebræ are entirely of cartilaginous origin; and 5, the cartilaginous visceral arches of the head probably do not correspond to the costal arches of the vertebræ, being formed in close connection with the wall of the alimentary canal, while the ribs are developed in the body-wall or somatopleure.

On the whole, it would appear, therefore, that the skeleton of the head and the skeleton of the trunk agree in being formed in continuous tissue lying between and surrounding the cerebro-spinal axis and the alimentary canal, and that the correspondence observed in their general construction is due to this community of origin and relations. But the several bones are developed independently, and in a different manner in the head and trunk, giving rise in the one case to the skull, in the other to the vertebral column; and although the head as a whole is undoubtedly derived in large part from a portion of the body that was primitively segmented, there is no evidence to show that the appearance of the skull has been preceded by a stage in which osseous or even cartilaginous vertebræ are developed in connection with these segments.[1] (Huxley, "Lectures on Comp. Anat.," 1864; Gegenbaur, "Elements of Comparative Anatomy," and Morph. Jahrb., xiii; O. Hertwig, "Lehrb. der Entwicklungsgeschichte.")

---

[1] The fœtal conditions referred to above are fully explained in the section on Embryology in Vol. I.

THE VARIOUS FORMS OF THE SKULL.

I. **Differences according to age.**—In the earlier stages of its development the posterior part of the cranium bears a very large proportion to the anterior part; so much so, that in the second month of fœtal life the line of the tentorium cerebelli is vertical to the basis cranii, and divides the cranial cavity almost equally into two parts. The parietal region then increases rapidly in volume, along with the greater development of the cerebral hemispheres; the frontal region next augments; and again, in the latter part of fœtal life, the occipital region increases as the cerebrum extends backwards (Cleland). At the time of birth the parietal region has reached its largest development in proportion to the occipital and frontal regions. The greatest frontal breadth is then smaller in proportion to that between the parietal eminences than afterwards. The base of the cranium is relatively small, and the great wing of the sphenoid and the temporal squama do not extend so far upwards as subsequently is the case. The petrous, which is, however, comparatively large, is inclined more forwards than in the adult. Other peculiarities, such as the existence of the fontanelles, the prominence of the frontal and parietal eminences, and the absence of the mastoid processes, have been referred to in describing the development of the several bones. The face at birth scarcely reaches an eighth of the bulk of cranium, while in the adult it is at least a half (Froriep). The skull grows rapidly during about the first seven years of life. By that time

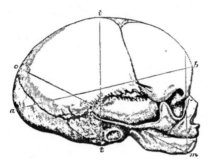

Fig. 83.—LATERAL VIEW OF THE CHILD'S SKULL AT BIRTH. (Leishman.) ½

This figure shows the elongated form of the skull in the infant, and the small proportion which the facial bears to the cranial part, and also the lateral fontanelles at the lower angles of the parietal bones. The lines indicate the various diameters.

certain parts, including the circumference of the occipital foramen, the body of the sphenoid, the cribriform plate, and the petrous division of the temporal, have attained their definitive size. The other regions also increase but little until the approach of puberty, when a second period of active growth begins, affecting especially the face and the frontal portion of the cranium, with which is associated the expansion of the frontal and other air-sinuses (Merkel). The face becomes elongated in the progress of growth, partly by increased height of the nasal fossæ and adjacent air-sinuses, partly by the growth of the teeth and the enlargement of the alveolar arches of the jaws. In old age the skull commonly becomes lighter and thinner, and often a little smaller; but in some cases it increases in thickness and weight owing to deposit of bone on the interior of the brain-case without a corresponding degree of absorption externally (Humphry). The proportion of the face to the cranium is also diminished by the loss of the teeth and absorption of the alveolar portions of the jaws. In consequence of this the upper jaw retreats, while in the lower jaw the same cause gives, especially when the mouth is closed, a greater seeming prominence to the chin. (Froriep, "Characteristik des Kopfes nach dem Entwickelungsgesetz desselben," 1845; Huschke, "Schädel, Hirn und Seele," 1854; Virchow, "Entwickelung des Schädelgrundes," 1857; Humphry, "A Treatise on the Human Skeleton," 1858, and "Old Age," 1889; Welcker, "Wachsthum und Bau des menschlichen Schädels," 1862; Cleland, "On the Variations of the Human Skull," Phil. Trans., 1869; Merkel, "Beitrag zur Kenntniss der postembryonalen Entwicklung des menschlichen Schädels," 1882.)

II. **Sexual differences.**—The female skull is, in general, smaller, lighter, and smoother than that of the male; the muscular impressions are not so strongly marked, the mastoid processes and the superciliary ridges are less prominent, and the frontal sinuses less developed. The cranial capacity is less, on the average, by one-tenth, than that of the male in the same race, and the frontal and occipital regions are less capacious in proportion to the parietal (Huschke). The face is smaller in proportion to the cranium, the zygomatic arches slender, and the jaws narrower and less prominent. The female skull resembles the young skull more than that of the adult male; but it must be admitted that it is often impossible to determine the sex by the appearance or form of a skull.

III. **Race differences, their measurement and classification. Craniometry.**—The most important measurements and characters in comparing skulls of different races are the cranial capacity, the circumference of the cranium, the relative length, breadth and height of the cranium, the degree of projection of the jaws, and the form of the nasal skeleton and the orbital opening.

The **capacity of the cranium** affords the most convenient indication of the development of the brain.[1] It is ascertained by filling the cranial cavity with shot, and then measuring the contained quantity in a properly graduated vessel, special precautions being taken to ensure as nearly as possible an equal pressure in both operations. The capacity of the normal human cranium varies from 1,000 to 1,800 cubic centimetres (about 60 to 110 cubic inches), with an average in all races of 1,400 cubic centimetres (85 cubic inches). Skulls with a capacity of from 1,350 to 1,450 cubic centimetres are placed in a middle group and termed *mesocephalic*, those exceeding 1,450 cubic centimetres in capacity are *megacephalic*, and those below 1,350 cubic centimetres are *microcephalic* (Flower). The following examples are of males only :—

	Cub. centim.	Cub. inches.
Eskimo . . .	1500	91·5
European . .	1480	90·3
Chinese and Mongols.	1430	87·3
African Negroes .	1350	82·4
Native Australians .	1300	79·3
Andaman Islanders .	1280	78·1

Before proceeding to the consideration of the linear measurements it is necessary to refer to certain definite points on the surface of the skull from which such measurements are

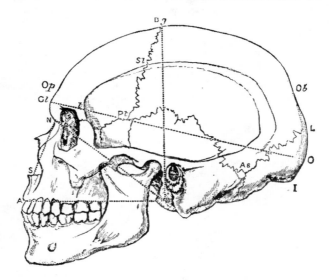

Fig. 84.—SIDE VIEW OF SKULL OF A MALE AUSTRALIAN. (After Flower.)

A, alveolar point ; S, sub-nasal point ; N, nasion ; Gl, glabella ; Op, ophryon ; Bg, bregma ; Ob, obelion ; L, lambda ; O, occipital point ; I, inion ; B, basion ; Pt, pterion ; St, stephanion ; As, asterion ; Gl O, length of cranium ; B N, basinasal length ; B A, basialveolar length ; N S, nasal height.

taken, or which have a particular importance as presenting varieties of more or less frequent occurrence, and to which special names have been given not of ordinary use in descriptive anatomy. These are :—

Alveolar point (fig. 84, A).—The centre of the anterior margin of the upper alveolar arch.

Subnasal or *spinal point* (S).—The middle of the inferior border of the anterior nasal aperture at the base of the nasal spine.

Nasion or *nasal point* (N).—The middle of the naso-frontal suture.

Ophryon or *supraorbital point* (Op).—The middle of the supraorbital line, which, drawn across the narrowest part of the forehead, separates the face from the cranium.

Bregma (Bg).—The point of junction of the coronal and sagittal sutures.

Obelion (Ob).—The region situated between the two parietal foramina where the sagittal suture is more simple than elsewhere, and where its closure generally commences.

Lambda (L).—The point of junction of the sagittal and lambdoid sutures.

Occipital point (O).—The point of the occiput in the median plane most removed from the glabella.

[1] According to Manouvrier (Mém. de la Soc. d'Anthrop. de Paris, 2 sér., t. iii, 1885), the weight of the brain in grammes may be approximately ascertained by multiplying the cranial capacity in cubic centimetres by ·87. But it is to be remarked that Manouvrier's capacities were obtained by Broca's method, which undoubtedly gives too high results. Welcker proposes (Arch. f. Anthrop., xvi, 51) a sliding scale, ranging from 91 gr. of brain-weight to 100 ccm. of cranial capacity for skulls with a capacity of 1200 ccm. to 95 gr. to 100 ccm. for skulls of 1600 ccm. capacity. Thus 1480 × ·938 = 1388 gr., which agrees closely with the average European brain-weight as ascertained by direct observation.

Inion (I).—The external occipital protuberance.

Opisthion.—The middle of the posterior margin of the foramen magnum.

Basion (B).—The middle of the anterior margin of the foramen magnum.

Pterion (Pt).—The region, near the anterior part of the temporal fossa, where the great wing of the sphenoid, the squamous, the parietal and the frontal bones approach each other, the exact disposition, however, varying in different individuals. In the most common condition the parietal and great wing of the sphenoid meet and form a short horizontal suture ; but it sometimes happens that these two bones are separated by the junction of the frontal and squamous, giving rise to a vertical fronto-temporal suture, generally continuing the line of the coronal suture. The latter form is especially frequent in some of the lower races of mankind, and is the rule in the gorilla and chimpanzee. There is often a small Wormian bone in this situation, the *epipteric bone* of Flower, and many cases of the occurrence of a fronto-temporal suture are attributable to the union of this piece of bone with the squamous or frontal.

Stephanion (St).—The point where the coronal suture crosses the temporal line.

Asterion (As).—The point where the lambdoid, parieto-mastoid and occipito-mastoid sutures meet. When a separate interparietal bone is present the suture dividing it from the supraoccipital runs transversely from asterion to asterion, which will in that case be the meeting point of four sutures.

Auricular point.—The centre of the orifice of the external auditory meatus.

The **circumference of the cranium** (horizontal) is taken in a plane passing anteriorly through the ophryon,[1] and posteriorly through the occipital point (fig. 84, O*p* O). This may exceed to a slight degree 550 millimetres (21·7 inches) or it may be as low as 450 mm. (17·7 inches). The average in the adult European male is 525 mm., in the female 500 mm. For comparison of the relative development of the anterior and posterior portions of the cranium, the preauricular part of the circumference is divided from the postauricular part by a line on each side passing from the auricular point to the bregma (*auriculo-bregmatic line*).

The **length of the cranium** (maximum) is measured from the most prominent point of the glabella to the occipital point (fig. 84, G*l* O), and this is made the standard = 100. The **breadth** (maximum) is the greatest transverse diameter of the cranium above the supramastoid ridges, measured perpendicularly to the median plane. The proportion of the latter to the length $\left(\dfrac{100 \times \text{breadth}}{\text{length}}\right)$ is the *index of breadth* or the *cephalic index*. Skulls with a breadth-index above 80 are *brachycephalic*, from 75 to 80 *mesaticephalic*, and below 75 *dolichocephalic*.

The **height of the cranium** is measured from the basion to the bregma, and the proportion of this to the length, calculated in the same way, is the index of height. It is subject to less variation than the breadth-index ; in some cases, especially in dolichocephalic skulls, it exceeds, but more frequently it falls below that index.

	Breadth-index.	Height-index.[2]
Mongolians of Siberia and Central Asia .	88	73
Andaman Islanders	82	77
Chinese	79	75
English	76	71
Native Australian	71	71
Fiji Islanders	66	74

For a more accurate determination of the form of the cranium other measurements are taken, such as the transverse circumference, passing through the auricular point on each side and the bregma above ; the longitudinal arc from the nasion to the opisthion, with its subdivisions into frontal, parietal and occipital arcs ; transverse arcs from the posterior root of the zygoma immediately above the auricular point of the one side to the other, across the most prominent parts of the frontal, parietal, and occipital bones respectively. The anteroposterior curve of the roof may also be indicated by a series of radii from the basion to the centre of the frontal bone, the bregma, the vertex and the lambda. Other features again are not capable of being expressed in terms of direct measurement, and must be described in each case ; for example, the form of the transverse arch of the cranium, which in the best shaped skulls is full and rounded, while in some races, notably in the Australian, the line of the sagittal suture is elevated, and the surface on each side flattened or even somewhat depressed, making the calvaria roof-shaped ; and this condition, combined with great prominence of the parietal eminences or of the temporal lines, gives the skull, when viewed from behind, a markedly pentagonal figure. The degree of complication and fusion of the sutures, the amount of projection of the glabella and of the inion, and other variable points, may be stated according to tables furnished by Broca in the work referred to below.

---

[1] Some anthropologists measure the circumference over the glabella (Turner, Schmidt).

[2] In these examples, which are taken from the Catalogue of the Museum of the Royal College of Surgeons, the indices are calculated from the ophryo-occipital length.

The situation and direction of the foramen magnum differ greatly, as was pointed out by Daubenton, in man and the lower animals, in connection with the altered position of the axis of the head in relation to that of the vertebral column. In man the foramen is placed in or near the centre of the base of the skull, and its plane looks mainly downwards; in quadrupeds it is placed on the posterior surface of the skull and looks backwards; while in the anthropoid apes it is intermediate in position and direction. But even in human skulls similar differences occur, though much less in degree. In the European the plane of the foramen is inclined upwards anteriorly, in the Australian and Negro it is horizontal or even inclined slightly upwards posteriorly. The degree of inclination requires for its determination a special "occipital goniometer" designed by Broca.

In the skeleton of the face the most striking differences are met with in the size of the jaws and the extent to which they project forwards. The human skull, in comparison with that of the lower animals, is especially distinguished by the great expansion of its cranial portion and the relatively small development of the face, the latter being extended vertically instead of horizontally, and thus brought downwards under the fore part of the cranium. A marked prominence of the jaws constitutes, therefore, an approach to the animal type of skull, and is to be regarded as a character of inferiority, particularly when it is accompanied, as is often the case, by a low and receding forehead. The degree of projection of the jaws beyond the cranium is most conveniently expressed by the *gnathic* or *alveolar index* of Flower, which is obtained by comparing the basialveolar length (fig. 84, BA) with the basinasal length (BN) = 100; skulls with a gnathic index below 98 are *orthognathous*, from 98 to 103 *mesognathous*, and above 103 *prognathous*.

$$\frac{BA \times 100}{BN}$$

	Gnathic Index
English	96
Chinese	99
Eskimo	101
Fiji Islanders	103
Native Australian	104

In the **form of the nasal skeleton** and the anterior nasal aperture variations are to be recognised corresponding to the external conformation of the nose. Of these, the height and width are capable of exact measurement, and the relation between the two, expressed by the *nasal index*, becomes a character of considerable importance. The height is measured from the nasion to the subnasal point (fig. 84, NS), the width is the greatest transverse diameter of the anterior nasal aperture, and the calculated proportion of this to the height = 100, is the index. With a nasal index below 48 a skull is *leptorhine*, from 48 to 53 *mesorhine*, above 53 *platyrhine*.

	Nasal Index.
Eskimo	44
English	46
Chinese	50
Native Australian	57

The **form of the orbit** also varies, but is a less significant character than that of the nose. The *orbital index* is the ratio of the vertical height of the base of the orbit to the transverse width = 100; if above 89 it is *megaseme*, between 89 and 84 *mesoseme*, and below 84 *microseme*.

	Orbital Index.
Andaman Islanders	91
Chinese	90
English	88
Native Australian	81
Guanches of Teneriffe	80

For an account of the variations in the form of the palate and of the mandible, as well as of the means of estimating the relative projection of the malar and nasal bones, and several other measurements of the face skeleton, reference must be made to the special treatises.

(For more detailed information on the foregoing subject consult Broca, "Instructions craniologiques et craniométriques," 1875; Flower, "Cat. of Museum of Roy. Coll. Surg. of Eng.," part i., 1879; de Quatrefages and Hamy, "Crania Ethnica," 1873–81; Topinard, "Éléments d'anthropologie générale;" Turner, "Challenger" Reports, Zoology, x; and Schmidt, "Anthropologische Methoden," 1888. References to earlier writings of importance are given in the last edition of this work.)

IV. Irregularities of form.—The most frequent irregularity in the form of the skull is want of symmetry. This sometimes occurs in a marked degree, and there is probably no skull perfectly symmetrical. The condition which has been observed to co-exist most frequently with irregular forms of skull is premature *synostosis* or obliteration of certain of the sutures.

The cranial bones increase in size principally at their margins; and when a suture is prematurely obliterated the growth of the skull in the direction at right angles to the line of suture may be supposed to be checked, and increased growth in other directions may take place to supply the defect. Thus, the condition known as *scaphocephaly* is found associated with absence of the sagittal suture, where, the transverse growth being prevented, a great increase takes place in the vertical, and especially the longitudinal directions, giving the vault of the skull a boat-like form. Similarly, *acrocephaly* is related to obliteration of the coronal suture, the compensatory growth taking place mainly upwards. Oblique deformity, or *plagiocephaly*, also is met with in connection with premature fusion of one half of the coronal or lambdoid suture; but independently of this a precisely similar deformity may be induced by rickets, wry-neck, or external pressure. (See Virchow, "Gesammelte Abhandlungen," 1856; Lucae, "Zur Architectur des Menschenschädels," 1857; W. Turner in Nat. Hist. Rev., 1864; J. Barnard Davis, "On Synostotic Crania," 1865; Topinard, *op. cit.*) Another series of irregular forms of skull is that produced by pressure artificially applied in early life, and is best exemplified from among those American tribes who compress the heads of their children by means of an apparatus of boards and bandages: it is also illustrated in a slighter degree by individual instances in which undue pressure has been employed unintentionally. (Gosse, "Essai sur les Déformations artificielles du Crâne," 1855; V. Lenhossék, "Die künstlichen Schädelverbildungen," &c., 1881.) Posthumous distortions likewise occur in long-buried skulls, subjected to the combined influence of pressure and moisture. (Wilson, "Prehistoric Annals of Scotland.")

IV.—THE BONES OF THE UPPER LIMB.

The upper limb consists of the shoulder, the arm, *brachium*, the forearm, *antibrachium*, and the hand, *manus*. The bones of the shoulder are the clavicle and scapula, which together form the pectoral arch or shoulder-girdle; in the arm is the humerus; in the forearm are the radius and ulna; and in the hand three groups of bones, viz., the carpus, metacarpus, and phalanges.

THE CLAVICLE.

The **clavicle** or collar-bone extends outwards and backwards, from the summit of the sternum to the acromion process of the scapula, and connects the upper limb with the trunk. It is curved like an italic *f*: the internal curve has its convexity

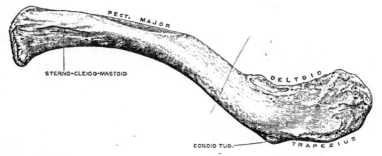

Fig. 85.—RIGHT CLAVICLE, FROM ABOVE.   (Drawn by T. W. P. Lawrence.) $\frac{2}{3}$

directed forwards, and extends over two-thirds of the length of the bone; the outer curve is concave forwards, corresponding to the hollow between the chest and shoulder.

The clavicle is broad towards its scapular end, being compressed from above downwards, but in the extent of its inner curve it is more or less prismatic or cylindrical. In its description, four surfaces may be distinguished, together with the two extremities.

The *superior surface* is broadest in its outer part; it is principally subcutaneous and smooth, but near the inner extremity presents a slight roughness, marking the clavicular attachment of the sterno-cleido-mastoid muscle. The *anterior surface* opposite the outer curve is reduced to a mere rough border, from which the deltoid muscle takes origin ; but in the inner half of its extent it is broadened out into an uneven space, more or less distinctly separated from the inferior surface, and giving attachment to the pectoralis major muscle. The *posterior surface* is broadest at the inner extremity, and smooth in the whole extent of the internal curvature ; but towards its outer extremity it forms a thick border which gives attachment to the trapezius muscle. About the middle of this surface is the aperture of a small canal for the medullary artery, directed outwards. On the *inferior surface*, at the sternal end is a rough impression for the attachment of the rhomboid ligament, by which the clavicle is bound down to the first rib ; more externally is a groove, extending somewhat

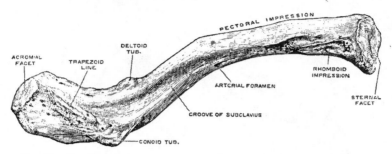

Fig. 86.—RIGHT CLAVICLE, FROM BELOW. (Drawn by T. W. P. Lawrence.) ⅔

beyond the middle third of the bone, in which the subclavius muscle is inserted ; behind this, projecting on the posterior border at the junction of the middle and outer thirds, is a well-marked eminence, the *conoid tubercle*, to which the conoid division of the coraco-clavicular ligament is attached, and from which the rough, generally raised. *trapezoid line*, for the trapezoid part of the same ligament, is directed outwards and forwards towards the end of the bone.

The *sternal end* is the thickest part of the clavicle. It presents a somewhat triangular concavo-convex surface, with its most prominent angle directed downwards and backwards. The *scapular end* is broad and flat, and articulates by a small oval surface with the acromion.

The clavicle is subcutaneous to a greater or less extent in its whole length ; the most prominent part is about the centre, corresponding to the intermuscular intervals, above between the sterno-mastoid and trapezius, and below between the pectoralis major and deltoid (*supra-* and *infraclavicular fossæ*). The outer extremity is a little higher than the upper surface of the acromion against which it fits, and forms a prominence on the upper part of the shoulder.

The interior of the clavicle contains coarse cancellated tissue in its whole extent, the principal lamellæ being directed longitudinally. The shell of compact tissue is for the most part very thick and dense, but it thins out gradually at the two ends of the bone.

Varieties.—At the inner part of the deltoid impression there is sometimes a flattened projection known as the *deltoid tubercle*. A small foramen for one of the supraclavicular nerves is occasionally found at the fore part of the upper surface of the bone about the middle.

THE SCAPULA.

The **scapula** is placed upon the upper and back part of the thorax, and forms the posterior part of the shoulder-girdle. It is not attached directly to the trunk, but is articulated with the outer end of the clavicle, and from it is suspended the humerus in the shoulder-joint.

It consists of a triangular blade or *body*, supporting two large processes. The surfaces of the body are anterior and posterior; the borders superior, internal or vertebral, and external or axillary; the angles superior, inferior, and external; the last being the thickest part of the bone, and bearing the large articular surface, is distinguished as the *head*, which is supported upon a *neck*. The processes are an anterior, *coracoid process*, and a posterior, the *spine*, which is produced into the *acromion*.

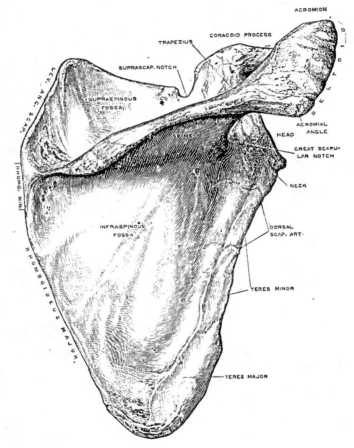

Fig. 87.—DORSAL VIEW OF RIGHT SCAPULA. (Drawn by T. W. P. Lawrence.) ⅔

The *anterior surface* or *venter*, looking also considerably inwards, presents a concavity, the *subscapular fossa*, occupied by the subscapularis muscle, and marked by three or four oblique prominent lines, converging upwards and outwards, which give attachment to the tendinous intersections of that muscle. Separated from this concavity, are two smaller flat surfaces, one in front of the superior angle and the other at the inferior angle; and these, together with the line running close to the vertebral border and uniting them, give attachment to the serratus magnus muscle.

The *posterior surface* or *dorsum* is divided by the spine into two unequal parts, the upper of which is the *supraspinous fossa*, and the lower, the *infraspinous fossa*. The supraspinous fossa is occupied by the supraspinatus muscle. The infraspinous fossa, much the larger, presents in the middle a convexity corresponding to the concavity of the venter, and outside this a concavity bounded by the prominent axillary border. It is marked near the inner border by short lines, corresponding to tendinous septa of the infraspinatus muscle, and is occupied by that muscle in the greater part of its extent. Adjacent to the axillary border, in its middle third, is a narrow area giving attachment to the teres minor muscle; and below this, extending over the inferior angle, is a raised oval surface, from which the teres major arises.

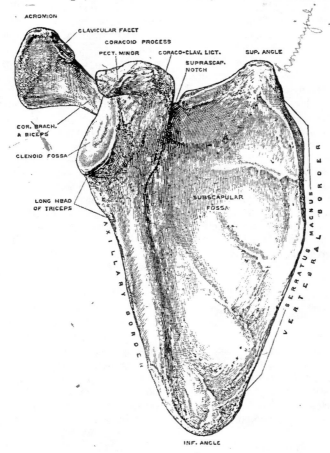

Fig. 88.—Right scapula, from before. (Drawn by T. W. P. Lawrence.) ⅔

These spaces are separated from each other, and from that of the infraspinatus muscle, by lines which give attachment to aponeurotic septa.

The *spine* of the scapula is a massive triangular plate of bone projecting backwards and upwards from the dorsum. Beginning internally near the upper fourth of the vertebral border, it extends outwards and a little upwards to the middle of the neck of the scapula; and becoming gradually elevated towards its outer extremity, it turns forwards and is continued into the acromion process. The upper and lower surfaces, smooth and concave, form part respectively of the supra- and infraspinous fossæ. It has two unattached borders, the more prominent of which is subcutaneous, and arises from the vertebral border of the bone by a smooth, flat, triangular surface, over which the tendon of the inferior part of the trapezius muscle glides, as it passes to be inserted into a rough thickening beyond.   In the rest of its extent this border is rough, broad, and serpentine, giving attachment by its superior margin to the trapezius, and by its inferior to the deltoid muscle.   The external border, short, smooth, and concave, arises near the neck of the scapula, and is continuous with the under surface of the acromion, enclosing the *great scapular notch* between it and the neck of the bone.

The *acromion process*, projecting outwards and forwards from the extremity of the spine over the glenoid cavity, forms the summit of the shoulder.   It is an expanded process, compressed from above downwards.   Its superior surface, rough and subcutaneous, is continuous with the prominent border of the spine ; while the inferior surface, smooth and concave, is continuous with the superior surface and external border of the spine.   On its internal border anteriorly is a narrow oval surface for articulation with the clavicle.   Its outer border gives origin to the acromial portion of the deltoid, and is marked by three or four tubercles from which tendinous processes of this part of the muscle spring : posteriorly it terminates in the prominent *acromial angle*, which overhangs the hinder margin of the glenoid cavity. The apex of the acromion projects beyond the end of the clavicle, and gives attachment to the coraco-acromial ligament.

The *head* bears the articular surface for the humerus, known as the *glenoid cavity*. This is a slightly concave surface, looking outwards, forwards, and slightly upwards. It is pyriform in shape, with the narrow end uppermost, and gently incurved in front.   Its rim is flattened, and in the recent state is covered by a fibrous band, the glenoid ligament, which deepens its concavity; at its upper extremity is a small mark indicating the attachment of the long head of the biceps muscle.

The *neck*, supporting the head, is most distinct behind, where it forms with the spine the *great scapular* or *acromio-scapular notch*, leading from the supraspinous to the infraspinous fossa ; its position is also marked above by the notch in the upper border of the bone.

The *coracoid process*, thick, strong, and hook-like, rises for a short distance almost vertically from the upper border of the head, and then bending at a right angle, is directed forwards and slightly outwards.   Its superior surface, towards the base, is rough and uneven, giving origin to the coraco-clavicular ligament ; on its outer border is attached the coraco-acromial ligament, at its extremity the coraco-brachialis muscle and short head of the biceps, and on the inner edge the pectoralis minor.

The *superior border* of the scapula is the shortest ; it extends from the superior angle outwards and downwards to the coracoid process, at the base of which it presents a rounded *suprascapular* or *coraco-scapular notch*, which is converted into a foramen by a ligament, or occasionally by a spiculum of bone, and is traversed by the suprascapular nerve.   The *axillary border* is the thickest; at the upper end, below the glenoid cavity, it presents a strong rough mark, above an inch long, to which the long head of the triceps muscle is attached ; and below this there is usually a slight groove, where the dorsal branch of the subscapular artery passes backwards ; on the ventral aspect of this edge in the greater part of its length is a marked groove in which a considerable part of the subscapularis muscle arises.   The *vertebral border*, called also the *base*, is the longest of the three, and is divisible into three parts, viz., a short one opposite the triangular surface of origin of the prominent border of the spine, and the portions above and below that space, both of which incline outwards as they recede from the spine.   The upper part gives attachment to the levator anguli scapulæ muscle, the middle to the rhomboideus minor, and the lower to the rhomboideus major muscle.

The subcutaneous parts of the scapula are the free border of the spine in nearly the whole of its length, the upper surface of the acromion, and a small part of the vertebral border in its lower half; the superior and axillary borders are entirely concealed by the muscles. The coracoid process projects in front beyond the clavicle, and can be readily felt inside the head of the humerus, but can be seen only in thin persons. With the arm hanging by the side, the scapula covers the ribs from the second to the seventh inclusive, sometimes the eighth; and the root of the spine and the lower edge of the glenoid cavity are on a level with the interval between the third and fourth dorsal spines. It must, however, be remembered that the bone changes its position with every movement of the arm.

The body of the scapula is in great part thin and translucent, and at these spots contains no cancellated tissue. The head, the coracoid and acromion processes, the prominent border of the spine, and the thick rib along the axillary border, derive their greater thickness and strength from increased thickness of the compact bony substance in some parts, and from cancellated tissue in others. Vascular foramina pierce the upper and lower surfaces of the spine, and others are to be found on the anterior surface of the bone, near the neck.

The morphological axis of the scapula corresponds to the line of attachment of the spine, extending from the glenoid cavity to the vertebral border of the bone. From this axis three laminæ radiate, the *prescapula*, *mesoscapula*, and *postscapula* of Parker, giving rise to the three scapular fossæ. The supraspinous angle (between the prescapula and mesoscapula) measures about 100°; the infraspinous and subscapular angles are each about 130°.[1] The scapula of man is remarkable for the great development of the postscapula, making the vertebral border very long and the inferior angle prominent. This is an adaptation to the freedom of movement possessed by the upper limb. The surface for attachment of the rotator muscles of the humerus is thus increased, and greater leverage is given to the lower part of the serratus magnus muscle, which rotates the scapula upwards. The relative length and breadth of the scapula are expressed by the *scapular index* =

$$100 \times \frac{\text{breadth}}{\text{length}}.$$

The index is higher in the infant than in the adult, and in Negroes than in Europeans. (Broca, Bull. Soc. Anthrop. Paris, 1878; Flower and Garson, Journ. Anat., xiv; Turner, "Challenger" Reports, Zoology, xvi; Dwight, "The Range of Variation of the Human Shoulder-Blade," Amer. Nat., 1887.)

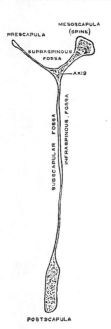

Fig. 89.—VERTICAL SECTION OF THE SCAPULA, PASSING THROUGH THE MIDDLE OF THE THREE FOSSÆ. (G. D. T.) ½

THE HUMERUS.

The **humerus** or arm-bone extends from the shoulder to the elbow, where it articulates with both bones of the forearm. It is divisible into the *superior extremity*, including the *head*, *neck*, and *great* and *small tuberosities*; the *shaft*; and the *inferior extremity*, including the *external* and *internal condyles*, and the *inferior articular surface*. In general form it is subcylindrical and slightly twisted.

The **superior extremity** is the thickest part of the bone. The *head* is a large hemispherical articular elevation, directed inwards, upwards, and backwards. The *neck*, as described by anatomists, is the short portion of bone which supports the head; inferiorly, it passes into the shaft; superiorly, it is a mere groove between the head and the great tuberosity. The *great tuberosity* is a thick projection, continued upwards from the external part of the shaft, and reaching nearly to the level of the upper margin of the head; it is surmounted by three flat surfaces, the uppermost of which gives attachment to the supraspinatus muscle, the lowest to the teres minor, and the intermediate one to the infraspinatus muscle. Separated from the great tuberosity by the commencement of the bicipital groove is the *small tuberosity*, oval and prominent; it looks forwards and gives attachment to the subscapularis muscle.

[1] See Ward's "Outlines of Human Osteology."

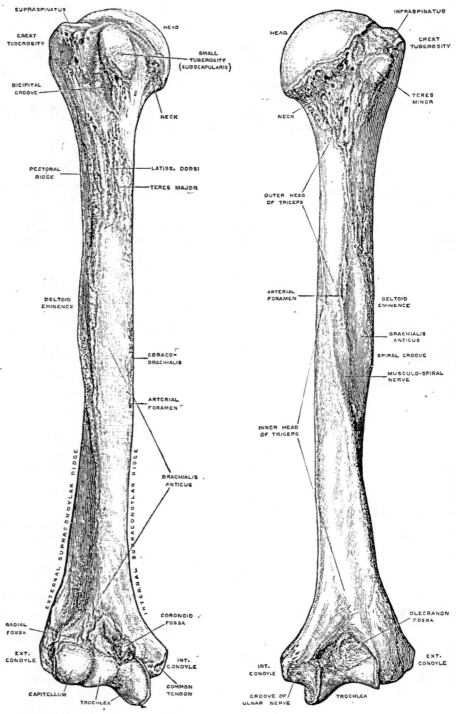

Fig. 90.—RIGHT HUMERUS, FROM BEFORE.
(Drawn by T. W. P. Lawrence.) $\frac{2}{3}$

Fig. 91.—RIGHT HUMERUS, FROM BEHIND.
(Drawn by T. W. P. Lawrence.) $\frac{2}{3}$

The **shaft** or **body**, thick and cylindrical above, becomes expanded transversely and somewhat three-sided below. It is divided into anterior and posterior faces by lateral lines, slightly marked in the upper part, but more prominent in the lower, where they pass into the supracondylar ridges. Superiorly, on its anterior aspect is the *bicipital groove*, so named from lodging the long tendon of the biceps muscle ; this groove, commencing between the tuberosities, descends with an inclination inwards, and is bounded by two rough margins, the external and more prominent of which, *pectoral ridge*, gives attachment to the pectoralis major muscle, the internal to the latissimus dorsi and teres major. To-wards the middle of the shaft, on the inner lateral line, is a rough linear mark where the coraco-brachialis muscle is inserted, and a little lower down is the foramen by which the chief medullary artery enters the bone, directed down-wards. On the external part of the shaft, near its middle, in a line anteriorly with the pectoral ridge, is a large, elevated, and rough surface, of a triangular shape, the *deltoid eminence*, for the insertion of the muscle of the same name. Below this, the ridge is continued into a smooth elevation which, descending on the front of the shaft to the inferior extremity, separates an

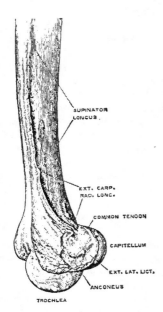

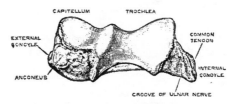

Fig. 92.—LOWER TWO-FIFTHS OF THE RIGHT HUMERUS, FROM THE OUTER SIDE. (Drawn by T. W. P. Lawrence.) ⅖

Fig. 93.—LOWER EXTREMITY OF THE RIGHT HUMERUS, FROM BELOW. (Drawn by T. W. P. Lawrence.) ⅔

external from an internal surface ; while at the sides these are separated from the flat posterior surface by the *supracondylar ridges*, which descend, the external more prominent than the internal, to the condyle on each side. About the middle of the shaft externally, a broad depression, the *spiral groove*, winds downwards and forwards, limited above by the deltoid eminence, and below by the external supracondylar ridge: the hollow is for the most part occupied by a process of the brachialis anticus muscle, but posteriorly, where there is often to be recognized a second smaller groove, the musculo-spiral nerve and superior profunda vessels rest against the bone. At the upper part of the groove there is generally a second foramen for a branch of the superior profunda artery.

The external and internal surfaces below the deltoid eminence are occupied by the origin of the brachialis anticus muscle. Posteriorly, the outer head of the triceps arises from the surface above the spiral groove, the inner head from the surface internal to and below the groove. The external supracondylar ridge gives origin in its upper two-thirds to the supinator longus, in its lower third to the extensor carpi radialis longior. The external and internal inter-muscular septa of the arm are also attached to the corresponding supracondylar ridges.

The **inferior extremity** is much enlarged laterally, flattened from before backwards, and curved slightly forwards. Projecting on either side are the *external* and *internal condyles* (the *epicondyle* and *epitrochlea* of Chaussier). The internal condyle is the more prominent, and is slightly inclined backwards, forming posteriorly a shallow groove in which the ulnar nerve lies: its extremity is marked anteriorly by an impression to which the common tendon of the superficial pronato-flexor muscles of the forearm is attached. On the external condyle are seen, 1, a mark for the common tendon of some of the muscles of the back of the forearm; 2, below and internal to this, a smaller impression for the anconeus; and 3, between the foregoing and the margin of the radial articular surface, a pit in which the external lateral ligament of the elbow-joint is attached. The *inferior articular surface* is divided into two parts. The external part, articulating with the radius, consists of a rounded eminence directed forwards, called the *capitellum*, and a groove internal to it; it does not extend to the posterior surface. The internal part, the *trochlea*, articulates with the ulna, and extends completely round from the anterior to the posterior surface of the bone; it is grooved in the middle like the surface of a pulley, and is somewhat broader behind than in front; anteriorly, its margins are inclined downwards and inwards; posteriorly, upwards and outwards, so that, seen from behind, it occupies the middle part of the bone. In front, the internal margin of the trochlea is the more prominent, and forms a convexity parallel to the groove; behind, the external margin is slightly more prominent. Above the trochlea posteriorly is a large and deep pit, the *olecranon fossa*, which receives the olecranon process of the ulna in extension of the forearm; and above it anteriorly, separated from the olecranon fossa only by a thin lamina of bone, is the much smaller *coronoid fossa*, which receives the coronoid process in flexion. Above the capitellum is a shallow depression—the *radial fossa*, into which the head of the radius is pressed in complete flexion.

The humerus, in its natural position with the arm hanging by the side, has a slight inclination from above downwards and inwards, and is also in a condition of what may be termed strong internal rotation, *i.e.*, the so-called anterior surface looks very much inwards, and the internal condyle is directed more backwards than inwards. The bone is almost completely covered by muscles; the upper extremity is thickly covered by the deltoid, which it pushes up, and thus gives roundness to the shoulder: the shaft is entirely surrounded: both condyles are subcutaneous, the internal being prominent, while the appearance of the external varies as the forearm is moved. When the elbow is bent the capitellum projects under its muscular covering, and forms the rounded prominence outside the point of the elbow.

The average length of the humerus in the adult male is about 13 inches, in the female 12 inches. It is nearly one-fifth of the stature of the individual, and somewhat more than twice as long as the clavicle.[1]

The major axes of the upper and lower extremities of the humerus do not lie in the same plane, but cross one another at an angle, known as the *angle of torsion*, which varies greatly in different individuals, but averages about 20° in Europeans, and 35° in Negroes. The axis of the upper end forms a smaller angle anteriorly with the sagittal plane than that of the lower end. In quadrupeds the torsion is usually about 90°. (Broca, Rev. d'Anthrop., 1881.)

Varieties.—A small hook-like process, with its point directed downwards, is not unfrequently found in front of the internal condylar ridge, the *supracondylar process*. From its

[1] On the length and proportions of the long bones in different races of men may be consulted Humphry, "A treatise on the human skeleton"; Topinard, "Éléments d'anthropologie générale"; Turner, "Challenger" Reports, Zoology, xvi; Rollet, "Mensuration des os longs des membres," 1889.

It may here be remarked also that the limb-bones of the two sides are seldom of equal length. In most cases the bones of the upper limb (humerus ± radius) are longer on the right side, the difference being commonly about one-third of an inch, and rising occasionally to three-quarters of an inch. The increased development is probably associated with the greater use of the right hand. In the lower limbs the differences are not so marked, and the excess appears to be more frequently on the left side. These differences do not exist at birth. (Garson, Journ. Anat., xiii, 502; Rollet, *op. cit.*; Gaupp, "Maass- und Gewichts- Differenzen zwischen den Knochen der rechten und linken Extremitäten," Diss., Breslau, 1889.)

extremity, a fibrous band, giving origin to the pronator radii teres muscle, descends to the internal condyle, and through the arch thus formed passes the median nerve, accompanied frequently by the brachial artery, or by a large branch rising from it. This process represents a portion of the bone enclosing a foramen in many animals. (Struthers, Edin. Med. Journ., 1848 ; Gruber, " Can. supracond. humeri," Mem. Acad. Imp. St. Petersburg, 1859.) The thin plate between the olecranon and coronoid fossæ is sometimes perforated, forming the *supra-trochlear* or *intercondylar foramen*.

THE ULNA.

The **ulna** is the internal of the two bones of the forearm, and is longer than the radius by the extent of the olecranon process. It is inclined downwards and outwards from the humerus in such a direction that a straight line passing from the great tuberosity of the humerus downwards through the capitellum would touch the lower end of the ulna.

The ulna articulates with the humerus and the radius : in the natural skeleton it is not in contact with the carpal bones, being excluded from the wrist-joint by an interarticular fibro-cartilage.

The **superior extremity** is much the larger, and articulates with the humerus by means of the *great sigmoid cavity*, which looks forwards and upwards, and is bounded in its posterior and upper part by the *olecranon*, a thick process continued upwards from the shaft, and in its lower part by the *coronoid process* projecting forwards. The *great sigmoid cavity* is concave from above downwards, and traversed by a longitudinal ridge. The part external to this ridge is broad and convex above, while the part internal to the ridge is concave and broader below : a slight constriction, and sometimes a groove of division, occurs across the middle of the cavity. Continuous with the great is the *small sigmoid cavity*, a small articular surface on the outer side of the base of the coronoid process, concave from before backwards, for the reception of the head of the radius. Superiorly, the *olecranon* is broad and uneven, terminating in front in an acute process or *beak*, which overhangs the great sigmoid cavity, and which in extension of the elbow passes into the olecranon fossa of the humerus, and behind in a rectangular prominence or *tuberosity*, which forms the point of the elbow, and gives attachment to the triceps extensor muscle. The posterior surface of the olecranon is subcutaneous and continuous with the posterior margin of the shaft of the ulna. The extremity of the *coronoid process* is sharp and prominent, and is received during flexion into the coronoid fossa of the humerus : its superior surface forms part of the surface of the great sigmoid cavity : the inferior or anterior surface rises gradually from the anterior surface of the bone, and is covered by a large triangular roughness, the inner part of which, together with the *tuberosity of the ulna* at the lower angle of the surface, gives insertion to the tendon of the brachialis anticus muscle.

The **body** or **shaft** tapers from above downwards, and in the upper three-fourths of its extent is three-sided, and slightly curved with the convexity backwards ; in the lower fourth it is slender and more cylindrical. It also presents a lateral curve, with the concavity inwards above, outwards below. The *anterior border*, continued downwards from the inner edge of the coronoid process, is thick and rounded. The *posterior border* begins a little below the olecranon process by the meeting of two lines which limit the triangular subcutaneous surface of the upper end of the bone, and runs with a sinuous course to the back of the styloid process : it is smooth and prominent in the upper two-thirds, rounded and ill defined in the lower third. The *external border* is in the middle three-fifths of the shaft a sharp rough edge which gives attachment to the interosseous membrane ; in the lower fifth it is only a faintly marked line. In the upper fifth this border is continued by two lines, one passing into the inner margin of the coronoid process, and the other to the posterior extremity of the small sigmoid cavity, near which it becomes very prominent as the

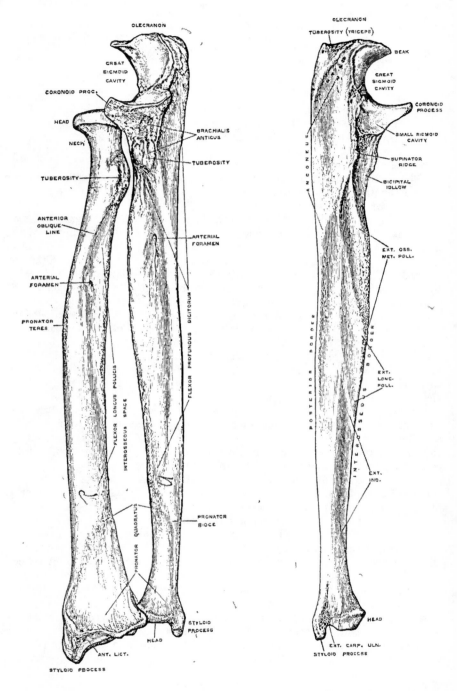

Fig. 94.—ANTERIOR VIEW OF THE RIGHT RADIUS AND ULNA IN SUPINATION OF THE HAND. (Drawn by T. W. P. Lawrence.) ⅔

Fig. 95.—RIGHT ULNA: POSTERO-EXTERNAL VIEW. (Drawn by T. W. P. Lawrence.) ⅔

supinator ridge, giving origin to a part of the supinator brevis muscle. Between these lines, and below the small sigmoid cavity, is a triangular hollow, the fore part of which lodges the tuberosity of the radius with the insertion of the biceps tendon in pronation of the hand, while in the hinder part fibres of the supinator brevis arise. The *anterior surface* is concave in the upper two-thirds, where the flexor profundus digitorum muscle takes origin, and in its lower third is marked by an oblique line— the *pronator ridge*, which joins the anterior border and limits the attachment of the pronator quadratus. Above the middle is a foramen for the medullary artery, directed upwards. The *internal surface* is smooth and convex, in the upper two-thirds giving attachment to the flexor profundus muscle, in the lower third subcutaneous. The *posterior surface*, more uneven, looks outwards and backwards ; an indistinct oblique line, descending from the supinator ridge to the posterior border at the junction of the upper and middle thirds of the shaft, limits a triangular area, which extends over the outer side of the olecranon and gives attachment to the anconeus muscle ; below this a longitudinal ridge divides the surface into an inner portion, smooth, and covered by the extensor carpi ulnaris, and an outer part, more irregular, and impressed by the extensor muscles of the thumb and index fingers.

The **inferior extremity** presents a rounded head, from the inner and back part of which a short cylindrical eminence, the *styloid process*, projects downwards, giving attachment in front and below to the internal lateral ligament of the wrist-joint, and externally to the triangular fibro-cartilage. The *head* bears two articular surfaces, an inferior, semilunar and flat-

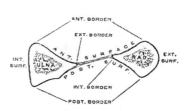

Fig. 96.—Transverse section through the middle of the bones of the forearm, with the interosseous membrane, in supination. (G. D. T.) ⅔

tened, upon which the triangular fibro-cartilage of the wrist plays ; and a lateral, narrow and convex, which is received into the sigmoid cavity of the radius. The head and the styloid process are separated posteriorly by a groove, which is traversed by the tendon of the extensor carpi ulnaris ; and inferiorly by a depression, into which also the triangular fibro-cartilage is inserted.

The ulna is placed in its whole length under the skin at the back of the forearm. The subcutaneous tract comprises the triangular surface on the back of the olecranon, the posterior border of the shaft, which lies at the bottom of a longitudinal groove between the flexor and extensor muscles, and, in the lower third, a narrow strip of the internal surface leading down to the styloid process : the latter projects in the supine position of the hand at the inner and posterior part of the wrist ; but when the hand is pronated, the outer and fore part of the head of the ulna becomes superficial and prominent between the tendons of the extensor carpi ulnaris and extensor minimi digiti muscles.

THE RADIUS.[1]

The **radius** is the external of the two bones of the forearm, and extends from the humerus to the carpus. It articulates with the humerus, the ulna, and the scaphoid and lunar bones of the carpus.

The **superior extremity** or **head**, is disc-shaped, with a smooth vertical

---

[1] In anatomical description the forearm is supposed to be placed in supination, with the thumb directed outwards and the palm of the hand looking forwards.

margin. It presents on its summit a depression, which articulates with the capitellum of the humerus, and is surrounded by a convex part, broadest internally where it glides upon the groove internal to the capitellum. The smooth, short, cylindrical surface of the vertical margin, likewise broadest internally, rotates in the small sigmoid cavity of the ulna, and within the orbicular ligament. The head is supported on a constricted portion, named the *neck*.

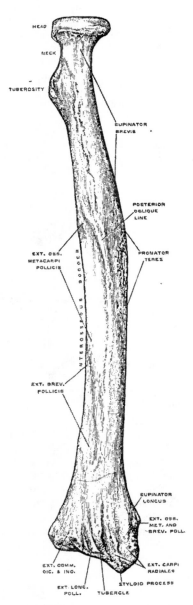

Fig. 97.—RIGHT RADIUS : POSTERIOR VIEW. (Drawn by T. W. P. Lawrence.) ⅔

The **shaft** or **body** is larger below than above, and slightly curved, with the convexity directed outwards and backwards. On its antero-internal aspect superiorly, where it is continuous with the neck, is the *bicipital tuberosity*, to the posterior rough portion of which is attached the tendon of the biceps muscle. Below the bicipital tuberosity the shaft has three surfaces, of which the external is only indistinctly marked off from the others by smooth, rounded *anterior* and *posterior borders*, while the anterior and posterior surfaces are separated in their middle three-fifths by a sharp, prominent *internal border* which gives attachment to the interosseous membrane. The *anterior surface* is limited above by the prominent *anterior oblique line*, running from the lower part of the tuberosity downwards and outwards to form the anterior border, and giving origin to a part of the flexor sublimis digitorum ; below this the surface is grooved longitudinally for the flexor longus pollicis muscle ; and at the lower end it is expanded, and presents a flattened impression for the insertion of the pronator quadratus, which also occupies a small triangular surface on the inner side of the bone in its lower fifth : above the middle of the anterior surface is the foramen for the medullary artery, directed upwards into the bone. The *posterior surface* is marked at the junction of its upper and middle thirds by the *posterior oblique line*, which limits superiorly the impression of the extensor ossis metacarpi pollicis ; below this is another small oblique impression for the extensor brevis pollicis. The *external surface* is convex transversely as well as longitudinally, and is marked near the middle, at its most prominent part, by a rough impression for the insertion of the pronator teres. Above this, the area between the anterior and posterior oblique lines gives insertion to the supinator brevis.

The **lower extremity** of the radius, broad and thick, presents inferiorly a large surface which articulates with the carpus, and internally a small one which articulates with the ulna. The *carpal articular surface,* concave and oblique, is divided by a line into a quadrilateral internal part which articulates with the lunar bone, and a triangular external part which articulates with the scaphoid bone. The *ulnar articular surface* is placed at a right angle with the inferior surface, and is concave from before backwards, forming the *sigmoid cavity,* which plays over the rounded head of the ulna. To the smooth border between the radial and ulnar articular surfaces the base of the triangular fibro-cartilage is attached. At the outer part of the inferior extremity the *styloid process* projects downwards, stout and pyramidal, giving attachment to the external lateral ligament of the wrist-joint. The posterior border of the lower articular surface descends farther than the anterior, and is roughened for ligamentous attachment. Anteriorly, a prominent transverse ridge forms the lower limit of the impression of the pronator quadratus, and between this and the scaphoid articular facet is a small triangular area occupied by a strong part of the anterior ligament of the wrist-joint. On its external and posterior aspects the inferior extremity of the radius is marked by grooves, which transmit the extensor tendons. Thus, on the external border is a flat groove directed downwards and forwards, which lodges the extensor ossis metacarpi and extensor brevis pollicis ; and on the posterior surface are three grooves, the middle one of which, oblique and narrow, and bounded externally by a prominent *tubercle,* lodges the extensor longus pollicis ; while of the two others, which are broad and shallow, the external, subdivided by a slight elevation, gives passage to the extensor carpi radialis longior and brevior, and the internal transmits the extensor communis digitorum and extensor indicis. Immediately above

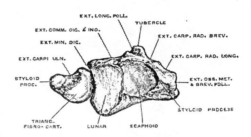

Fig. 98.—LOWER EXTREMITIES OF RIGHT RADIUS AND ULNA, IN SUPINATION, FROM BELOW. (Drawn by T. W. P. Lawrence.) ⅔

The dorsal surface is uppermost.

the first mentioned groove on the outer side is a small triangular mark, into which the tendon of the supinator longus is inserted.

The outermost groove is separated anteriorly from the impression of the pronator quadratus by a prominent edge which is continued upwards from the transverse ridge of the front of the lower extremity, and to which the posterior annular ligament is attached, while posteriorly it is limited by a less marked elevation descending on the back of the styloid process. The groove of the extensor longus pollicis is bounded externally by the tubercle, internally by a small, often indistinct, ridge ; and a sharp border projects between the innermost groove and the sigmoid cavity. The several prominences give attachment to fibrous septa, which with the annular ligament convert the grooves into canals for the passage of the tendons.

The radius is for the most part deeply placed. The head and shaft are entirely covered by muscles. At the lower end the styloid process comes to the surface between the tendons of the extensor muscles of the thumb and forms a projection on the outer side of the wrist, lower down than the styloid process of the ulna : the tubercle on the back of the lower end of the bone may also be readily felt beneath the skin.

The relative length of the forearm to the arm is expressed by the *humero-radial* or *anti-brachial index* $\left(\dfrac{\text{length of radius} \times 100}{\text{length of humerus}}\right)$, the range of variation of which in man and the anthropoid apes is shown by the following examples, viz.—Eskimo, 71 ; European, 74 ; Australian, 77 ; Negro, 79 ; Andamanese, 81 ; gorilla, 80 ; chimpanzee, 90 ; and orang, 100. The index is higher in the fœtus and infant, and diminishes during the period of growth.

THE CARPUS.

The **carpus** is composed of eight short bones, which are disposed in two rows, four in each. Enumerated from the radial to the ulnar side, the bones which constitute the first or superior row are named *scaphoid, lunar, pyramidal,* and *pisiform ;* those of the second or inferior row are the *trapezium, trapezoid, os magnum,* and *unciform.*

The dorsal surface of the carpus is convex, the palmar is concave from side to side, the concavity being bounded by four prominences, one at the outer and one at

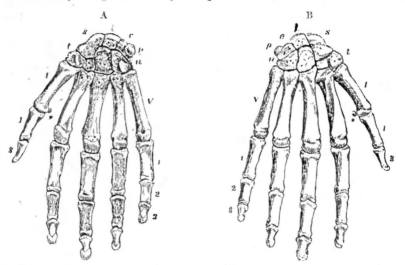

Fig. 99.—The bones of the right hand: A, from before; B, from behind. (Allen Thomson.) ½

s, scaphoid ; *l,* lunar ; *c,* pyramidal ; *p,* pisiform ; *t,* trapezium ; next to it the trapezoid, and then the os magnum, both not lettered ; *u,* unciform.

I to V, the metacarpal bones ; 1, 3, first and second phalanges of the thumb ; 1, 2, 3, the first, second, and third phalanges of the little finger, and similarly for the other three fingers, not marked ; * one of the sesamoid bones of the thumb seen sideways.

the inner extremity of each row. The anterior annular ligament is stretched across between these prominences, so far as to form a canal for the transmission of the flexor tendons.

The superior surfaces of the scaphoid, lunar, and pyramidal bones form, when in apposition, a continuous convexity which corresponds with the concavity presented

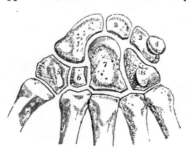

Fig. 100.—Semi-diagrammatic view of the right carpus and part of the metacarpal bones, from before, the carpal bones being slightly separated to show the mode of their connection with each other. (Allen Thomson.) ⅔

1, scaphoid bone ; 2, lunar ; 3, pyramidal ; 4, pisiform ; 5, trapezium, the figure is placed upon the ridge, to the inside of which is the groove for the tendon of the flexor carpi radialis ; 6, trapezoid ; 7, os magnum ; 8, unciform, the figure is placed on the unciform process. The articulation of the fourth metacarpal bone with the os magnum is represented somewhat too large.

by the radius and the triangular fibro-cartilage, while the pisiform bone is attached in front of the pyramidal, with which alone it articulates. The line of articulation between the superior and inferior rows is concavo-convex from side to side, the trapezium, trapezoid and os magnum bounding a cavity which lodges the external part of the scaphoid, and the os magnum and unciform rising up in a convexity, which is received into a hollow formed by the scaphoid, lunar, and pyramidal bones.

The **scaphoid bone**, the largest and most external of the first row, lies with its long axis directed outwards and downwards. It has a concave surface, which looks downwards and inwards, and rticulates with the os magnum ; on the opposite side are two convex articular surfaces, an upper for the radius, and a lower for the trapezium and trapezoid bones of the second row ; these approach so near to one another behind, that the dorsal free surface is reduced to a narrow grooved ·transverse strip, to which the posterior ligaments of the wrist are attached.

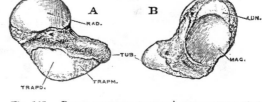

Fig. 101.—RIGHT SCAPHOID BONE : A, FROM OUTER SIDE AND BEHIND : B, FROM BEFORE AND INNER SIDE. (G. D. T.)

At the inner extremity is a small crescentic surface for articulation with the lunar bone ; while the outer end is produced into a stout conical *tuberosity*, which projects forwards and gives attachment to the annular ligament. The scaphoid articulates with five bones, viz., the radius, lunar, trapezium, trapezoid, and os magnum.

The **lunar bone** (*semilunar*), irregularly cubic, is characterized by the deep concavity from before backwards of its inferior surface, which rests on the head of the os magnum, and commonly also by a bevelled edge slightly on the unciform bone. Its external surface is crescentic and vertical, and articulates with the scaphoid bone : its internal surface looks downwards and inwards, is much deeper and narrower than the external, and articulates with the pyramidal. The convex superior surface, which articulates with the radius, extends like that of the scaphoid farther backwards than forwards, and hence the anterior free surface is deeper than the posterior. The lunar articulates with five bones, viz., the radius, scaphoid, pyramidal, os magnum, and unciform.

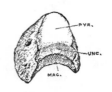

Fig. 102.—RIGHT LUNAR BONE, FROM THE INNER SIDE AND BELOW. (G. D. T.)

The **pyramidal bone** (*cuneiform*) is situated with its blunted apex directed downwards and inwards : the base has the shape of a half-oval, and articulates with the lunar bone. There are three surfaces : the inferior, concavo-convex from without inwards, articulates with the unciform bone ; the anterior is distinguished by having a smooth circular facet on its inner half for articulation with the pisiform bone ; and the supero-posterior presents at the base a small articular facet entering the wrist-joint, but is for the most part rough for the attachment of ligaments. The pyramidal articulates with three bones, viz., the lunar, pisiform, and unciform.

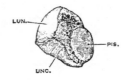

Fig. 103.—RIGHT PYRAMIDAL BONE, FROM BEFORE AND OUTER SIDE. (G. D. T.)

The **pisiform bone** lies on a plane anterior to the other bones of the carpus. In form it is spheroidal, with its longest diameter directed vertically. On its posterior aspect is an oval articular surface for the pyramidal

Fig. 104.—RIGHT PISIFORM BONE, FROM THE OUTER SIDE AND BEHIND. (G. D. T.)

bone : this surface does not extend the whole length of the pisiform bone, but leaves a small free projecting portion below. The inner side of the bone is generally convex and somewhat rough. The outer side is smoother and slightly concave.

The **trapezium** is the most external of the second row of carpal bones. It presents a rhombic form when seen in its dorsal or palmar aspect, but with the lower angle much produced and truncated. Its anterior surface is marked by a vertical groove traversed by the tendon of the flexor carpi radialis muscle, and externally to the groove by a ridge or *tuberosity*, one of

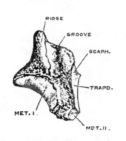

Fig. 105.—Right trapezium, from before. (G. D. T.)

the four prominences which give attachment to the anterior annular ligament. Of the internal sides of the rhomb, the superior articulates with the scaphoid and the inferior with the trapezoid ; while a small facet on the prominent lower angle is for the second metacarpal bone. Of the external sides, the superior is free, and the inferior presents a smooth surface, convex from behind forwards, and concave from without inwards, which articulates with the metacarpal bone of the thumb, and is separated by a small interval from the surface for the second metacarpal bone. The trapezium articulates with four bones, viz., the scaphoid, trapezoid, and first and second metacarpals.

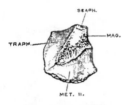

Fig. 106.—Right trapezoid bone : palmar aspect. (G. D. T.)

The **trapezoid bone** is considerably smaller than the trapezium. Its longest diameter is from before backwards. Its posterior free surface is much larger than the anterior. The external inferior angle of the anterior surface is distinguished by being prolonged a little backwards between the articular surfaces for the trapezium and second metacarpal bone. The superior surface articulates with the scaphoid ; the external with the trapezium ; the internal with the os magnum ; and the inferior by a large surface convex from side to side with the second metacarpal bone. The trapezoid articulates with four bones, viz., the scaphoid, trapezium, os magnum, and second metacarpal bone.

The **os magnum** is the largest of the carpal bones. In form it is elongated vertically, nearly rectangular below, rounded above. The upper extremity or *head*

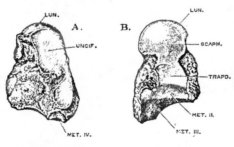

Fig. 107.—Right os magnum : A, inner view; B, outer view. (G. D. T.)

articulates superiorly with the lunar bone by a convex surface, extending farther down behind than in front, and prolonged on the outer side for the scaphoid. A *neck* is formed beneath by depressions on the anterior and posterior surfaces. The anterior surface of the bone is much narrower than the posterior. The posterior surface projects downwards at its internal inferior angle. On the outer side, below the surface for the scaphoid, is a short surface for the trapezoid bone ; and on the inner side is a vertically elongated surface which articulates with the unciform bone. Inferiorly, this bone articulates by three distinct surfaces, of which the middle is much the largest, with the second, third, and fourth metacarpal bones. The os magnum articulates with seven bones, viz., the scaphoid, lunar, trapezoid, unciform, and second, third, and fourth metacarpal bones.

The **unciform bone** is readily distinguished by the large hook-like process, projecting forwards and curved slightly outwards, on its anterior surface. Seen from the front or behind, it has a triangular form. Its external surface is vertical, and articulates with the os magnum ; its inferior surface is divided into two facets which articulate with the fourth and fifth metacarpal bones ; its superior surface, meeting the pyramidal, is concavo-convex, inclines upwards and outwards towards the head of the os magnum, and is separated internally by a rough border from the inferior surface. At the upper angle, externally, there is usually a narrow facet which touches the lunar bone. The

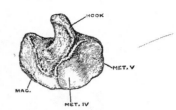

Fig. 108. — RIGHT UNCIFORM BONE, FROM THE OUTER SIDE AND BELOW. (G. D. T.)

unciform articulates with five bones, viz., the os magnum, lunar, pyramidal, and fourth and fifth metacarpal bones.

Varieties.—An increase in the number of carpal bones is occasionally met with. This may arise from the division of one of the normal bones, as has been seen in the case of the scaphoid, lunar, trapezoid, and magnum ; or it may be due to the persistence of an additional element, the *os centrale*, which is placed on the dorsal aspect of the hand between the scaphoid, magnum and trapezoid, and which is normally present as a cartilaginous rudiment in the fœtus (p. 143). Another form of supernumerary ossicle results from the separation of the styloid process of the third metacarpal bone. (W. Gruber, " Ueber das Os centrale Carpi des Menschen," 1883 ; Leboucq, " De l'augmentation numérique des os du carpe humain," Ann. de la Soc. de Méd. de Gand, 1884.)

THE METACARPUS.

The **metacarpus,** the part of the hand supporting the fingers, consists of five long bones, which diverge slightly from each other, and are numbered from without inwards.

The metacarpal bones are placed in a segment of an arch transversely, and being at the same time slightly curved longitudinally, they present a concavity directed forwards. They are terminated at their carpal extremities by expanded bases of different forms, and at the digital ends by large rounded heads. The first metacarpal bone is broader and shorter than the others. The second is the longest of all, the third, fourth, and fifth decrease regularly in length, according to their position from without inwards.

The *shaft* of the first metacarpal bone is somewhat compressed from before backwards ; the dorsal surface is slightly convex ; on the palmar aspect is a rounded longitudinal ridge, placed nearer to the inner than the outer border. The shafts of the others are three-sided, presenting a surface towards the back of the hand, and towards the palm a smooth margin between the two lateral surfaces. They are most slender near the carpal extremity, and become gradually thicker towards the head. The dorsal surface of each is triangular, being bounded by lines which, proceeding from the sides of the head, pass upwards and converge in the second, third, and fourth metacarpal bones opposite the middle of the carpal extremity, and in the fifth towards its inner side.

The *heads* articulate with the proximal phalanges. Their smooth, rounded surfaces are broader, and extend farther, on the palmar than on the dorsal aspect of the bones ; and on each side is a tubercle with a hollow below it for the attachment of the lateral ligament.

The *carpal extremity* presents distinctive peculiarities in each metacarpal bone. That of the first has a saddle-shaped articular surface, concave from before backwards, and convex from side to side, for articulation with the trapezium, and

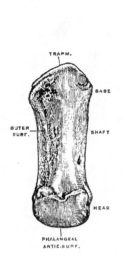

Fig. 109.—First metacarpal bone of the right hand : palmar aspect. (G. D. T.

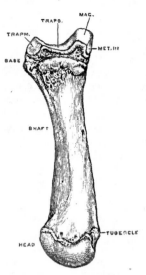

Fig. 110.—Second metacarpal bone of the right hand : palmar aspect. (G. D. T.)

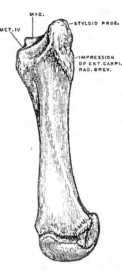

Fig. 111.—Third metacarpal bone of the right hand, from behind. (G. D. T.)

Fig. 112.—Fourth metacarpal bone of the right hand : radial side. (G. D. T.

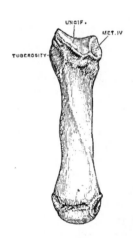

Fig. 113.—Fifth metacarpal bone of the right hand : dorsal aspect. (G. D. T.)

externally a slight prominence, to which the extensor ossis metacarpi pollicis is attached. The second is notched to receive the trapezoid bone ; on the radial side is a small facet for the trapezium ; the more prominent ulnar lip articulates superiorly by a narrow surface with the os magnum, and internally with the third metacarpal bone ; and posteriorly, close to the articulation with the trapezium, is a rounded mark where the extensor carpi radialis longior is inserted.

The third bone articulates above with the os magnum, and on the sides with the contiguous metacarpal bones ; at its posterior and outer angle it forms a projection upwards, *styloid process,* immediately below which, on the dorsal aspect, is an impression for the insertion of the extensor carpi radialis brevior. The fourth articulates principally with the unciform bone above, but also by a small facet at the posterior and outer corner with the os magnum : on its radial side are two small rounded facets, and on the ulnar side a slightly concave semi-elliptical surface, for articulation with the adjacent metacarpal bones. The fifth articulates above with the unciform bone by means of a saddle-shaped surface directed slightly outwards, and externally with the fourth metacarpal bone ; while on its ulnar side there is a broad tuberosity for the insertion of the extensor carpi ulnaris.

THE DIGITAL PHALANGES

The **phalanges** (*internodia*) are fourteen in number, three for each finger, but only two for the thumb.

Those of the *first row* are slightly curved like the metacarpal bones. Their dorsal surfaces are smooth and transversely convex ; the palmar are flat from side to side, and bounded by rough margins, which give insertion to the fibrous sheaths of the flexor tendons. Their proximal extremities are thick, and articulate each by a transversely oval concave surface with the corresponding metacarpal bone. Their distal extremities, smaller and more compressed antero-posteriorly, are divided by a shallow groove into two condyles.

Those of the *middle row* are four in number. Smaller than those of the preceding set, they resemble them in form, with this difference, that their proximal extremities present, on the articular surface, a slight middle elevation and two lateral depressions, adapted to articulate with the condyles of the first phalanges.

The *terminal* or *ungual* phalanges, five in number, have proximal extremities similar to those of the middle row, but with a depression in front, where the deep flexor tendon is inserted. They taper towards their somewhat flattened and expanded free extremities, which are rough and raised round the margins and upon the palmar aspect in the so-called *ungual process.*

Fig. 114.—THE PHALANGES OF THE MIDDLE FINGER: PALMAR ASPECT. (G. D. T.)

In each digit the proximal phalanx is the longest, and the distal phalanx the shortest. Collectively, the phalanges of the middle finger are the longest ; then follow in order, the ring, the index, and the little fingers, and lastly the thumb. The greater prominence of the index in relation to the ring finger, which is observed sometimes in the complete hand, is due entirely to the length of the metacarpal bone (Braune and Fischer, Arch. f. Anat., 1887).

SESAMOID BONES.—A pair of sesamoid bones is placed in the palmar wall of the metacarpo-phalangeal articulation of the thumb ; and similar nodules, single or double, are sometimes found in the corresponding joint of one or more of the other fingers, most frequently of the index and little fingers.

OSSIFICATION OF THE BONES OF THE UPPER LIMB.

With the exception of the clavicle, all the bones of the upper limb begin to ossify in cartilage

The **clavicle** begins to ossify before any other bone in the body. Its ossification commences before the deposition of cartilage in connection with it, but afterwards progresses in cartilage at both ends, as well as in fibrous substance. It is formed from one principal

Fig. 115.—OSSIFICATION OF THE CLAVICLE. (R. Quain.)

a, the clavicle of a fœtus at birth, osseous in the shaft, 1, and cartilaginous at both ends.

b, clavicle of a man of about twenty-three years of age; the shaft, 1, fully ossified at the acromial end; the sternal epiphysis, 2, is represented rather thicker than natural.

centre, appearing about the 6th week, to which is added an epiphysis at the sternal end. The epiphysis appears from the 18th to the 20th year, and is united to the shaft about the 25th year.

The **scapula** is ossified in two principal pieces, one forming the body or scapula proper, and the other the coracoid process, which is generally regarded as representing the independent

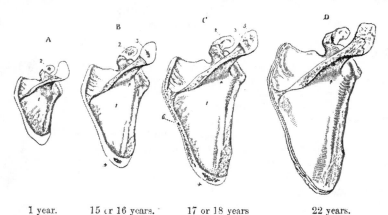

A	B	C	D
1 year.	15 or 16 years.	17 or 18 years	22 years.

Fig. 116.—OSSIFICATION OF THE SCAPULA. (R. Quain.)

1, scapula proper, including the body and spine; 2, coracoid ossification; 3, 5, nuclei of acromion; 4, epiphysis at the lower angle; 6, epiphysis on vertebral border.

In A, ossification has commenced in the coracoid process. In B the coracoid process (represented as too little ossified in the figure) is now partially united at its base, and centres have appeared in the acromion and at the lower angle. In C, a second point has appeared in the acromion, and a long epiphysis on the vertebral border. In D, the acromion, and the epiphysis of the vertebral border are still separate.

and often largely developed *coracoid* bone of the monotremata and lower vertebrates. The centre of the body appears near the head, about the 7th or 8th week, and gives rise to a triangular plate of bone, towards the upper margin of which, about the 3rd month, the spine appears as a slight ridge. At birth, the coracoid and acromion processes, the base and inferior angle, the edges of the spine and of the glenoid cavity are cartilaginous. The greater part of the coracoid process is formed from a centre which appears in the first year, but a small part at the base of the process, including the upper extremity of the glenoid cavity, is a separate ossification (*subcoracoid*), commencing about the tenth year.[1] The coracoid process joins the body about the age of puberty, and at this time epiphyses make their appearance. In the acromion two, sometimes three, nuclei appear between the 14th and 16th years; they soon coalesce, and the resulting epiphysis is united to the spine from the 22nd to the 25th year. The cartilage of the base, which it may be noticed corresponds to a more largely developed

---

[1] It is believed by some anatomists that the subcoracoid ossification is the true coracoid element of the shoulder-girdle, and that the coracoid process represents the precoracoid of reptiles (Sabatier) or the epicoracoid of monotremes (Howes).

permanent cartilage or bone, *suprascapular*, found in many animals, becomes the seat of ossification about the 16th to the 18th year, by the appearance of a nucleus at the inferior angle, and thereafter of a line of osseous deposit extending upwards throughout its length. A

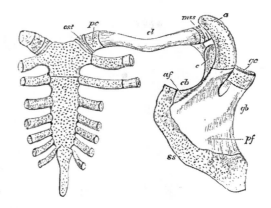

Fig. 117.—Posterior aspect of the sternum and right shoulder-girdle from a fœtus of about four months. (Flower after Parker.) $1\frac{1}{2}$

The dotted parts are cartilaginous; *ost*, omosternum of Parker, lateral part of episternum of Gegenbaur, afterwards becoming the interarticular fibro-cartilage; *pc*, precoracoid of Parker; *a*, acromion; *cl*, shaft of clavicle; *mss*, mesoscapular segment of Parker; *c*, coracoid; *gc*, glenoid cavity; *gb*, glenoid border; *cb*, coracoid border; *af*, anterior or supraspinous fossa; *pf*, posterior or infraspinous fossa; *ss*, suprascapular border.

thin lamina, in two pieces, is also added along the upper surface of the coracoid process, and another at the margin of the glenoid cavity. These epiphyses are united about the 25th year.

In the **humerus** a nucleus appears near the middle of the shaft in the 8th week. It gradually extends, until at birth only the ends of the bone are cartilaginous. In the 1st year the nucleus of the head appears, and during the 3rd year that for the great tuberosity.

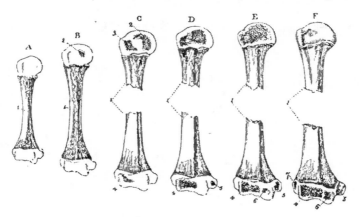

Fig. 118.—Ossification of the humerus. (R. Quain.)

A, from a full-grown fœtus; B, in the second year; C, at three years; D, at the fifth year; E, at about the twelfth year; F, at the age of puberty.

1, the primary centre for the shaft; 2, nucleus for the head; 3, that for the great tuberosity; 4, for the capitellum and adjacent part of the trochlea; 5, for the internal condyle; 6, for the inner part of the trochlea; 7, for the external condyle. In this and the following figures the more advanced bones are shown on a smaller scale than the earlier ones.

The lesser tuberosity is either ossified from a distinct nucleus which appears in the 5th year, or by extension of ossification from the great tuberosity. These nuclei join together about the 6th year to form an epiphysis, which is not united to the shaft till the 20th year. In the cartilage of the lower end of the bone four separate nuclei are seen, the first appearing in the capitellum in the 3rd year. The nucleus of the internal condyle appears in the 5th year, that of the trochlea in the 11th or 12th year, and that of the external condyle in the 13th or 14th year. The nucleus of the internal condyle forms a distinct epiphysis which unites with the shaft in the 18th year; the other three nuclei coalesce to form an epiphysis, which is united to the shaft in the 16th or 17th year.

The **radius** is developed from a nucleus which appears in the middle of the shaft in the 8th week, and from an epiphysial nucleus in each extremity which only appears some time after birth. The nucleus in the carpal extremity appears at the end of the 2nd year, while that of the head is not seen till the 5th or 6th year. The superior epiphysis and shaft unite about the 17th or 18th year; the inferior epiphysis and shaft unite about the 20th year.

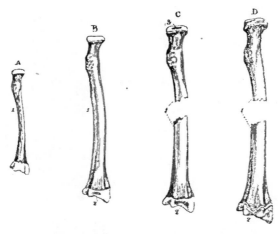

Fig. 119.—OSSIFICATION OF THE RADIUS. (R. Quain.)

A, the radius of a full-grown foetus; B, at about two years of age; C, at five years; D, at about eighteen years.

1, shaft; 2, ossific point of the lower epiphysis; 3, that of the upper end. In D, the upper epiphysis is united to the shaft, while the lower is still separate.

The ulna is ossified similarly to the radius, but begins a little later. The nucleus of the shaft appears about the 8th week, that of the carpal extremity in the 4th or 5th year. The upper extremity grows mainly from the shaft, but at the end of the olecranon a small epiphysis is formed from a nucleus which appears in the 10th year. This epiphysis is united to the shaft about the 17th year; the inferior epiphysis about the 20th year.

From what is stated above it appears that in the bones of the arm and forearm the epiphyses which meet at the elbow-joint begin to ossify later, and unite with their shafts earlier, than those at the opposite ends of the bones, whereas in the bones of the thigh and leg

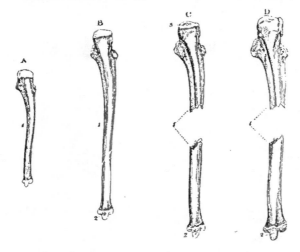

Fig. 120.—OSSIFICATION OF THE ULNA. (R. Quain.)

A, the ulna at birth; B. at the end of the fourth year; C. of a boy of about twelve years of age; D, of a male of about nineteen or twenty years.

1, shaft; 2, nucleus of the lower epiphysis; 3, nucleus of the upper epiphysis. In D, the upper epiphysis is united to the shaft, while the lower is still separate.

the epiphyses at the knee-joint are the soonest to ossify (except in the fibula) and the latest to unite with their shafts. In the bones of the arm and forearm the arterial foramina are directed towards the elbow; in those of the thigh and leg they are directed away from the knee. Thus, in each bone the epiphysis of the extremity towards which the canal of the medullary artery is directed is the first to be united to the shaft. It is found also that, while the elongation of the long bones is chiefly the result of addition to the shaft at the epiphysial synchondroses, the growth takes place more rapidly, and is continued longer, at the end where the epiphysis is last united; and the oblique direction of the vascular canals is due to this inequality of growth, which causes a shifting of the investing periosteum, and so draws the proximal portion of the medullary artery towards the more rapidly growing end.

The carpus is entirely cartilaginous at birth. Each carpal bone is ossified from a single nucleus. The nucleus of the os magnum appears in the 1st year; that of the unciform in the 1st or 2nd year; that of the pyramidal in the 3rd year; those of the trapezium and the lunar bone in the 5th year; that of the scaphoid in the 6th or 7th year; that of the trapezoid in the 7th or 8th year; and that of the pisiform in the 12th year.

The **metacarpal bones and phalanges** are usually formed each from a principal centre for the shaft and one epiphysis. The ossification of the shaft begins about the 8th or 9th week. In the inner four metacarpal bones the epiphysis is at the distal extremity, while in the metacarpal bone of the thumb and in the phalanges it is placed at the proximal extremity. In many instances, however, there is also a distal epiphysis visible in the first metacarpal bone at the age of 7 or 8 years, and there are even traces of a proximal epiphysis in the second metacarpal. In the seal and some other animals there are always two epiphyses in these bones. The epiphyses begin to be ossified from the 3rd to the 5th year, and are united to their respective shafts about the 20th year. The terminal phalanges of the digits present the remarkable peculiarity that the ossification of their shafts commences at the distal extremity, instead of in the middle of their length, as is the case with the other phalanges and with the long bones generally (Schäfer and Dixey, Proc. Roy. Soc. xxx, 550, and xxxi, 63).

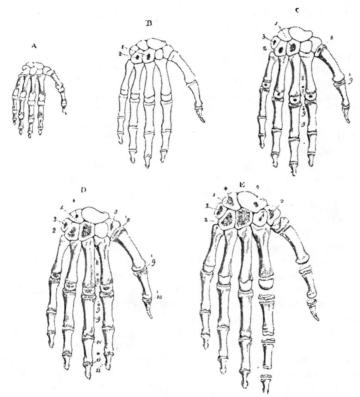

Fig. 121.—OSSIFICATION OF THE BONES OF THE HAND. (R. Quain.)

A, the condition at birth. The carpus is entirely cartilaginous. Each of the metacarpal bones and digital phalanges has its shaft ossified.

B, at the end of the first year. The os magnum and unciform have begun to ossify.

C, about the third year. Centres of ossification are seen in the pyramidal and in the proximal epiphysis of the first and distal epiphyses of the other four metacarpal bones, and in the proximal epiphyses of the first row of phalanges.

D, at the fifth year. Centres have been formed in the trapezium and later in the lunar bone, and in the epiphyses of the middle and distal phalanges : (the figure does not show them distinctly in the middle phalanges).

E, at about the ninth year. Centres have been formed in the scaphoid and trapezoid bones, and the more developed epiphyses of the metacarpal bones and phalanges are shown in the first and second digits separately.

1, os magnum ; 2, unciform ; 3, pyramidal ; 4, lunar ; 5, trapezium ; 6, scaphoid ; 7, trapezoid ; 8, metacarpal bones, the principal pieces ; 8*, four metacarpal epiphyses ; 8′, that of the thumb ; 9, first phalanges ; 9*, their epiphyses ; 9′, that of the thumb ; 10, second phalanges ; 10′, epiphysis of terminal phalanx of thumb ; 11, terminal phalanges of the fingers ; 11*, their epiphyses.

V.—THE PELVIS AND LOWER LIMB.

The divisions of the lower limb are the haunch or hip, thigh, leg, and foot. In the haunch is the hip-bone, which enters into the formation of the pelvis ; in the thigh is the femur ; in the leg the tibia and fibula ; and at the knee a large sesamoid bone, the patella. The foot is composed of three parts, viz., the tarsus, metatarsus, and phalanges.

THE HIP-BONE.

The **hip-bone**, *os coxæ*, or innominate bone, with its neighbour of the opposite side and the addition of the sacrum and coccyx, forms the pelvis ; it transmits the weight of the body to the lower limb. It is constricted in the middle and expanded above and below, and is so curved that, while the upper part is nearly vertical, the lower part is directed inwards. On the external aspect of the constricted portion is the *acetabulum,* a cavity which articulates with the femur, and perforating the inferior expansion is a large opening, the *thyroid* or *obturator foramen.* The superior wider part of the bone forms part of the abdominal wall ; the inferior enters into the formation of the true pelvis. The hip-bone articulates with its fellow of the opposite side, with the sacrum, and with the femur.

In the description of this bone it is convenient to recognise as distinct the three parts of it which are separate in early life, viz., the *ilium, os pubis* and *ischium.* These three portions meet at the acetabulum, in the formation of which they all take part ; and the os pubis and ischium also meet on the inner side of the obturator foramen.

The **ilium** constitutes the superior expanded portion of the bone, and forms a part of the acetabulum by its inferior extremity. Above the acetabulum it is limited anteriorly and posteriorly by margins which diverge at right angles one from the other, and superiorly by an arched thick border, *the crest of the ilium.* Viewed from above, the *crest* is curved like the letter *f,* the fore part being concave inwards, the hinder part concave outwards : it is narrow in its middle third, broadened in front and behind, and forms a marked projection externally in its anterior third : on it may be distinguished external and internal lips and an intermediate ridge. The anterior extremity of the crest forms a projection forwards called the *anterior superior spine of the ilium,* and, separated from it by a concave border, and placed immediately above the acetabulum, is another eminence called the *anterior inferior spine :* the projecting posterior extremity of the crest forms the *posterior superior spine,* and separated from it by a small notch is the *posterior inferior spine,* below which the posterior border of the bone is hollowed out into the *ilio-sciatic* (or *great sciatic*) *notch.* The external surface or *dorsum* of the ilium is convex in front, below the prominence of the crest, and concave behind this. It is traversed by three curved *gluteal lines,* which limit the areas of attachment of the gluteal muscles. The *posterior* or *superior gluteal line* leaves the iliac crest about one-fourth of its length from the posterior superior spine, and curves downwards and forwards towards the hinder part of the ilio-sciatic notch : the *middle gluteal line* begins in front at the iliac crest, about one inch and a half from its anterior extremity, and arches backwards and downwards to the upper margin of the ilio-sciatic notch : the *inferior gluteal line,* less strongly marked than the middle, commences at the anterior border of the ilium, just above the anterior inferior spine, and is continued backwards nearly parallel to the margin of the acetabulum to the fore part of the ilio-sciatic notch. Behind the posterior gluteal line is a narrow semilunar surface, the upper portion of which is rough and gives attachment to the gluteus maximus muscle, while the lower part is smooth and free from muscular attachment.   The sickle-shaped space between the iliac crest and posterior gluteal line above and the middle gluteal line below is occupied by the gluteus medius ; and the surface between the middle and inferior gluteal lines gives

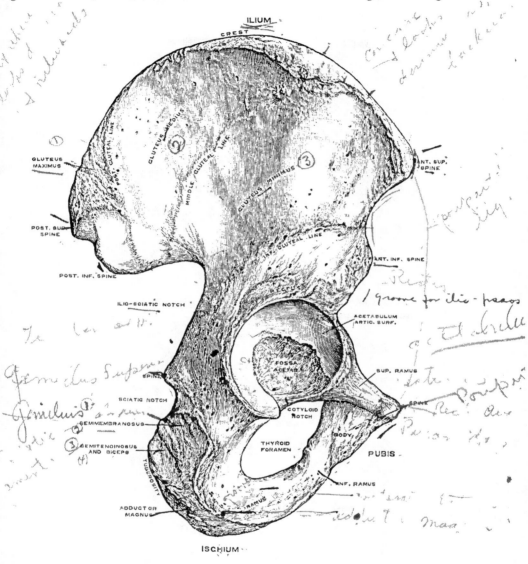

Fig. 122.—RIGHT HIP-BONE OF MALE : OUTER VIEW.   (Drawn by T. W. P. Lawrence.)   ⅓

origin to the gluteus minimus.   On the lowest part of this surface, immediately above the margin of the acetabulum, is a rough elongated mark where the reflected head of the rectus femoris is attached.

The internal surface of the ilium is divided into two parts.   The anterior of these (*iliac surface*) is the larger : it is smooth and concave, occupied by the iliacus muscle, and is known as the *iliac fossa*.   Inferiorly, the fossa terminates above the margin of the acetabulum, and to the inner side of the anterior inferior iliac spine, in a groove which lodges the ilio-psoas muscle as it passes from the abdomen into the thigh. The inner boundary of the groove is formed by an elevation, the *ilio-pectineal eminence*, marking the place of junction of the pubis and ilium.

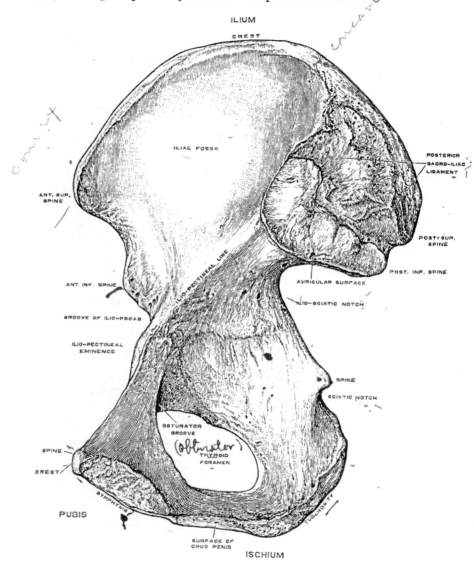

Fig. 123.—RIGHT HIP-BONE OF MALE : INNER VIEW.   (Drawn by T. W. P. Lawrence.) ⅔

The posterior part (*sacral surface*) is again subdivided, presenting from below upwards—1, a smooth surface entering into the formation of the true pelvis, and continuous with the pelvic surfaces of the pubis and ischium, only a faint line indicating in the adult the place of union ; this gives origin to a part of the obturator internus muscle, and is separated from the iliac fossa by a smooth rounded border, the *iliac portion of the ilio-pectineal line* ; 2, the uneven *auricular surface*, in the recent state covered with cartilage, for articulation with the sacrum, broad in front, and extending on to the posterior inferior spine behind ; 3, some depressions for the attachment of the posterior sacro-iliac ligament ; and 4, a rough surface reaching up to the hinder portion of the iliac crest, and giving origin to parts of the erector and multifidus spinæ muscles.

The iliac crest gives attachment by its outer lip to the tensor vaginæ femoris, obliquus externus, and latissimus dorsi muscles, and the gluteal fascia; by its middle ridge to the internal oblique ; and by its inner lip to the transversalis, quadratus lumborum, and erector spinæ muscles, and the iliac fascia. To the anterior superior spine are attached the tensor vaginæ femoris externally, the sartorius in front, and Poupart's ligament internally. The anterior inferior spine gives origin to the straight head of the rectus femoris muscle. Between this and the margin of the acetabulum is an impression where the ilio-femoral ligament is fixed to the bone. The iliac part of the ilio-pectineal line gives attachment to the iliac and obturator fasciæ, and the tendon of the psoas parvus when that muscle is present.

The **os pubis** forms the anterior wall of the pelvis, and bounds the thyroid foramen in the upper half of its extent. At its outer and upper extremity it forms a part of the acetabulum ; at its inner extremity it presents an elongated oval surface which forms the articulation with the bone of the opposite side, the junction being called the *symphysis pubis*. The part which passes downwards and outwards below the symphysis is called the *inferior* or *descending ramus*, the upper part is called the *superior* or *ascending ramus*, and the flat portion between the rami is the *body*. The deep or pelvic surface of the body is smooth ; the anterior or femoral surface is roughened near the symphysis by the attachments of muscles. At the superior extremity of the symphysis is the *angle of the pubis*, and extending outwards from this on the superior border is the rough *pubic crest*, terminating in the projecting *spine*. The inferior ramus is thin and flattened, and joins the ramus of the ischium. The superior ramus becomes prismatic, and increases in thickness as it passes upwards and outwards. Its superior border is the *pubic portion of the ilio-pectineal line*, a sharp ridge continued from the iliac portion of the line downwards and inwards to the pubic spine. The triangular surface in front of this line is covered by the pectineus muscle ; it is bounded externally by the ilio-pectineal eminence, and below by the prominent *obturator crest*, which extends from the pubic spine to the acetabular margin at the anterior extremity of the cotyloid notch. Behind the outer part of the crest, on the inferior surface of the ramus, is the deep *obturator groove*, directed from behind forwards and inwards, for the obturator vessels and nerve.

The pubic crest gives origin to the rectus abdominis and pyramidalis muscles. The pubic spine serves for the insertion of Poupart's ligament ; and for a short distance outside this Gimbernat's ligament and the conjoined tendon of the internal oblique and transversalis muscles are fixed to the ilio-pectineal line. Along the front of the pubic portion of the ilio-pectineal line the pectineus muscle arises, and to the line itself the pubic portion of the fascia lata is attached. From the front of the pubis the adductor longus muscle arises in the angle between the crest and symphysis, and below this the adductor brevis and upper part of the adductor magnus. Internally to these the gracilis is attached to the prominent edge of the surface, and externally the obturator externus. Along the margin of the symphysial surface is a small rough area, which is occupied by the anterior ligament of the articulation, and is wider in the female than in the male bone (Cleland). The posterior surface of the pubis gives attachment to part of the obturator internus muscle ; and above this, where a faint line may sometimes be recognized passing obliquely from the upper margin of the obturator foramen to the lower end of the symphysis, the levator ani and obturator and recto-vesical fasciæ are fixed together to the bone.

The **ischium** forms the posterior and inferior part of the hip-bone, and bounds the thyroid foramen in the lower half of its extent. Superiorly it enters into the acetabulum : inferiorly it forms a thick projection, the *tuberosity*, and this part, diminishing in size, is continued forwards into the *ramus*. On its posterior border, behind the acetabulum, a sharp process, the *spine*, projecting with an inclination inwards, forms the inferior limit of the *ilio-sciatic notch*, and is separated from the tuberosity by a short interval, the *sciatic* (or *small sciatic*) *notch*, against the smooth margin of which, covered in the recent state with cartilage, the tendon of the obturator internus muscle glides. In front of this, on the external surface, a horizontal groove, occupied by the upper border of the obturator externus muscle, lies between the inferior margin of the acetabulum and the tuberosity. The tuberosity presents

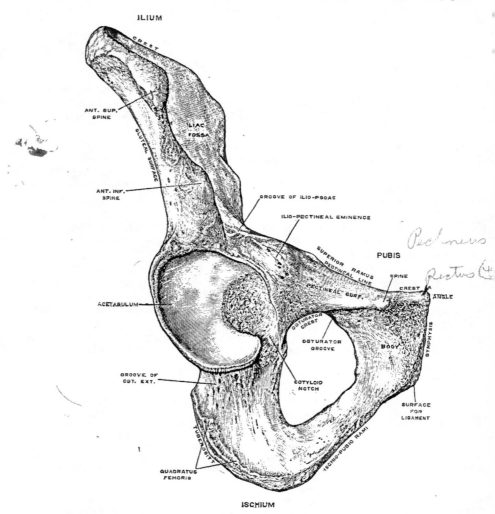

Fig. 124.—Right hip-bone of male, from before and below. (Drawn by T. W. P. Lawrence.)

a rough pyriform surface continuous with the internal margin of the ramus, on the broader superior portion of which are two impressions placed side by side, the outer for the semimembranosus, the inner for the conjoined origins of the biceps and semitendinosus, while the lower part is ridged and gives attachment to the adductor magnus muscle; the inner border is sharp and prominent where the great sacro-sciatic ligament is attached; and along the outer margin is a faint elongated impression marking the place of origin of the quadratus femoris muscle. The ramus of the ischium is flattened like the inferior ramus of the pubis, with which it is continuous on the inner side of the thyroid foramen.

The ischial spine gives attachment posteriorly to the small sacro-sciatic ligament, externally to the superior gemellus, and internally to the coccygeus and the hinder fibres of the levator ani. The inferior gemellus arises from the upper margin of the tuberosity, below the sciatic notch ; and the inner surface of the ischium gives origin to part of the obturator internus. On the conjoined ischio-pubic rami, immediately above the inner margin, in the male bone, is an oval surface to which are attached the crus penis, surrounded by the ischio-cavernosus muscle, and more deeply the transversus perinei and constrictor urethræ muscles. The smaller and less distinct surface in the female gives attachment to the crus clitoridis and corresponding muscles.

The *acetabulum*, or *cotyloid cavity*, is a cup-shaped hollow, looking outwards, downwards, and forwards, and surrounded in the greater part of its circumference by an elevated margin, which is most prominent at the posterior and upper part ; while at the opposite side, close to the obturator foramen, it is deficient, forming the *cotyloid notch*. Its lateral and upper parts present a broad horseshoe-shaped smooth surface, which articulates with the head of the femur, and in the recent state is coated with cartilage ; but the central part of the cup and the region of the notch are depressed below the level of the articular surface (*fossa acetabuli*), lodge a mass of fat and the interarticular ligament, and have no cartilaginous coating. Rather more than two-fifths of the acetabulum are formed from the ischium, less than two-fifths from the ilium, and the remainder from the pubis. The iliac portion of the articular surface is the largest, the pubic the smallest : the non-articular surface belongs chiefly to the ischium.

The *thyroid* or *obturator foramen*, also called *foramen ovale*, is internal and inferior to the acetabulum. In the male it is nearly oval, with the long diameter directed downwards and backwards ; in the female it is broader and more triangular. In the recent state it is closed by a fibrous membrane, except in the neighbourhood of the groove in its upper margin.

The crest of the ilium is subcutaneous, and forms the boundary between the abdomen and the region of the hip. In front the pubic spine is to be felt through the integuments, and lower down the inner margin of the united rami of the ischium and pubis can be followed to the ischial tuberosity, dividing the perineum from the thigh. The remainder of the bone is thickly covered by muscles.

The hip-bone varies greatly in thickness at different parts. The strongest portions are found along the lines of greatest pressure ; these are, a very thick bar in the ilium between the auricular surface and the acetabulum, through which the weight of the body is transmitted to the thigh-bones, and a second formed by the ischium, ending in the tuberosity, which supports the body in the sitting posture. The ilium has also a thick rib running from the acetabulum to the most prominent portion of the iliac crest, while the bone between this and the auricular surface, corresponding to the deepest part of the iliac fossa, is very thin. The floor of the non-articular portion of the acetabulum is also a thin plate of bone, and this, as well as the thin part of the ilium, is occasionally perforated. The chief vascular foramina penetrate the bone where it is thickest, viz., in the iliac fossa near the auricular surface, on the pelvic surface of the ilium near the ilio-sciatic notch, on the outer surface of the ilium between the inferior gluteal line and the acetabulum, and on the ischium between the acetabulum and tuberosity.

THE PELVIS.

The hip-bones with the sacrum and coccyx form the pelvis.

This part of the skeleton may be considered as divided into two parts by a plane passing through the sacral promontory, the ilio-pectineal lines, and the upper border of the symphysis pubis. The circle thus completed constitutes the *brim* or *inlet* of

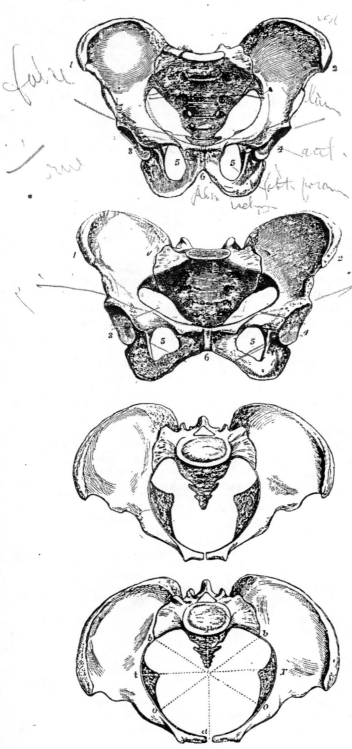

the lower or *true pelvis*; the space above it, between the iliac fossæ, belongs really to the abdomen, but has been

Fig. 125.—ADULT MALE PELVIS SEEN FROM BEFORE, IN THE ERECT ATTITUDE OF THE BODY. (Allen Thomson.) ¼

1, 2, anterior extremities of the iliac crests in front of the greatest transverse diameter of the false pelvis; 3, 4, acetabula; 5, 5, thyroid foramina; 6, subpubic angle or arch.

Fig. 126.—ADULT FEMALE PELVIS. (Allen Thomson.) ¼

Similarly placed with that shown in the preceding figure, and illustrating by comparison with it, the principal differences between the male and female pelvis. The numbers indicate the same parts as in the preceding figure.

called the upper or *false pelvis*. The inferior circumference, or *outlet* of the pelvis, presents three large bony eminences, the coccyx and the tuberosities of the ischia. Between the tuberosities of the ischia in front is the *subpubic arch*, which bounds an angular space extending forwards to the symphysis, and is formed by the inferior

Figs. 127 and 128.—THE MALE AND FEMALE PELVIS, AS SEEN PERPENDICULARLY TO THE PLANE OF THE BRIM. (Allen Thomson.)

In Fig. 128 of the female pelvis the lines are shown in which the dimensions of the pelvis are usually measured at the brim.

a, p, antero-posterior or conjugate diameter; *t, r*, transverse or widest diameter; *o, b, o, b*, oblique diameters.

rami of the pubes and the rami of the ischia. The interval between the sacrum and coccyx and the ischium on each side (*sacro-sciatic notch*) is bridged over in the recent state by the great sacro-sciatic ligaments, which therefore assist in bounding the outlet of the pelvis.

Position of the pelvis.—In the erect attitude of the body, with the heels in contact and the toes directed outwards, the pelvis is so inclined that the plane of

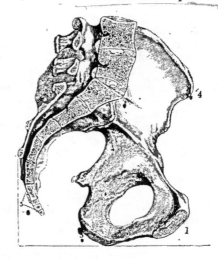

Fig. 129.—MEDIAN SECTION OF A FEMALE PELVIS. (Reduced from Nägele.) ⅓

1, symphysis pubis ; 2, promontory of the sacrum ; 3, coccyx ; 4, anterior superior spine of ilium ; 5, tuberosity of ischium ; 6, spine of ischium (the thyroid foramen is not represented so pointed below as it generally is in females). The vertical and horizontal lines in the lower part of the figure will assist the eye in judging of the degree of inclination of the pelvis, as illustrated by the next figure.

the brim of the true pelvis forms an angle with the horizontal, which varies in different individuals from 50° to 60°. The base of the sacrum is then about 3½ inches above the upper margin of the symphysis pubis, and the tip of the coccyx from half an inch to an inch above the apex of the subpubic arch. The inclination of the pelvis varies with the position of the lower limbs, and the angle is generally somewhat greater in the female than in the male.[1] The pelvic surface of the sacrum, near its base, looks much more downwards than forwards, hence the sacrum appears at first sight to occupy the position of the keystone of an arch ; but being in reality broader

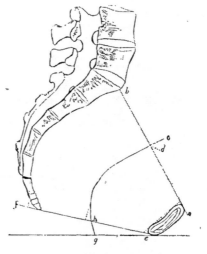

Fig. 130.—SKETCH OF PART OF THE PRECEDING FIGURE, SHOWING THE INCLINATION OF THE BRIM OF THE PELVIS AND ITS AXIS IN THE ERECT POSTURE. ⅓

a, b, line of inclination of the brim of the true pelvis ; e, f, a line inclining backwards and upwards, touching the lower edge of the symphysis pubis and point of the coccyx ; c, d, axis of the brim at right angles to the plane of the brim ; d, h, g, curved axis of the cavity and outlet.

at its pelvic than on its dorsal aspect, it is a keystone inverted, or having its broad end lowest, and is supported in its place chiefly by ligaments, but also to a slight extent by the inward projection of the anterior margin of the iliac articular surface. The line of pressure of the weight of the body on the sacrum is directed downwards towards the symphysis pubis, and the resistance of the head of the thigh-bone on each side is directed upwards and inwards.

The *axis of the pelvis* is the name given to a line drawn at right angles to the planes of the brim, cavity and outlet, through their central points. The

[1] Nägele, "Das weibliche Becken," &c., 1825 ; Wood, art. "Pelvis," in Cyclop. of Anat. and Phys. ; G. H. Meyer, Arch. f. Anat., &c., 1861 ; Fürst, "Die Maass- und Neigungs-Verhältnisse des Beckens," 1875.

posterior wall, formed by the sacrum and coccyx, being about five inches long and concave, while the anterior wall at the symphysis pubis is only one and a half or two inches long, the axis is curved ; it is directed at the inlet upwards and forwards towards the umbilicus, and at the outlet downwards and a little backwards or forwards according to the level of the coccyx.

Differences according to sex.—The size and form of the pelvis differ markedly in the two sexes. In the female the constituent bones are more slender and the muscular impressions less marked : the height is less, and the breadth and capacity of the true pelvis greater ; the ilia however are more vertical, and thus the false pelvis is relatively narrower than in the male ; the inlet of the true pelvis is more regularly oval, the sacral promontory projecting less into it ; the sacrum is flatter and broader ; the depth of the symphysis pubis is less ; the subpubic arch is much wider, and the space between the tuberosities of the ischia greater.

The average dimensions of the pelvis, as measured in a number of full-sized males and females, may be stated as follow, in inches :—

	MALE.			FEMALE.		
Greatest distance between the crests of the ilia externally	$11\frac{1}{4}$			11		
Distance between the anterior superior spines of the ilia	$9\frac{1}{2}$			$9\frac{1}{4}$		
Distance between the front of the symphysis pubis and the first sacral spine . . .	$7\frac{1}{4}$			7		
TRUE PELVIS.	Brim.	Cavity.	Outlet.	Brim.	Cavity.	Outlet.
Transverse diameter	5	$4\frac{3}{4}$	$3\frac{1}{2}$	$5\frac{1}{4}$	5	$4\frac{3}{4}$
Oblique diameter	$4\frac{3}{4}$	$4\frac{1}{2}$	4	5	$5\frac{1}{4}$	$4\frac{1}{2}$
Antero-posterior diameter	4	$4\frac{1}{4}$	$3\frac{1}{4}$	$4\frac{1}{2}$	5	4[1]

The human pelvis, compared with that of the lower animals, is characterised by its shallowness and breadth, and by the great capacity of the true pelvis ; by the expansion of the ilia. the length and sigmoid curve of their crests, the massiveness and straightness of the ischial tuberosities, and the shortness of the symphysis. Similar, although much slighter, variations in the form of the pelvis are to be recognized in the different races of mankind, the most important of which is in the relation of the antero-posterior to the transverse diameter, and is expressed by what is termed the *pelvic index*. This is measured at the pelvic brim ; the transverse diameter is taken as the standard = 100, and the proportion of the antero-posterior diameter to this gives the index. For this purpose the pelves of the two sexes must necessarily be grouped separately, and the male is usually selected for comparison. The following examples of the average pelvic index in the male of four races will show the range of variation :—European, 80 ; Negro, 93 ; Australian, 97 ; Andamanese, 99. Pelves with an index above 95 are *dolichopellic*, from 95 to 90 *mesatipellic*, and below 90 *platypellic* (Turner). (Verneau, "Le bassin dans les sexes et dans les races," 1875 ; Garson, Journ. Anat., xvi ; Turner, Journ. Anat., xx, and " Challenger " Reports, Zoology, xvi.)

THE FEMUR.

The **femur** or thigh-bone, situated between the hip-bone and the tibia, is the largest and longest bone of the skeleton. In the erect position of the body it inclines inwards and slightly backwards as it descends, so as to approach inferiorly its fellow of the opposite side, and to have its upper end a little in advance of the lower. It is divisible into the *superior extremity*, including the *head* and *neck* and two eminences called *trochanters* ; the *shaft* ; and the *inferior extremity*, expanded into an *external* and an *internal condyle*.

At the **superior extremity** of the bone, the *neck* extends inwards, upwards,

[1] This diameter may be increased to the extent of one inch or more by movement of the coccyx.

and slightly forwards, being set upon the shaft at an angle of about 125°. The neck is expanded from above down at its base, where it meets the shaft obliquely, but compressed from before back, so that the vertical diameter greatly exceeds the antero-posterior ; the summit becomes more rounded, and is somewhat enlarged again as it joins the head. It is shorter above and in front than below and behind. On its posterior surface there may usually be recognized a shallow horizontal groove, in which the tendon of the obturator externus lies. The *head* forms more than half a sphere, and is covered with cartilage in the fresh state. Behind and below its central point is a small oval depression, the fore part of which gives attachment to the interarticular ligament of the hip-joint. In the hollow there are often one or two small vascular foramina.

The *great trochanter* is a thick truncated process prolonged upwards in a line with the external surface of the shaft. In front it is marked by the insertion of the gluteus minimus. Externally an oblique line directed downwards and forwards indicates the inferior border of the insertion of the gluteus medius muscle ; and lower down the surface is bounded by a horizontal line, which is continued upwards on the front of the trochanter to an eminence at the junction with the neck, the *tubercle of the femur ;* this line marks the upper limit of the vastus externus. Internally at its base, and rather behind the neck, is the *trochanteric* or *digital fossa,* which gives attachment to the obturator

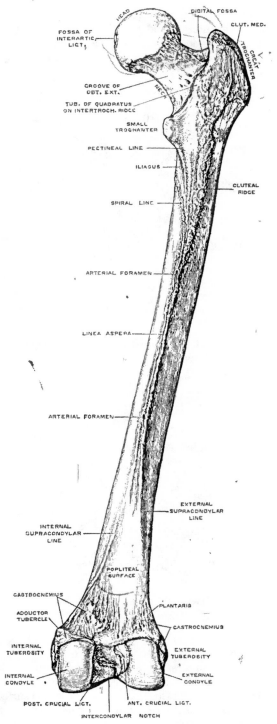

Fig. 131.—RIGHT FEMUR, FROM BEHIND. (Drawn by T. W. P. Lawrence.) ⅖.

externus muscle, while close above and in front of this is the impression of the obturator internus and gemelli muscles. The upper border of the great trochanter is narrow, and presents an oval mark for the insertion of the pyriformis. The

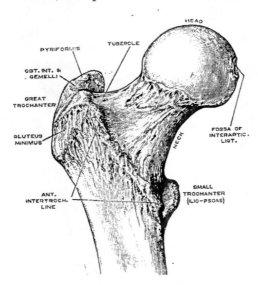

Fig. 132.—UPPER PORTION OF RIGHT FEMUR, FROM BEFORE. (Drawn by T. W. P. Lawrence.) ⅔

posterior border is prominent, and continued into a strong rounded elevation, the *inter-trochanteric ridge* or *posterior intertrochanteric line*, which passes downwards and inwards to the small trochanter, and limits the neck posteriorly : above the centre the ridge is thickened, marking the attachment of the upper part of the quadratus femoris ; the enlargement is termed the *tubercle of the quadratus.*

The *small trochanter*, a pyramidal eminence, projects from the posterior and inner aspect of the bone at the junction of the neck with the shaft ; its rounded summit gives attachment to the tendon of the ilio-psoas muscle. The neck is separated from the shaft anteriorly by the *anterior intertrochanteric line*, or upper part of the *spiral line*, a broad rough line commencing at the tubercle of the femur and directed obliquely downwards and inwards a finger's breadth in front of the small trochanter ; it indicates the attachment of the thick anterior portion of the capsular ligament of the hip-joint and the upper border of the united crureus and vastus internus muscles.

The **shaft** is arched from above downwards, with the convexity forwards. It is somewhat narrowed in the middle third, and becomes considerably expanded below. Towards the centre it is nearly cylindrical, but with a

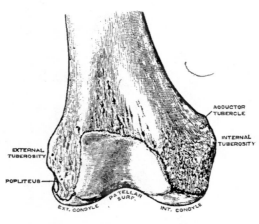

Fig. 133.—LOWER END OF RIGHT FEMUR, FROM BEFORE. (Drawn by T. W. P. Lawrence.) ⅔

tendency to the prismatic form, due to the projection of the linea aspera behind, and a slight flattening of the surface in front ; so that it may conveniently be regarded as presenting an anterior and two lateral surfaces, although definite lines separating the surfaces do not exist. All three surfaces, smooth and uniform, are covered by the crureus and vasti muscles. The lateral surfaces in the middle of their extent approach one another behind, being only separated by the linea aspera. The *linea aspera* is a prominent ridge, extending along the central third of the shaft posteriorly, and bifurcating above and below. It presents two sharp margins or lips separated by a narrow interval. The external lip is prolonged up to the great trochanter, and in its course is strongly marked for about three inches where the gluteus maximus is attached, constituting the *gluteal ridge*. The internal lip is continued, winding in front of the small trochanter, to the anterior intertrochanteric line, and forms the lower part of the *spiral line;* it marks the attachment of the vastus internus. In the interval between the two diverging branches of the linea aspera a less distinct line, which gives attachment to the pectineus, is seen passing to the small trochanter. Inferiorly the two lips are prolonged to the condyles under the name of *internal* and *external supracondylar lines,* enclosing between them a flat triangular surface of bone, the *popliteal surface of the femur,* which forms the floor of the upper part of the popliteal space. The internal supracondylar line is interrupted at the upper part where the femoral vessels lie against the bone; it terminates below in a small sharp projection, the *adductor tubercle,* giving attachment to the tendon of the adductor magnus. Above the centre of the linea aspera is the foramen for the medullary artery, directed upwards into the bone ; a second foramen is frequently to be seen near the lower end of the line.

To the inner lip of the linea aspera are attached the vastus internus, adductor longus and adductor magnus muscles, the last also extending upwards on the inner side of the gluteal ridge, and downwards along the internal supracondylar line. The outer lip of the linea aspera and the external supracondylar line give attachment to the short head of the biceps and the external intermuscular septum of the thigh. The adductor brevis is inserted into the upper third of the shaft externally to the pectineal line. Running downwards from the tubercle of the quadratus to the level of the small trochanter there is sometimes to be seen a faint *linea quadrati,* marking the insertion of the quadratus femoris. A small triangular area below the lesser trochanter, between the pectineal and spiral lines, gives insertion to the outer fibres of the iliacus. At the lower part of the popliteal surface is a slight roughness on each side, above the corresponding condyle, where fibres of the two heads of the gastrocnemius, and externally also the plantaris, arise.

The **inferior extremity** presents two rounded eminences, the *condyles,* united in front, but separated behind by a deep *intercondylar fossa* or *notch.* Their greatest prominence is directed backwards, and their curve, as it increases towards that part, may be compared to that of a partially uncoiled piece of watch-spring. The external condyle is the broader and more prominent in front : the internal is the longer and more prominent laterally. In the natural position of the femur, however, the inferior surfaces of the two condyles are on the same level. One large articular surface, coated continuously with cartilage, extends over both condyles ;

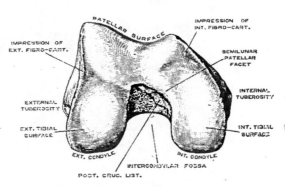

Fig. 134.—Lower extremity of right femur, from below. (Drawn by T. W. P. Lawrence.) ⅔

but opposite the front of the intercondylar fossa it is divided by two irregular, slightly marked transverse grooves into three parts, a convex surface on each side of the fossa for articulation with the tibia ; and a grooved anterior surface for the patella. The *patellar surface* is of a trochlear form, being marked by a vertical hollow and two prominent lips ; the external portion of this surface is wider and more prominent, and rises higher than the internal. The *tibial surfaces* are nearly

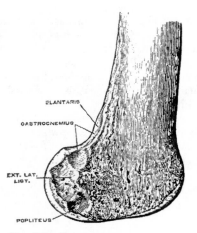

PLANTARIS

GASTROCNEMIUS

EXT. LAT. LIGT.

POPLITEUS

Fig. 135.—LOWER PORTION OF RIGHT FEMUR : OUTER VIEW. (Drawn by T. W. P. Lawrence.)

parallel, except in front, where the internal turns obliquely outwards to reach the patellar surface. On the exposed lateral surface of each condyle is a rough *tuberosity*, giving attachment to the respective lateral ligament of the knee-joint. The external tuberosity is the smaller of the two ; above it is a roundish impression for the outer head of the gastrocnemius, and below and behind it an oblique groove, ending inferiorly in a pit, in which the popliteus muscle takes origin : the tendon of the muscle plays over the smooth hinder edge of the groove, and sinks into the hollow when the knee-joint is fully bent. On the upper part of the internal condyle, between the adductor tubercle and the articular surface, is an impression for the internal head of the gastrocnemius. The floor of the intercondylar fossa is rough, and presents two impressions where the crucial ligaments are attached :

Fig. 136.—CORONAL SECTION OF THE UPPER END OF THE FEMUR. (Zaaijer.)

that of the anterior ligament occupies the hindmost part of the inner surface of the external condyle, while that of the posterior ligament is at the inner and fore part of the fossa, above the curved portion of the internal tibial articular surface.

The head and neck of the femur are deeply placed ; the great trochanter is covered only by the aponeurosis of the gluteus maximus, and is readily felt, forming the most prominent part of the hip. The shaft is thickly surrounded by muscles. The condyles are subcutaneous on each side of the knee, the internal being especially prominent ; the trochlear surface is concealed by the patella during extension, but in the flexed limb its form can be traced pushing up the muscular covering.

The arrangement of the cancellous tissue at the upper end of the femur is shown in fig. 136. A system of "pressure-lamellæ," springing from the compact wall of the lower side of the neck and the upper end of the shaft internally, ascends radiating inwards to the head and outwards to the great tro-chanter ; those passing to the head are especially dense. These are crossed at right-angles by a set of "tension-la-mellæ," which start from the outer side of the shaft, and arch upwards and inwards to the head and inner side of the neck. The concave side of the neck is farther strengthened by a nearly vertical plate of compact tissue (calcar femorale[1]), which projects upwards into the spongy substance a little in front of the small trochanter. At the lower end of the bone the chief lamellæ run vertically from the compact wall of the shaft to the tibial articular surfaces.

The average length of the femur in the European male is a little more than 18 inches, in the female about 17 inches. It equals about ·275 of the stature, and its proportion to the humerus is as 100 : 71.

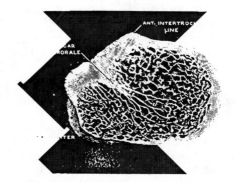

Fig. 137.—TRANSVERSE SECTION OF THE FEMUR IMMEDIATELY ABOVE THE SMALL TROCHANTER. (G. D. T.)

In the erect attitude the inclination of the femur is such that the shaft forms an angle of about 9° with the sagittal plane, and 5° with the frontal plane ; the former angle is larger in the female than in the male. The femur also exhibits a torsion similar to that of the humerus, but usually in the opposite direction, the head being inclined forwards from the transverse axis of the lower extremity : the angle of torsion varies within wide limits, but is in the majority of cases between 5° and 20° (Mikulicz, Arch. f. Anat., 1878).

The angle between the neck and shaft of the femur varies much in different individuals, ranging in the adult from 110° to 140°. It is as a rule smaller in short than in long thigh-bones, and in women than in men. It is more open in the fœtus and child, and decreases during the period of growth under the influence of the weight of the body ; but it does not appear to undergo any change after growth is completed (Humphry, Journ. Anat., xxiii, 273).

Varieties.—The upper part of the gluteal ridge is sometimes very prominent, forming a *third trochanter* similar to the process so named in the horse and some other animals. In some cases there is a hollow, *fossa hypotrochanterica,*[2] in place of or in addition to the ridge. A marked development of the linea aspera gives rise to the condition known as the *pilastered femur.* The adductor tubercle may be of unusual size, and has been seen forming a projection three-quarters of an inch in length.

[1] Merkel, Virchow's Archiv, lix.
[2] Houzé, Bull. de la Soc. d'Anthrop., Bruxelles, 1883.

THE PATELLA.

The **patella**, *rotula*, or knee-pan, situated at the front of the knee-joint, is a sesamoid bone developed in the tendon of the quadriceps extensor cruris. It is compressed from before backwards, and somewhat triangular in shape, with the apex below. Its anterior surface is convex and longitudinally striated, being covered by a fibrous prolongation from the extensor tendon; it presents a few

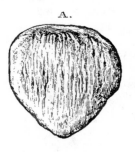
A.

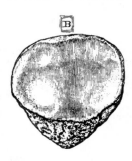
B

Fig. 138.—RIGHT PATELLA : A, FROM BEFORE ; B, FROM BEHIND. (Drawn by T. W. P. Lawrence.) ⅔

In B, the articular surface is seen, divided by a ridge into a smaller internal and a larger external part. On each of these three facets may be recognized, of which the middle is the largest and the lower the smallest, while along the inner margin there is a narrow seventh facet.

vascular foramina, and is separated from the skin by one or more bursæ. The superior border is broad, and sloped from behind downwards and forwards; it is occupied, except near the posterior margin, by an impression into which the common (suprapatellar) tendon of the quadriceps is inserted. The deep surface is for the most part coated with cartilage for articulation with the femur, and is divided by a vertical elevation into two parts, the external of which is the larger and transversely concave, while the internal is convex : below the articular surface is a triangular depressed and roughened area, covered in the recent state by a mass of fat ; and from the lower angle and sharp margins of this part of the bone the infrapatellar tendon or ligamentum patellæ springs, by which the patella is attached to the tibia.

THE TIBIA.

The **tibia**, or shin-bone, is, next to the femur, the longest bone in the skeleton. It is the anterior and inner of the two bones of the leg, and alone communicates the weight of the trunk to the foot. It articulates with the femur, fibula, and astragalus.

The **superior extremity** or **head** is thick and expanded, broader from side to side than from before back, and inclined somewhat backwards from the direction of the shaft. It forms on each side a massive eminence or *tuberosity*, on the upper aspect of which is a slightly concave articular surface for the corresponding condyle of the femur. The *internal tuberosity*, somewhat larger than the external, is rounded, and marked posteriorly by a horizontal groove for the insertion of the semimembranosus muscle. The *external tuberosity* forms at the junction of its anterior and outer surfaces a broad prominent tubercle, into which the ilio-tibial band of the fascia lata is inserted ; at its posterior and under part is a small flat surface for articulation with the head of the fibula. The *internal condylar surface* is oval in shape, larger than the external, and slightly more hollowed. The *external condylar surface* is more nearly circular, and concave from side to side, but rather concavo-convex (in some cases altogether convex) from before backwards, and is prolonged for a short distance on the posterior surface of the tuberosity where the tendon of the popliteus glides. The peripheral part of each articular surface is flattened, and separated from the condyle of the femur by a semilunar interarticular fibro-cartilage. Between the condylar surfaces is an irregular

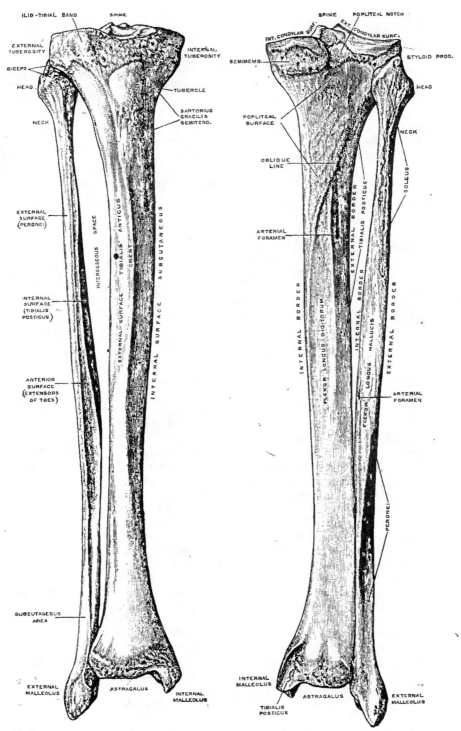

Fig. 139.—RIGHT TIBIA AND FIBULA, FROM
BEFORE. (Drawn by T. W. P. Lawrence.) ½

Fig. 140.—RIGHT TIBIA AND FIBLUA, FROM
BEHIND. (Drawn by T. W. P. Lawrence.) ½

interval, depressed in front and behind, where it gives attachment to the crucial ligaments and the semilunar fibro-cartilages of the knee-joint, and elevated in the middle, thus forming the *spine*, which is received into the intercondylar notch of the femur. The summit of the spine presents two compressed tubercles, with a slight intervening hollow, and the condylar articular surfaces are prolonged upwards on the sides of the process. The depressed surface behind the spine is continued into a shallow excavation—the *popliteal notch*, which separates the tuberosities on the posterior aspect of the head. Lower down on the front of the bone, at the junction of the head and shaft, is situated the *tubercle* or *anterior tuberosity*, marked by the attachment of the ligamentum patellæ.

The **shaft** of the tibia is three-sided, and diminishes in size as it descends for about two-thirds of its length, but increases somewhat towards its lower extremity. The *internal surface* is convex and for the most part subcutaneous ; at the upper

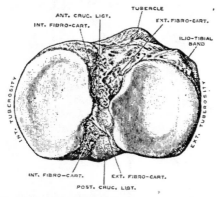

Fig. 141.—Upper extremity of the right tibia, from above. (Drawn by T. W. P. Lawrence.) ⅔

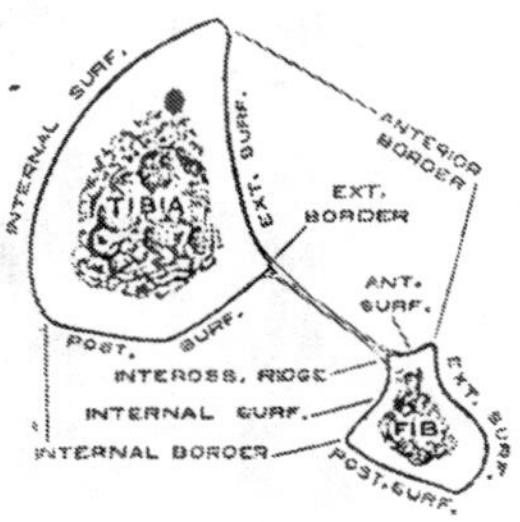

Fig. 142.—Transverse section through the middle of the bones of the leg, with the interosseous membrane. (G. D. T.) ⅔

end, by the side of the tubercle, is a slight roughness where the tendons of the sartorius, gracilis and semitendinosus muscles are inserted. It is separated from the external surface by the *anterior border*, which runs with a sinuous course from the tubercle to the front of the internal malleolus, having its concavity directed outwards above, and inwards below ; in its upper two-thirds it forms a sharp ridge known as the *crest of the tibia* ; in its lower third it is smooth and rounded. The *external surface* is slightly hollowed in its upper two-thirds, where it lodges the belly of the tibialis anticus muscle ; but below the point where the crest disappears it turns forwards, becomes convex, and is covered by the extensor tendons. The *posterior surface* is crossed obliquely in its upper third by the rough *popliteal* or *oblique line*, which runs downwards and inwards from the outer tuberosity, and gives origin to the soleus muscle : above this is a triangular area occupied by the popliteus muscle ; while below the line, in the middle third of the shaft, a longitudinal ridge divides the surface into two portions, an inner giving origin to the flexor longus digitorum, and an outer, larger, to the tibialis posticus. A little below the oblique line, and external to the longitudinal ridge, is a large foramen for the medullary artery, directed downwards into the bone. The posterior surface is separated from the internal by the *internal border*, which is most distinct in the middle third of the bone, being rounded off above and below, and from the outer surface by the *external border* or *interosseous ridge*, a prominent edge or line, inclined forwards above, to which the interosseous membrane is attached.

The **inferior extremity**, much smaller than the superior, is expanded transversely, and projects downwards on its inner side, so as to form a thick process, the *internal malleolus*. Inferiorly it presents for articulation with the astragalus a cartilaginous surface, which is quadrilateral, concave from before backwards, and having its posterior border narrower and projecting farther downwards than the anterior ; internally the cartilaginous surface is continued down in a vertical direction upon the internal malleolus, clothing its outer surface somewhat more deeply in front than behind. The external surface is hollowed for the reception of the fibula, and rough for the attachment of ligament, except over a small part along the lower border. The posterior surface of the internal malleolus is marked by a groove for the tendon of the tibialis posticus, and more externally is a slight depression where the tendon of the flexor longus hallucis lies.

Both tuberosities of the tibia are subcutaneous, the external forming a well-marked prominence at the outer and fore part of the knee. The internal surface of the shaft is thinly covered for a short distance at the upper part by the tendons of the sartorius, gracilis, and semitendinosus, but in the rest of its extent it is subcutaneous, together with the continuous surface of the internal malleolus. Anteriorly, the tubercle gives rise to a slight elevation below the knee, on which the body is supported in, kneeling, and running down from this the crest is to be followed, constituting the shin.

The *femoro-tibial index* $\left(\dfrac{\text{length of tibia} \times 100}{\text{length of femur}}\right)$ is about 81 in the European, 83 in the Negro, and 86 in the Bushman. The tibia is twisted so that when the upper extremity has its longest diameter directed transversely, the internal malleolus is inclined forwards : the *angle of torsion* is commonly between 5° and 20°, but it may range from 0 to 48° (Mikulicz, Arch. f. Anat., 1878).

Varieties.—The shaft of the tibia is sometimes much compressed laterally, and expanded from before back, the posterior longitudinal ridge being very prominent, so that a transverse section at the junction of the upper and middle thirds has the form of a narrow lozenge : such a bone is said to be *platycnemic*. A facet at the anterior margin of the lower extremity for articulation with the neck of the astragalus in extreme flexion of the ankle-joint is rare in Europeans, but common in some lower races. (Manouvrier, " Sur le platycnémie," &c., Mém. Soc. d'Anthrop. Par., 1888 ; A. Thomson, " Influence of posture on the form of the tibia," &c., Journ. Anat. xxiii and xxiv.)

THE FIBULA.

The **fibula**, or *peroneal bone*, is situated on the outer side of the leg ; it is nearly equal to the tibia in length, but is much more slender. Its inferior extremity is placed a little in advance of the superior ; and its shaft is slightly curved, so as to have the convexity directed backwards, and, in the lower half, slightly inwards towards the tibia.

The **superior extremity**, or **head**, somewhat expanded, is produced upwards at its hindmost part into a conical eminence, known as the *styloid process ;* in front of, and inside this is a small oval cartilage-covered facet, looking upwards, inwards and forwards, for articulation with the outer tuberosity of the tibia ; while more externally is a slightly excavated surface where the tendon of the biceps femoris is inserted : the outer side of the head is smooth and subcutaneous. The somewhat constricted part below the head is distinguished as the *neck*.

The **inferior extremity**, or **external malleolus**, is longer and more prominent than the internal malleolus ; internally it forms the outer limit of the ankle joint, and presents a triangular smooth surface for articulation with the astragalus, behind which is a rough depression where the posterior band of the external lateral ligament is attached : its anterior border, after projecting rather abruptly forwards, slopes downwards and backwards : posteriorly it is marked by a shallow groove traversed

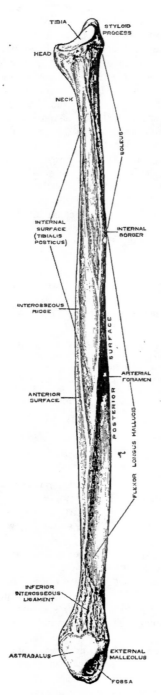

Fig. 143.—Right fibula : inner view. (Drawn by T. W. P. Lawrence.) ½

by the tendons of the peroneus longus and brevis muscles : externally it is convex and subcutaneous ; and a triangular subcutaneous surface is continued up from it for two or three inches on the shaft.

The **shaft** has four surfaces, separated by as many prominent lines. Three of these lines are known as borders, the fourth is the interosseous ridge. The *anterior border* is the most prominent ; it commences at the fore part of the neck, and takes a straight course down the front of the bone as far as the lower fifth, where it bifurcates, the one line running to the front of the malleolus, the other to the back, and enclosing between them the triangular subcutaneous surface. Immediately internal to this is the *interosseous ridge*, so named from giving attachment to the interosseous membrane ; it is close to the anterior border above, but gradually diverges from that as it passes downwards ; it terminates about an inch and a half above the ankle-joint in the apex of a triangular surface, convex and roughened by the inferior interosseous ligament, fixing it to the tibia. The *external border* extends the whole length of the bone, from the styloid process to the back of the malleolus, inclining inwards in its lower half. The remaining border, *internal*, commences at the inner side of the neck, runs down the shaft for two-thirds of its length, and then ends by joining the interosseous ridge. The surfaces are :—the *anterior*, between the anterior border and the interosseous ridge, narrow above, wider below ; it gives origin to the extensor muscles of the toes and the peroneus tertius : the *external*, broadest of all, somewhat hollowed at the upper part, and turning below to the back of the malleolus, thus indicating the course of the peronei muscles, by which it is completely covered : the *posterior*, which winds to the inner side of the bone in its lower half ; in its upper third it is rough, giving origin to the soleus, while the rest of its extent is occupied by the flexor longus hallucis : and the *internal*, between the internal border and the interosseous line, a fusiform surface over the upper two-thirds only of the shaft, and giving origin to the tibialis posticus ; it is often traversed by an oblique ridge which gives attachment to a tendinous septum in the muscle. The foramen of the medullary artery is small, placed on the internal or posterior surface, about the middle, and is directed downwards.

The head of the fibula projects under the skin at the outer and back part of the knee, behind and somewhat below the level of the prominent outer tuberosity of the tibia. The shaft is covered by muscles, except over the triangular surface above mentioned. The external malleolus descends lower and projects farther backwards than the internal, its point being nearer to the heel by about three-quarters of an inch.

THE TARSUS.

The **tarsus** is composed of seven bones, viz., the calcaneum, astragalus, navicular, three cuneiform, and cuboid.

The **calcaneum** or **os calcis** is the largest bone of the foot. Projecting downwards and backwards, it forms the heel. Above, it articulates with the astragalus, and in front with the cuboid bone. Its principal axis extends forwards and outwards from its posterior extremity to the cuboid bone.

The large *posterior extremity*, or *tuberosity*, presents inferiorly two *tubercles*, which rest upon the ground, and of which the internal is the larger : its hinder surface is

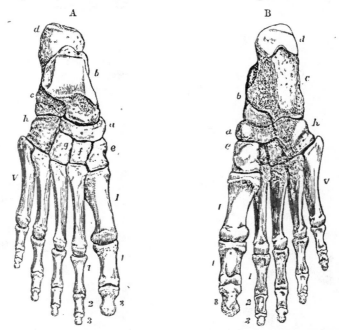

Fig. 144.—THE BONES OF THE RIGHT FOOT : A, FROM ABOVE ; B, FROM BELOW. (Allen Thomson.) ¼

a, navicular bone ; *b*, astragalus ; *c*, os calcis ; *d*, its tuberosity ; *e*, internal cuneiform ; *f*, middle cuneiform ; *g*, external cuneiform ; *h*, cuboid bone ; I to V, the metatarsal bones ; 1, 3, first and last phalanges of the great toe ; 1, 2, 3, first, second, and third phalanges of the second toe.

divided into an upper part, smooth and separated by a bursa from the tendo Achillis, a middle part for the attachment of the tendon, and a lower part, convex and roughened, continued below onto the tubercles, and covered by the thick skin and fatty pad of the heel. The part in front of the tuberosity forms a slightly constricted *neck*. The *internal surface* of the bone is deeply concave, and its concavity is surmounted in front by a flattened process, the *sustentaculum tali*, which projects inwards near the anterior extremity of the bone on a level with its upper surface, and presents inferiorly a groove occupied by the tendon of the flexor longus hallucis. The *upper surface* has two articular facets for the astragalus, separated by an oblique groove in which the interosseous ligament is attached ; the anterior facet, often subdivided into two, is placed over the sustentaculum, and is concave ; the other, posterior and external to this, and larger, is convex from behind forwards and outwards : the outer end of the groove is much widened, and at its fore part is a

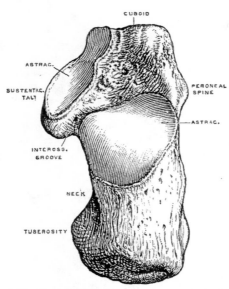

rough surface where the extensor brevis digitorum takes origin. The *anterior extremity* articulates with the cuboid bone by a surface concave from above, downwards and outwards, and convex in the opposite direction ; and internal to this, along the front of the sustentaculum tali, the internal calcaneo-navicular ligament is attached. The *under surface,* projecting in a rough *anterior tubercle,* gives attachment to the inferior calcaneo-cuboid ligaments. The *external surface* is on the whole flat, but often presents at its fore part an oblique ridge, the *peroneal spine,* separating two slight grooves, the upper for the tendon of the peroneus brevis, the lower for the peroneus longus.

The **astragalus**, or *talus,* second in size of the tarsal bones, receives the weight of the body from the leg. It articulates with the tibia above and internally, the fibula externally, the os calcis below, and the navicular in front. Its longest axis is directed forwards and inwards. Its main part is called the *body,* the convex anterior extremity is the *head,* and the grooved part behind this is the *neck.* The *superior articular surface* occupies the whole of the upper aspect of the body, and sends a prolongation downwards on each of the lateral surfaces of the bone. The middle part, looking upwards to the tibia, is convex from before backwards, broader in front than behind, with its outer margin longer than the inner, and curved, while the inner is straight. The inner lateral part is narrow, sickle-shaped,

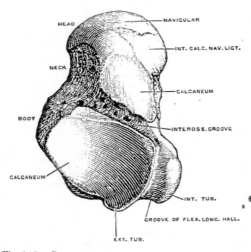

and articulates with the internal malleolus ; the outer lateral part, much deeper, triangular, and concave from above down, articulates with the external malleolus. *Inferiorly,* there are two smooth surfaces, which articulate with the calcaneum. The posterior of these, the larger, concave from within outwards and forwards, is separated by a rough depression for the interosseous ligament from the convex anterior surface, which rests on the sustentaculum tali. The rounded anterior surface of the head articulates with the navicular bone ; and at the lower and inner part, between this and the anterior articulation with the os calcis, is a facet which rests upon the internal calcaneo-navicular ligament, the three forming one continuous articular surface. The *posterior surface* is of small extent, and marked at its inner part by a groove for the flexor longus hallucis, which is continuous below with that of the sustentaculum tali. Bounding the groove are two *tubercles*, of which the *internal* is usually but little marked, while the *external* is more prominent and gives attachment to the posterior band of the external lateral ligament of the ankle-joint.

The **navicular** or **scaphoid bone** is placed at the inner side of the foot between the astragalus and the cuneiform bones. It is elongated transversely, and compressed from before backwards. It presents *posteriorly* an articular concavity for the head of the astragalus, and *anteriorly* a convex surface divided by two lines converging below into three facets, which articulate respectively with the three cuneiform bones. Its *upper surface* is convex from side to side ; the *lower* is narrower and very uneven. On the outer end there is in some instances a small articular surface for the cuboid bone ; the *inner end* forms the prominent *tuberosity*, directed downwards, and giving insertion to the tendon of the tibialis posticus muscle.

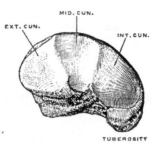

Fig. 147.—RIGHT NAVICULAR BONE, FROM BEFORE. (G. D. T.)

The **cuneiform bones** are known as first, second, and third, from within outwards, or internal, middle and external. They are placed between the navicular bone and the inner three metatarsal bones, and present anteriorly and posteriorly smooth surfaces for articulation with those bones. The internal cuneiform bone is the largest, the

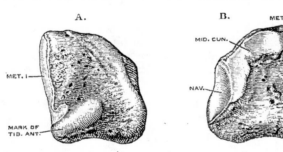

Fig. 148.—RIGHT INTERNAL CUNEIFORM BONE : A, INNER VIEW ; B, OUTER VIEW. (G. D. T.)

middle is the smallest. The proximal ends of the three bones are in the same transverse line ; but at their distal ends the internal and external project forwards beyond the middle one, and thus form a deep recess into which the base of the second metatarsal bone is received.

The **internal cuneiform bone** has its sharp border directed upwards, and the thick rounded base of the wedge projects downwards on the inner border of the foot. The *anterior articular surface*, for the first metatarsal bone, is much larger than the *posterior*, is kidney-shaped and convex. The *internal surface* is free, rather uneven, and marked by an oblique groove for the tendon of the tibialis anticus muscle, ending below in an oval facet where the larger part of the tendon is inserted. On the *outer side*, along the posterior and superior borders, is an L-shaped surface, which articulates with the middle cuneiform, and at its anterior extremity with the second metatarsal bone.

The **middle cuneiform bone** has its base directed upwards, and the sharp edge downwards towards the sole. The *posterior end* is somewhat broader than the *anterior.* On the *inner side* is an L-shaped articular surface, corresponding to that on the internal cuneiform bone ; and on the *outer side* is a smaller facet, at the posterior part, for the external cuneiform bone.

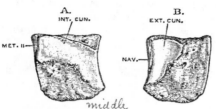

Fig. 149.—Right ~~internal~~ *middle* cuneiform bone : A, inner view ; B, outer view. (G. D. T.)

The **external cuneiform bone** is also situated with its base upwards. At its *anterior end* is a triangular articular surface for the third metatarsal bone, and continuous with this are small facets on the fore part of each lateral surface, for the second and fourth metatarsal bones. On the *internal surface*, at the posterior part, is an articular facet for the middle cuneiform bone, and on the *outer surface* a much larger one for the cuboid bone.

The **cuboid bone** is situated on the outer side of the foot, between the

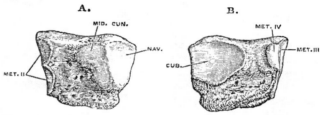

Fig. 150.—Right external cuneiform bone : A, inner view ; B, outer view. (G. D. T.)

calcaneum and the fourth and fifth metatarsal bones. It deviates from the cuboid form and becomes rather pyramidal, by the sloping of four of its surfaces towards the short, rounded external border. *Posteriorly* it articulates with the os calcis, and the lower internal corner projects backwards as a conical process beneath the anterior

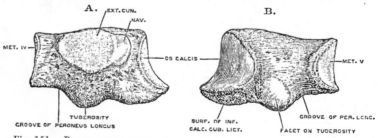

Fig. 151.—Right cuboid bone : A, inner view ; B, outer view. (G. D. T.)

extremity of that bone. Its *anterior surface*, smaller than the posterior, is divided into an internal quadrilateral and an external triangular facet, articulating with the fourth and fifth metatarsal bones. On its *internal aspect*, in the middle, and reaching the superior border, is a surface for articulation with the external cuneiform bone ; and behind this, in many instances, is a smaller facet articulating with the navicular, while the remainder is rough for ligaments. The *superior surface*, looking upwards and outwards, is on the whole flat, but rather rough. On the *inferior surface* is a thick oblique ridge or *tuberosity*, the outer end of which presents a smooth facet, covered with cartilage in the recent state, where the tendon of the peroneus longus turns round into the sole. Between the tuberosity and the anterior margin of this surface is a deep groove, beginning at a notch in the outer border of the bone, for the reception of the tendon. Behind the tuberosity is a triangular depressed area occupied by the plantar calcaneo-cuboid ligament.

Varieties.—Instances are recorded in which the number of tarsal bones is reduced owing to congenital synostosis of the os calcis and navicular, of the astragalus and os calcis, or of the astragalus and navicular. An increase in number may arise from the separation of the external tubercle at the back of the astragalus (*os trigonum*—Bardeleben), or of the tuberosity of the navicular bone, from the division of the internal cuneiform bone into dorsal and plantar pieces, and from the presence of a supernumerary ossicle at the fore and inner part of the os calcis, or between the internal cuneiform and second metatarsal bones. (H. Leboucq, " De la soudure congénitale de certains os du tarse," Bull. de l'Acad. Roy. de Méd. de Belgique, 1890, 103 ; L. Stieda, " Der Talus und das Os trigonum Bardelebens beim Menschen," Anat. Anzeiger, 1889, 305 ; W. Gruber, " Os cuneiforme I. bipartitum beim Menschen," Mém. Acad. St. Petersburg, 1877 ; Hartmann et Mordret, " Anatomie du premier cunéiform," Bull. Soc. Anat. de Paris, 1889, 71.)

THE METATARSUS.

The five **metatarsal bones** are distinguished by numbers, according to their position from within outwards. They resemble the metacarpal bones of the hand in being long bones, slightly convex from end to end on the dorsal aspect, in having differently shaped bases, three-sided shafts, and rounded heads which articulate with the phalanges. They also agree with the metacarpal bones in the number of bones with which each articulates.

The **first metatarsal bone** is the shortest, but is much thicker and more massive than the others. On its *base* is a large kidney-shaped surface, slightly concave, for articulation with the internal cuneiform bone, and sometimes there occurs a small facet on the outer side for the second metatarsal bone. The lower part of the base forms the *tuberosity*, which projects downwards and outwards in the sole, and is marked on its outer side by a rounded impression for the peroneus longus : on the inner side is a smaller mark where a slip of the tibialis anticus is inserted. Of the three surfaces

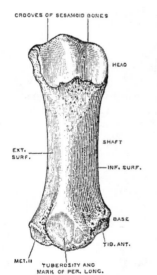

Fig. 152.—First metatarsal bone of right foot : plantar aspect. (G. D. T.)

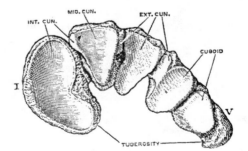

Fig. 153.—Bases of the metatarsal bones, from behind. (G. D. T.)

of the *shaft*, the *superior*, which looks also inwards, is oblong and convex, the *inferior* is concave, and the *external*, the largest, is triangular and flattened. The *head* is large, and has on its under surface a median ridge, separating two grooves in which the sesamoid bones glide.

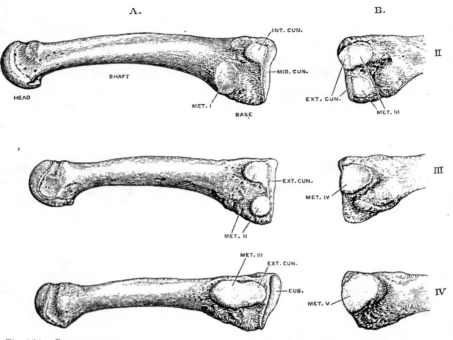

Fig. 154.—Second, third, and fourth metatarsal bones of the right foot : A, from inner side ; B, from outer side. (G. D. T.)

Fig. 155.—Fifth metatarsal bone of right foot: dorsal aspect. (G.D.T.)

The remaining four bones are distinguished from the metacarpal bones by being more slender and compressed from side to side, corresponding to the narrower form of the foot compared with that of the hand. The second is the longest ; the others diminish gradually to the fifth. Their *shafts* present in the greater part of their extent a prominent border looking upwards, which in the middle three appears on the back of the foot between the dorsal interosseous muscles on each side. Their *heads* are elongated from above down, and terminate below in two small projections ; on each side is a tubercle and depression for the attachment of the lateral ligament. The *bases* differ in the several bones, and thus furnish distinctive characters between them. The **second** has a triangular base, which articulates with the middle cuneiform bone ; on the inner side is a small facet for the internal cuneiform, and sometimes, below and in front of this, a less distinct surface for the first metatarsal bone ; on the outer side there are usually two small surfaces, an upper and a lower, each again subdivided into two, thus making four facets, of which the two posterior articulate with the external cuneiform, and the two anterior with the next metatarsal bone. The **third** has also a triangular base articulating with the external cuneiform bone ; on the inner side are usually two facets for the second, and on the outer side a single larger facet for the fourth metatarsal bone. The base of the **fourth** is oblong or oval, and articulates with the cuboid ; on the inner side is generally a double facet for the third metatarsal and the external cuneiform bones, but the articulation with the latter is sometimes absent ; and on the outer side is a single surface for the fifth metatarsal bone, with a deep groove below it.   The **fifth** articulates by its base with the cuboid, and internally with the fourth metatarsal bone, while externally it projects in a large rough *tuberosity*, into which the peroneus brevis muscle is inserted.

Variety.—In some rare cases an independent ossicle has been found taking the place of the tuberosity of the fifth metatarsal bone (W. Gruber, Virchow's Archiv, xcix, 460 ; Ch. Debierre, Bull. Soc. Anat. de Paris, 1888, 392).

THE PHALANGES.

The **phalanges** of the toes correspond so nearly in general conformation with those of the fingers that it will only be necessary in this place to state the points in which they differ from the latter.

The phalanges of the four outer toes are much smaller than the corresponding phalanges of the hand ; but those of the great toe are larger than those of the thumb. The shafts of the first row of phalanges in the four outer toes are compressed laterally and narrowed in the middle ; those of the second row, more especially in the fourth and fifth toes, are very short, their length scarcely exceeding their breadth. The last two phalanges of the little toe are frequently connected by bone into one piece.[1]

SESAMOID BONES.—Two sesamoid bones, developed in the tendons of the flexor brevis hallucis, lie side by side in the plantar wall of the first metatarso-phalangeal joint, and glide in the grooves on the head of the first metatarsal bone. Small sesamoid bones sometimes occur in the corresponding joints of the other toes.

Fig. 156. — PHALANGES OF SECOND TOE : PLANTAR ASPECT. (G.D.T.)

THE BONES OF THE FOOT AS A WHOLE.

The foot is narrowest at the heel, and as it passes forwards becomes broader as far as the heads of the metatarsal bones. The posterior extremity of the calcaneum is inclined slightly inwards.   The astragalus, overhanging the sustentaculum tali, inclines inwards from the calcaneum so much that its external superior border is directly over the middle line of the calcaneum, and hence the internal malleolus appears more prominent than the external.   The foot is arched from behind forwards, the posterior pier of the arch being formed by the heel, the anterior by the heads of the metatarsal bones.   The arch, indeed, may be considered as double in front, with a common support behind.   The internal division of the arch is that which bears the greater part of the weight of the body, and is most raised from the ground ; it consists of the posterior two-thirds of the calcaneum, the navicular and cuneiform bones, and the three inner metatarsal bones : the outer arch is formed by the calcaneum in its whole length, the cuboid bone, and the fourth and fifth metatarsal bones. Besides being arched longitudinally, the foot presents likewise a transverse arch, formed behind by the cuboid and three cuneiform bones, and in front by the metatarsal bones.

[1] W. Pfitzner found this union in about 36 per cent., and as frequently in infants as in adults (Arch. f. Anat., 1890, 12).

OSSIFICATION OF THE BONES OF THE LOWER LIMB.

Hip-bone.—The hip-bone is formed from the three principal pieces previously mentioned, viz., the ilium, ischium, and os pubis, and from various others of an epiphysial nature. Ossification commences in the cartilage of the ilium a little later than in other large bones, the deposit of bone beginning above the ilio-sciatic notch in the 8th or 9th week. This is followed

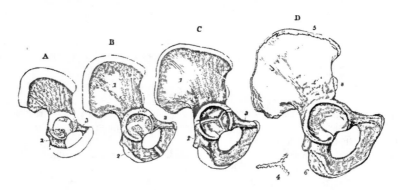

Fig. 157.—Ossification of the hip-bone. (R. Quain.)

A, the condition of the bone at birth. Bone has spread from three nuclei into the ilium, ischium, and pubis, which meet in the cartilage of the acetabulum.

B, from a child under six years of age. The rami of the ischium and pubis are farther ossified, but still separate.

C, a bone of two or three years later, in which the rami are united.

D, the bone of the right side from a person of about twenty years. Union has taken place in the acetabulum, and the additional epiphyses are seen on the crest of the ilium, the anterior inferior spine, the ischial tuberosity, and the margin of the symphysis pubis.

In A, B, and C, 1, ilium ; 2, ischium ; 3, pubis ; in D, 5, epiphysis of the crest ; 6, that of the tuberosity of the ischium ; 7, that of the symphysis pubis ; 8, that of the anterior inferior spine of the ilium.

by similar deposits in the thick part of the ischium below the acetabulum in the 3rd month, and in the superior ramus of the pubis in the 4th or 5th month. At birth the greater part of the acetabulum, the crest of the ilium, the tuberosity and ramus of the ischium, the body and inferior ramus of the pubis are still cartilaginous ; ossification from the three primary centres has however extended into the margin of the acetabulum. In the 7th or 8th year the rami of

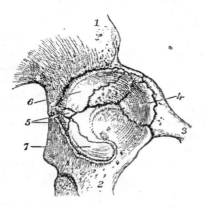

Fig. 158.—Acetabular region of the hip-bone at 14 years of age. (G. D. T.) ½

1, ilium ; 2, ischium ; 3, pubis ; 4, os acetabuli ; 5, bony nodules between ilium and ischium ; 6 and 7, epiphysial laminæ on ilium and ischium.

the ischium and pubis become completely united by bone. In the acetabulum the three parts are still separated by a Y-shaped strip of cartilage, which is continuous with that lining the cavity. This cartilage begins to be ossified from several centres about the 12th year. The most constant of these gives rise to a triangular piece of bone at the fore part of the acetabulum, which is known as the *os acetabuli*,[1] and forms the whole of the so-called pubic portion of the articular cavity. It becomes united first with the pubis, and later with the ilium and ischium. Between the ilium and ischium there are only some irregular nodules of bone, and other small osseous points form a more or less perfect lamina over the iliac and ischial portions of the articular surface. The union of the several portions in the acetabulum is completed from the 18th to the 20th year.

[1] W. Leche, Internat. Monatschr. f. Anat. u. Histol., 1884, 363 ; W. Krause, *ib.*, 1885, 150.

Epiphyses are likewise formed in the cartilage of the crest of the ilium, the tuberosity of the ischium, the anterior inferior spine of the ilium, and the symphysis pubis. These begin to ossify soon after puberty, and unite with the main bone from the 23rd to the 25th year.

The *pelvis* of the fœtus and young child is of very small capacity in proportion to the size of the body, and those viscera which are afterwards contained for the most part in the true

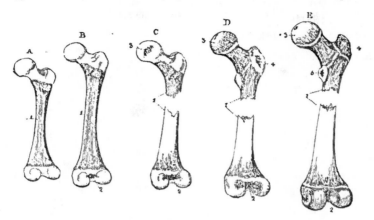

Fig. 159.—OSSIFICATION OF THE FEMUR.   (R. Quain.)

A, from a fœtus under eight months ; the body is osseous, both ends are cartilaginous.
B, from a child at birth, showing a nucleus in the lower epiphysis.
C, from a child of about a year old, showing a nucleus in the head.
D, at the fifth year ; a nucleus has appeared in the great trochanter.
E, near the age of puberty, showing a nucleus in the lesser trochanter.
1, shaft ; 2, lower extremity ; 3, head ; 4, great trochanter ; 5, small trochanter.
C, D, & E are represented considerably, A & B very little, under the natural size.

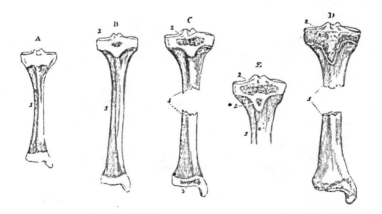

Fig. 160.—OSSIFICATION OF THE TIBIA.   (R. Quain.)

A, some weeks before birth ; the shaft is ossified, the ends are cartilaginous.
B, at birth, showing a nucleus in the upper epiphysis.
C, at the third year, showing the nucleus of the lower epiphysis.
D, at about eighteen or twenty years, showing the lower epiphysis united, while the upper remains separate.   The upper epiphysis is seen to include the tubercle.
E, shows an example of a separate centre for the tubercle.
1, shaft ; 2, superior epiphysis ; 2*, separate centre for the tubercle ; 3, inferior epiphysis.

pelvis occupy a part of the abdominal cavity. The inclination of the pelvis is considerably greater in early life than in the adult.

The **femur** is developed from one principal ossific centre for the shaft which appears in the

7th week, and from four epiphyses, the centres for which appear in the following order :—A single nucleus for the lower extremity appears shortly before birth, one for the head appears in the 1st year, one for the great trochanter in the 4th year, and one for the small trochanter in the 13th or 14th year. These epiphyses become united to the shaft in an order the reverse of that of their appearance. The small trochanter is united about the 17th year, the great trochanter about the 18th year, the head from the 18th to the 19th year, and the lower extremity soon after the 20th year. The neck of the femur is formed by extension of ossification from the shaft.

The **patella** is formed in the 3rd month by a deposit of cartilage in the tendon of the quadriceps extensor cruris muscle. In this cartilage ossification begins from a single centre during the 3rd year, and is completed about the age of puberty.

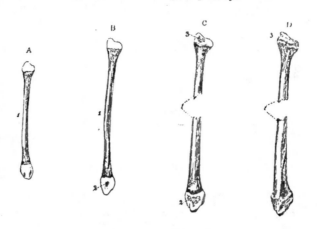

Fig. 161.—Ossification of the fibula. (R. Quain.)

A, at birth ; the shaft is ossified, the ends are cartilaginous.
B, at two years, showing a nucleus in the lower epiphysis.
C, at about four years, showing the nucleus of the upper epiphysis ; the lower ought to have been shown as more advanced.
D, at about twenty years ; the lower end is complete, but the upper epiphysis is still separate.
1, shaft ; 2, lower epiphysis ; 3, upper epiphysis.

The **tibia** and **fibula** each present, besides the principal centre for the shaft, a superior and an inferior epiphysis. In the tibia the centre for the shaft appears in the 7th week ; that for the upper extremity, including both tuberosities and the tubercle, appears most frequently before, but sometimes after birth ; and that for the inferior extremity and internal malleolus appears in the 2nd year. The tubercle is occasionally formed from a separate centre. The lower epiphysis and shaft unite in the 18th or 19th year, the upper epiphysis and shaft in the 21st or 22nd year. In the fibula the centre for the shaft appears rather later than in the tibia ; that for the lower extremity appears in the 2nd year, and that for the upper, unlike that of the tibia, not till the 3rd or 4th year. The lower epiphysis and shaft unite about the 21st year, the upper epiphysis and shaft about the 24th year.

The fibula in the embryo at an early period is nearly as large as the tibia, and also articulates with the femur. The tibial malleolus on the other hand is up to the seventh month of foetal life longer than the fibular ; and the marked preponderance of the fibular malleolus, which is peculiar to man, is only acquired after birth (Gegenbaur).

The **tarsal bones** are ossified in cartilage each from a single nucleus, with the exception of the os calcis, which in addition to its proper osseous centre, has an epiphysis upon its posterior extremity. The principal nucleus of the os calcis appears in the 6th month of foetal life ; its epiphysis begins to be ossified in the 10th year, and is united to the tuberosity in the 15th or 16th year. The nucleus of the astragalus appears in the 7th month ; that of the cuboid about the time of birth ; that of the external cuneiform in the 1st year ; that of the internal cuneiform in the 3rd year ; that of the middle cuneiform in the 4th year ; and that of the navicular in the 4th or 5th year.

The **metatarsal bones** and **phalanges** agree respectively with the corresponding bones of the hand in the mode of their ossification. Each bone is formed from a principal piece and one epiphysis ; and while in the four outer metatarsal bones the epiphysis is at the distal extremity, in the metatarsal bone of the great toe and in the phalanges it is placed at the proximal extremity. In the first metatarsal bone there is frequently, as in the first metacarpal (see p. 109), also a second or distal epiphysis; and in some instances a proximal epiphysis is formed on the tuberosity of the fifth metatarsal bone (Gruber). In the metatarsal bones the

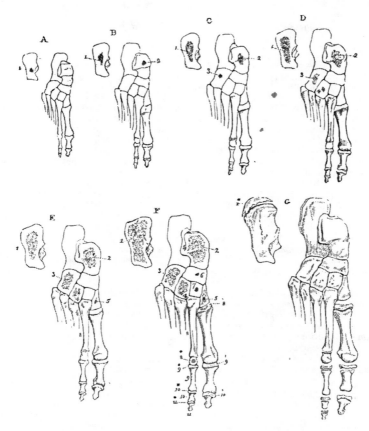

Fig. 162.—OSSIFICATION OF THE BONES OF THE FOOT. (R. Quain.)

A, right foot of a fœtus of six months; the metatarsal bones and digital phalanges have each their shafts ossified from their primary centres; the tarsus is wholly cartilaginous, excepting the os calcis, in which the nucleus of bone has just appeared.

B, foot of a fœtus of seven or eight months; the astragalus shows a nucleus.

C, from a child at birth; the cuboid has begun to ossify.

D, about a year old, showing a nucleus in the external cuneiform.

E, in the third year; ossification has reached the internal cuneiform.

F, about four years old, showing ossification in the middle cuneiform and navicular bones, and in the epiphyses of the metatarsal bones and phalanges.

G, about the age of puberty; ossification is nearly complete in the tarsal bones; an epiphysis has been formed on the tuberosity of the os calcis, and the epiphyses of the metatarsal bones and phalanges are shown separate.

1, nucleus of the os calcis; 1* in G, the epiphysis of the os calcis; 2, nucleus of the astragalus; 3, of the cuboid; 4, of the external cuneiform; 5, of the internal cuneiform; 6, of the navicular; 7, of the middle cuneiform; 8, metatarsal bones; 8*, distal epiphysis of the second metatarsal bone; 8', proximal epiphysis of the first; 9, first phalanx of the second toe; 9*, proximal epiphysis of this phalanx; 9', that of the first phalanx of the great toe; 10, second phalanx; 10*, the epiphysis of this phalanx; 10', epiphysis of the terminal phalanx of the great toe; 11, terminal phalanx; 11*, its epiphysis.

nuclei of the shafts appear in the 8th or 9th week. The epiphyses appear from the 3rd to the 8th year, and unite with the shafts from the 18th to the 20th year. The nuclei of the shafts of the phalanges appear in the 9th or 10th week. The epiphyses appear from the 4th to the 8th year, and unite with the shafts from the 19th to the 21st year.

In the infant the head of the astragalus is directed more inwards than in the adult, and the foot is naturally inverted. The first metatarsal bone is also relatively short in the fœtus, and at first is inclined inwards from the internal cuneiform bone, the distal articular surface of which is oblique. In these respects the young foot is more like that of the ape. (Leboucq. "Le développement du premier metatarsicn et de son articulation tarsienne chez l'homme," Arch. de Biologie, iii, 335.)

MORPHOLOGY OF THE BONES OF THE LIMBS.

Relation to the axial skeleton.—Anatomists have generally agreed to look upon the relation which the bones of the limb bear to the rest of the skeleton as that of appendages to the trunk, and most are also disposed to regard these appendages as similar radiations or extensions from one or more of the vertebral segments in two determinate situations of the trunk. But opinions are much divided as to the typical number of the vertebral segments which are involved, and as to the exact morphological nature of the parts which form the radiations. The quinquifid division of the peripheral parts of both limbs in man and many animals appears favourable to the view that each has the elements of five segments prolonged into it; but of late years attention has been specially directed by K. Bardeleben and others to certain marginal structures which are interpreted as vestiges of more or less completely suppressed digits, and there seems reason for believing that the pentadactyle extremity has been preceded by a heptadactyle form. In association with this it may be noticed also that the nerves entering into the proper limb-plexuses are in each case seven, viz., the 4th. 5th, 6th, 7th and 8th cervical, with the 1st and 2nd dorsal, in the brachial plexus, and the 2nd, 3rd, 4th and 5th lumbar, with the 1st, 2nd and 3rd sacral in the crural plexus. It is farther generally held that the constituent elements follow each other in a similar order in the two limbs from the cephalic to the caudal part of the vertebral axis, so that the pollex and radial elements occupy the cephalic side of the upper, while the hallux and tibia take the same place in the lower limb.

Homological comparison of upper and lower limbs.—A certain anatomical correspondence between the upper and lower limbs, which is apparent to common observation, is admitted in even a fuller degree by most anatomists as a result of a careful comparison of the form and relations of their bones, as well as of their other parts, in both their embryonic and fully formed conditions; and the general conclusion has been formed that the thoracic and pelvic limbs are constructed on the same general type in man and animals, both as regards the attaching girdles of the shoulder and pelvis, and in the three several sections of which each limb is composed. There are, however, certain modifications of that general plan, leading to considerable differences in the form, size, and number of the individual parts in different animals, which appear to be in a great measure related to the different uses to which the upper and lower limbs are respectively applied; as, for example, in the upper limb of man, the breadth of the shoulders, caused by the interposition of the clavicle, the greater extent of motion in the shoulder-joint, the eversion of the humerus, and the forward flexed attitude of the elbow-joint, the arrangements for pronation and supination by rotation of the radius and hand, and the opposability of the thumb, all have reference to the freedom, versatility, and precision of the movements of the upper limb as an organ of prehension and touch.; while in the lower limb, the comparatively fixed condition and arched form of the pelvic girdle, the greater strength of the bones, the close-fitting of the hip-joint, the inversion of the femur, the backward flexure of the knee-joint, the arched form of the foot, and non-opposability of the great toe, have all manifest relation to the support of the trunk and pelvis, and their movements upon the lower limbs. In the lower animals, greater modifications in the form of both limbs are to be observed, obviously adapted to their different functions in each case.

Without attempting to follow out this subject by any detailed reference to comparative anatomy or development, it may be useful to state here shortly the more probable conclusions which have been formed with respect to the homological correspondence of the several parts of the upper and lower limbs.

Shoulder and pelvic girdles.—In each of these a division is to be recognized at the place of attachment of the limb-stalk (shoulder and hip-joints) into a dorsal and a ventral section. The dorsal section in the upper limb is the scapula, in the lower limb the ilium, which accordingly correspond, the chief difference between them consisting in the scapula being free from articulation with the vertebral column, and therefore capable of a considerable degree of motion, while the ilium is firmly jointed to the lateral mass of the sacrum. The ventral section is in each case double, including the clavicle and coracoid in the shoulder-girdle, and the pubis and ischium in the pelvic girdle. It is generally admitted that the coracoid and ischium are corresponding structures, the coracoid being reduced to a relatively small process in man and most mammals, but forming a large and important bone which reaches the sternum in monotremata and many lower vertebrates. The pubis appears to be represented most closely by the precoracoid of reptiles and amphibia, while the clavicle is not

Figs. 163 & 164.—SKETCH OF THE BONES OF THE THORACIC AND PELVIC LIMBS, SO PLACED AS TO SHOW CORRESPONDING PARTS IN BOTH. (Allen Thomson.)

The preaxial borders of both limbs are towards the reader's right hand, and the original dorsal or extensor surfaces are shown throughout their whole extent. The somewhat artificial representation given in these figures cannot be obtained from a single view of the specimens in one position, but it is easily brought out by slightly shifting the bones or changing the point of view. The humeral tuberosities are separated so as to show them on the borders of the bone. Fig. 163. Thoracic limb; *ssp*, supraspinous or prescapular fossa; *isp*, infraspinous or postscapular fossa; *ssc*, a small part of the subscapular fossa; *bs*, base of scapula; *sa*, superior angle; *ia*, inferior angle; *sp*, spine; *ac*, acromion; *cr*, coracoid process; *gb*, glenoid border with place of attachment of triceps muscle; *gc*, glenoid cavity; *h*, humerus, preaxial border; *tm*, large or preaxial tuberosity; *tp*, small or postaxial tuberosity; *cr*, radial condyle; *cu*, ulnar condyle; *r*, radius; *u*, ulna; *o*, olecranon; *px*, pollex and preaxial side; *pi*, pisiform and postaxial side of hand. Fig. 164. Pelvic limb; *ss*, sacral surface of ilium; *il*, iliac fossa; *di*, a small part of the dorsum ilii or gluteal surface; *ic*, crest of ilium; *as*, anterior superior spine; *ipl*, ilio-pectineal line; *ep*, ilio-pectineal eminence; *is*, anterior inferior spine and attachment of rectus muscle; *cc*, cotyloid cavity; *sp*, symphysis pubis; *isc*, ischium; *f*, femur, its preaxial border; *trp*, lesser or preaxial trochanter; *trm*, greater or postaxial trochanter; *ct*, tibial condyle; *cf*, fibular condyle; *p*, patella; *t*, tibia; *tt*, tubercle of tibia; *fi*, fibula; *hx*, hallux and preaxial side of foot; *ca*, calcaneal tuberosity.

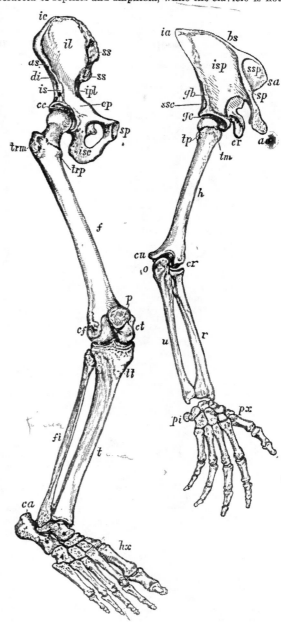

repeated in the pelvic girdle; it is, however, held by many anatomists that the mammalian clavicle corresponds morphologically to the reptilian precoracoid, and therefore is also the representative of the pubis.

With regard to the comparison to be established between the individual parts of the scapula and ilium there is much difference of opinion, but an examination of the simpler forms of these bones in some of the lower animals, and a general consideration of their relations give support to the view adopted by Flower as the more probable.[1] The scapula and

[1] Flower, Journ. Anat., iv, and "Osteology of the Mammalia." For different views, see Humphry,

ilium may be regarded as consisting essentially of three-sided prismatic rods, in the primitive position of which an internal or vertebral surface is separated from two external surfaces by preaxial and postaxial ridges, and the two external surfaces are separated by an external ridge, which descends from the dorsal extremity of the bone to the joint-socket. It is on this external ridge, *glenoid* in the scapula and *cotyloid* in the ilium, that in each case the long head of the great extensor muscle of the limb is attached. The primitive arrangement is modified in two ways, viz., 1st, by the outgrowth to a greater or less extent of the edges of the rod, thus giving rise to fossæ in the situation of the original surfaces, and 2nd, by the occurrence of a rotation in different directions in the two limbs, the scapula outwards,

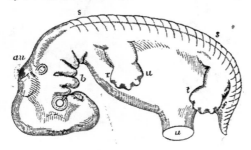

Fig. 165.—Diagram of an early human embryo, showing the rudimentary limbs in their second position. (Allen Thomson.)

r, preaxial or radial and pollex border of the thoracic limb ; *u*, its postaxial or ulnar and little finger border ; *t*, preaxial or tibial and hallux border of the pelvic limb : *f*, its postaxial or fibular and little toe border.

the ilium inwards, in accordance with the rotation which takes place during the course of development in the free part of the limb. The primitive vertebral surface of the scapula becomes the prescapular or supraspinous fossa, while in the ilium the corresponding surface is the sacral, which, being connected to the vertebral column, undergoes but little change in position. The postscapular or infraspinous fossa of the scapula is accordingly represented by the iliac fossa of the ilium, and the subscapular fossa by the gluteal surface. (See the table of homologous parts below.)

Bones of the limbs.—In making the comparison of the bones composing the limbs themselves, it is necessary to revert to the simpler relations subsisting between the limbs and the trunk or vertebral axis of the body in embryonic life. In the earliest stage the limbs may be said to bud out from the side of the trunk as flattish semilunar flaps, so that they present a

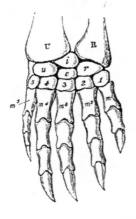

Fig. 166.—Dorsal surface of the right manus of a water tortoise. (Gegenbaur.)

R, radius ; U, ulna ; *r*, radiale ; *i*, intermedium ; *u*, ulnare ; *c*, centrale ; 1—5, five carpal bones of the distal row ; m^1—m^5, five metacarpals.

dorsal and a ventral surface, coinciding with these respective surfaces of the trunk ; but in the next stage, when the limbs come to be folded against the body in the ventral direction, although the original relation to the trunk is undisturbed, their axes have now come to lie nearly perpendicularly to the coronal plane of the vertebral axis, and the position of the limbs is such that in each there is one border which looks towards the head, and another which looks towards the tail. To these borders of the limbs the names of preaxial and postaxial are given respectively, as indicating their position before and behind the limb-axis. When at a somewhat later stage of development the divisions of the limbs make their appearance, and more especially when the quinquifid division of the digits in the hand and foot becomes perceptible, it is obvious that the thumb and radius in the one limb, and the great toe and tibia in the other, occupy corresponding cephalic and preaxial situations ; and it is not difficult to trace from these the corresponding relations of the parts in the upper division of the limbs. Thus, the radial condyle of the humerus with the great tuberosity are preaxial, while the lesser tuberosity, ulnar condyle, ulna, and little finger are postaxial. In the lower limb, the small trochanter, internal condyle, tibia and great toe are preaxial, while the great trochanter, external condyle, fibula, and little toe, are postaxial. And at the same time the dorsal or extensor surface of the limbs is external, and the ventral or flexor surface is internal.

Journ. Anat., v, 67 ; Sabatier, "Comparaison des ceintures et des membres antérieurs et postérieurs dans la série des vertébrés," Montpellier, 1880.

Very soon, however, in the higher animals and in man, farther changes operate in bringing about the permanent condition. The humerus is folded backwards against the trunk, and at the same time undergoes a rotation outwards, so that the radial (preaxial) condyle becomes external, and the extensor aspect of the elbow is directed backwards. The femur, on the other hand, is inclined forwards and rotated inwards, thereby bringing the tibial (preaxial) condyle to the inner side, and the extensor aspect of the knee forwards. The rotation of the humerus outwards in man amounts to about 45°, so that the axis of the elbow-joint is placed obliquely to the median plane, but in quadrupeds the rotation takes place through 90°, and thus the axis of the elbow-joint becomes transverse. The rotation inwards of the femur is about 90°, and the axis of the knee-joint is therefore placed transversely, in both man and quadrupeds. In the upper limb of man, the radius being in semipronation, no material change occurs in the position of the hand, the thumb hanging naturally forwards ; but in animals destined to rest on the palmar aspect of the hand or digits, important changes occur in the position of the radius by which, as this bone is brought forwards upon the humerus, and its lower end carried inwards, the manus or its elements are placed permanently in the prone position, with the

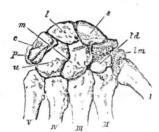

Fig. 167.—Dorsal surface of the right carpus of man. (Flower.)

s, scaphoid ; l, lunar ; c, cuneiform or pyramidal ; p, pisiform ; tm, trapezium ; td, trapezoid ; m, magnum ; u, unciform ; I—V, five metacarpals.

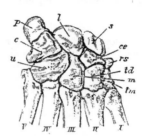

Fig. 168.—Dorsal surface of the carpus of a baboon. (Flower.)

s, scaphoid ; l, lunar ; c, cuneiform or pyramidal ; p, pisiform ; tm, trapezium ; td, trapezoid ; m, magnum ; u, unciform ; rs, radial sesamoid ; ce, os centrale ; I—V, five metacarpals.

first or radial digit inwards. In the foot no such change is required, as already by the internal rotation of the femur at its upper part, the conditions for plantar support have been secured, and the first or tibial digit is on the inner side. Farther, in man, as the body attains its full development, both limbs are extended in a line parallel to the axis of the trunk, the upper dropping loosely from the shoulder-joint with the greatest freedom of motion ; the lower more closely articulated in the hip-joint, and suited to give firm support to the body in the erect posture.

Hand and foot.—The similarity of the digital and metacarpal bones of the hand with those of the foot in number, form, and connections is so great that the homodynamous correspondence of these bones is immediately recognised. The main differences between them consist in the greater length of the fingers, and the opposability of the thumb to the other digits through its mobility at the carpo-metacarpal articulation, in adaptation to the function of the hand as a grasping organ.

The morphological construction of the carpus and tarsus is only to be understood by reference to a more generalized form, such as is met with in the carpus of the water-tortoise (fig. 166) and in the tarsus of certain amphibia. Here nine elements are seen, arranged in a proximal series of three, which are named respectively *radiale* or *tibiale*, *intermedium*, and *ulnare* or *fibulare*, a distal series of five, named *carpalia* or *tarsalia* I—V, counting from the preaxial border, and an interposed *centrale*.[1] In man, as in nearly all mammals, the distal row of the carpus and tarsus comprises only four bones, the unciform and cuboid, which support the postaxial two digits, being generally regarded as formed by the fusion of the fourth and fifth elements. Of the proximal elements of the carpus, the radiale is represented in the scaphoid, the intermedium in the lunar, and the ulnare in the pyramidal. The centrale appears to be absent in the carpus of man, although it occurs as a distinct bone in nearly all apes. In the human fœtus, however, at the latter part of the second month, a rudiment of the centrale is present as a small cartilaginous nodule, which in the course of the third month becomes fused with the cartilage of the scaphoid.[2] The latter bone must therefore be regarded

[1] Gegenbaur, "Untersuch. zur vergleich. Anat. ; I. Carpus und Tarsus," Leipzig, 1864.
[2] Leboucq, "Recherches sur la morphologie du carpe chez les mammifères," Arch. de Biologie, v, 35

as composed of the radiale and the centrale. Traces of the centrale are often to be recognized in the adult scaphoid, and it may in rare cases be developed as a separate bone. In the proximal series of the tarsus the course of development is somewhat different. The astragalus results from the union of the tibiale and intermedium, although the latter occasionally remains distinct as the *os trigonum* (p. 133): at the back of the posterior articular surface on the under aspect of the astragalus there is often to be seen a slight groove, indicative of this separation (fig. 146). The fibulare forms the greater part of the os calcis, and the centrale of the navicular bone. The pisiform bone has been considered a sesamoid bone (*ulnare sesamoideum*) developed in the tendon of the flexor carpi ulnaris, but recent investigations tend to show that it is a vestige of a suppressed ray (digitus postminimus): the corresponding structure of the tarsus enters into tuberosity of the os calcis. On the outer margin of the carpus there is in some animals another bone (*radiale sesamoideum*), which, if represented in man, seems most nearly to correspond to the tuberosity of the scaphoid; and the tuberosity of the navicular bone of the tarsus may be the representative of a similar element (*tibiale sesamoideum*) in the foot. These so-called "sesamoid" ossifications are also regarded by Bardeleben as vestiges of a suppressed digit (prepollex or prehallux).[1]

The following tables present a synoptical view of the probable corresponding or homologous bones and their parts in the thoracic and pelvic limbs :—

I.—TABLE OF THE HOMOLOGOUS BONES IN THE THORACIC AND PELVIC LIMBS.

THORACIC LIMB.	PELVIC LIMB.
Scapula	Ilium.
Precoracoid	Pubis.
Coracoid	Ischium.
Glenoid cavity	Cotyloid cavity.
Clavicle	*Absent.*
Humerus	Femur.
Great tuberosity	Small trochanter.
Small tuberosity	Great trochanter.
External condyle and capitellum	Internal condyle.
Internal condyle and trochlea	External condyle.
Absent	Patella.
Radius	Tibia.
Ulna	Fibula.
Carpus	Tarsus.
Metacarpus	Metatarsus.
Pollex	Hallux.
Digital phalanges	Digital phalanges.

II.—TABLE OF THE HOMOLOGOUS BONES OF THE CARPUS AND TARSUS.

CARPUS.		*Typical names.*		TARSUS.
Pyramidal	Ulnare	Fibulare	}	Os calcis
Pisiform	Ulnare sesamoideum (?)	Fibulare sesamoideum (?)	}	
Lunar	Intermedium	Intermedium	}	Astragalus
Scaphoid	{ Radiale	Tibiale	}	
	{ Radiale sesamoideum (?)	Tibiale sesamoideum (?)	}	Navicular
	{ Centrale	Centrale	}	
Trapezium	Carpale I.	Tarsale I.		Int. Cuneiform.
Trapezoid	—— II.	—— II.		Mid. Cuneiform.
Magnum	—— III.	—— III.		Ext. Cuneiform.
Unciform	{ —— IV.	—— IV.	}	Cuboid.
	{ —— V.	—— V.	}	

[1] According to another view, which is supported by Baur and Leboucq, the "tibial sesamoid" is the tibiale, and the astragalus the intermedium only.

III.—TABLE OF THE HOMOLOGOUS PARTS OF THE SCAPULA AND ILIUM (ACCORDING TO FLOWER).

SCAPULA.	Primitive condition.	ILIUM.
Supraspinous fossa . . .	Vertebral surface . . .	Sacral surface.
Infraspinous fossa . .	Preaxial surface . . .	Iliac fossa.
Subscapular fossa . . .	Postaxial surface . . .	Gluteal surface.
Spine and acromion . .	Preaxial border . . .	Ilio-pectineal line.
Superior or coracoid border .	Postaxial border . . .	Posterior or ischial border.
Axillary or glenoid border .	External border . . .	Anterior or cotyloid border.
Base	Dorsal extremity . . .	Iliac crest.
Superior angle . . .		Posterior superior spine.
Inferior angle . . .		Anterior superior spine.

ADAPTATION OF THE SKELETON TO THE ERECT ATTITUDE.

The axial skeleton of man is, for the purposes of station and progression, raised more fully to the vertical position than is the case in any other animal; and along with this the lower limbs are extended in lines parallel to the axis of the trunk. The feet rest on the ground by the contact of the heel and the heads of the metatarsal bones, the centre of gravity of the body falling within the basis of support. For the maintenance of this attitude, the constant action of the muscles passing over the ankle-joint is more immediately necessary. But at the knee-and hip-joints it is mainly by the mechanism of the ligaments and other parts of the joints, and less directly by muscular action, that the erect attitude is maintained, as will be more fully shown in the description of the different articulations.

There are, besides, many peculiarities in the construction of the body, and especially of the skeleton, which are associated with the assumption of the erect posture, and although many of them have been noticed in the description of the bones, it may still be useful to re-capitulate the chief ones briefly in this place.

It may first be remarked that the full development of these peculiarities belongs to the adult condition. In the infant, while still unable to walk, the large proportional size of the head, amounting to nearly a fifth of the whole body, the comparative straightness of the vertebral column, or absence of the curves which characterise the spine of the adult, the short-ness of the lower limbs, and incompleteness of their structure, all contribute to render the assumption of the erect attitude by the child, for a time, difficult and insecure. Thus the middle distance between the vertex of the head and the sole of the foot in an infant is situated somewhat above the umbilicus, while in the adult it is generally at the upper border of the pubis, or even lower, in some part of the symphysis. In the child also, from the large dimensions of the head and upper part of the body, the centre of gravity is carried to a considerably higher point than in the adult.

The skull of man differs from that of other animals in being nearly balanced on the vertebral column, the condyles of the occipital bone being brought forwards to near the middle of the base by the comparative shortness of that part of the skull which lies in front of the foramen magnum, and the projection backwards of that which lies behind it. In quadrupeds the skull extends forwards from the extremity of the column, and is sustained by the elastic ligamentum nuchæ, represented in man by a comparatively feeble structure which passes between the external occipital protuberance, and the spinous processes of the cervical vertebræ. Together with this altered relation of the head to the spine, the plane of the foramen magnum, which in quadrupeds is vertical, becomes in man horizontal, or even inclined somewhat upwards anteriorly.

The spinal column, by its pyramidal form, is fitted to sustain the weight which bears down upon its lower part, and by means of its different curvatures possesses elasticity and strength combined, and allows considerable range of motion to the trunk, without removal of the centre of gravity from within its base. The strong and expanded sacrum is the immediate means of transferring the weight of the trunk to the hip-bones and lower limbs.

The thorax in man is comparatively short, compressed in the sagittal direction, and ex-panded transversely, whereby the centre of gravity is carried backwards, nearer to the spine.

The pelvis is of peculiar breadth in man, presenting an upper and a lower arch which meet at the hip-joints, and is so inclined that a vertical line descending from the centre of gravity of the body is in a plane slightly behind the centres of motion of the hip-joints. The breadth of the pelvis enables the balance to be more easily maintained in lateral movements of the body by compensating inclinations of different parts to opposite sides of the basis of support, and the long neck of the femur gives an advantageous insertion to the muscles by which the balance of the body is principally preserved. The hip-bone is mainly distinguished from the same bone in animals by the breadth of its iliac portion, which gives support to the abdominal viscera, and attachment to the greatly developed iliac and gluteal muscles.

The lower limbs are remarkable for their length and strength. The femur is greatly elongated, its length considerably exceeding that of the tibia,—a condition which is requisite not only to give a sufficient extent of stride, but also to enable the body to be balanced in different degrees and varieties of stooping. The foot of man alone among animals has an arched instep, and it likewise presents a great breadth of sole. The great toe is distinguished by its full development, and especially from that of the apes, by its want of opposability, being constructed, not for grasping, but for supporting the weight of the body, and giving spring to the step.

While stability and strength are thus provided in the lower limbs, mobility and lightness are secured in the upper. This is apparent on comparison of the shoulder, elbow, and wrist, with the hip, knee, and ankle. In the hand, also, the freely moveable phalanges are as long as the carpal and metacarpal bones taken together, while in the foot they are not a third of the length of the tarsal and metatarsal bones.